Rebellion in the University

Books by Seymour Martin Lipset

Agrarian Socialism

With Martin Trow and James S. Coleman: *Union Democracy*

With Reinhard Bendix: *Social Mobility in Industrial Society*

Political Man: The Social Bases of Politics

The First New Nation: The United States in Historical and Comparative Perspective

Estudiantes universitarios y política en el Tercer Mundo

Revolution and Counterrevolution

With Earl Raab: *The Politics of Unreason: Right-Wing Extremism in America, 1790–1970*

With Gerald M. Schaflander: *Passion and Politics: Student Activism in America*

Edited by Seymour Martin Lipset

With Sheldon S. Wolin: *The Berkeley Student Revolt*

Student Politics

With Philip G. Altbach: *Students in Revolt*

Rebellion in the University

Seymour Martin Lipset

Harvard University

Little, Brown and Company   Boston

LIBRARY OF CONGRESS CATALOG CARD NO. 70–185920

FIRST PRINTING

Published simultaneously in Canada
by Little, Brown & Company (Canada) Limited

PRINTED IN THE UNITED STATES OF AMERICA

Dedication

To the memory of
Richard Hofstadter, Joseph Levenson,
Robert S. Lynd, and Robert McCloskey

Acknowledgments

This volume is an outgrowth of a program of studies of problems of the university and of student unrest undertaken at the Center for International Affairs at Harvard University and supported by a grant from the Hazen Foundation. Other books in this program, which will be published in 1972, are *Latin American Students* by Arthur Liebman, Kenneth Walker and Myron Glazer, *Higher Education in a Transitional Society* by Philip G. Altbach, and *Higher Education in India* edited by Amrik Singh and Philip G. Altbach. Earlier books sponsored by the Center's research program dealing with student activism were written under grants for comparative and international research made by the Ford Foundation and the Carnegie Corporation and that of the Hazen Foundation. These include:

Seymour Martin Lipset, ed. *Student Politics*. New York: Basic Books, 1967.

Philip G. Altbach. *Student Politics in Bombay*. Bombay: Asia, 1968.

————, ed. *Turmoil and Transition*. New York: Basic Books, 1968.

Seymour Martin Lipset and Philip G. Altbach, eds. *Students in Revolt.* Boston: Houghton Mifflin, 1969. Paperback ed.: Boston: Beacon, 1970.

Philip G. Altbach, ed. *Student Revolution: A Global Analysis.* Bombay: Lalvani, 1970.

Arthur Liebman. *Politics of Puerto Rican Students.* Austin: University of Texas Press, 1970.

Philip G. Altbach. *Student Politics and Higher Education in the U.S.: A Select Bibliography.* Cambridge: Center for International Affairs, Harvard University, 1968.

_____. *A Select Bibliography on Students, Politics and Higher Education.* Cambridge: Center for International Affairs, Harvard University, 1968.

_____. *Higher Education in Developing Countries: A Select Bibliography.* Cambridge: Center for International Affairs, Harvard University, 1970. Occasional Paper 24.

Various individuals and institutions contributed to making this book possible. William Creed, Fred Rackmil, and Bartley Horwitz were particularly helpful as research assistants. Mrs. Meena Vohra helped supervise the production of different drafts. I am particularly grateful to a number of executives of various American polling organizations for furnishing me with detailed reports of their national surveys of college students. These include Dr. Irving Crespi of the American Institute of Public Opinion Research (the Gallup Poll); Dr. Daniel Yankelovich of Daniel Yankelovich Associates; Louis Harris of Louis Harris Associates; Burns Roper of the Roper Organization; and George Mihaly of Gilbert Youth Research. Access to the findings of studies completed for projects associated with the White House was made possible through the good offices of the staff of the President's Commission on Campus Unrest, particularly Dr. Richard Braungart. Some of the material in Chapters 2 and 3 was initially written as research memoranda for the Commission, and has been substantially revised since. Other parts of the book have drawn upon articles published earlier. All of the previously published material has been substantially rewritten and revised. The articles include:

"Youth and Politics." In Robert K. Merton and Robert Nisbet, eds., *Contemporary Social Problems*. 3rd ed. New York: Harcourt, Brace and Jovanovich, 1971. Pp. 743–791.

"The Possible Effects of Student Activism on International Politics." In Seymour Martin Lipset and Philip G. Altbach, eds., *Students in Revolt*. Boston: Houghton Mifflin, 1969. Pp. 495–524.

"The Activists: A Profile." *The Public Interest* (Fall 1968), pp. 38–50.

"Student Opposition in the United States." *Government and Opposition* 1 (April 1966), pp. 351–374.

I would also like to acknowledge the helpful advice in my efforts to make sense out of the events and research in this area of my colleagues, Chaim Adler of the Hebrew University, Philip Altbach of the University of Wisconsin, Arthur Liebman of the State University of New York at Binghamton, and Nathan Glazer of Harvard University. My principal intellectual debt, however, is to the large number of students who have sought in different ways to describe the way in which they and their peers see the world.

Seymour Martin Lipset

Contents

Introduction

The American university has been a place of turmoil since the Berkeley revolt of 1964–65. A literal flood of books and articles has poured forth seeking to describe, advocate, or analyze different modes of campus behavior. These analyses have ranged from those that place the responsibility for campus discontent on aspects of the social structure to some that see the university itself as the source. Still others argue that specific political events, especially the war in Indo-China and the civil rights struggles, are the principal energizing factors. These theories, of course, are not mutually exclusive. Each of them would appear to contain some validity.

The approaches which stress societal factors include the proposition that changes in child-rearing and educational practices have produced a generation of students who combine belief in equalitarian doctrines with an insistence on instant gratification. The scions of the liberal segment of the upper-middle class were reared by parents who did not discipline them strongly for fear of injuring their personalities, and sent them to "progressive" private or suburban public schools. These parents also accepted the belief, as David Cohen has argued, that youth should not be restrained or coerced, that education should reflect the desires of the students, that education (and work) should be play, that is, should be unalienated behavior reflecting the free choice of the individual. And it follows from this analysis that when these students came of age, they began to insist that the rest of the world conform to the idealistic state of freedom and comparative equality which they had experienced. The year 1965 is twenty years after the end of World War II, and therefore corresponds to the time in which one would expect the children of the parents of the liberalizing thirties to have come of age.

There are, of course, other structural change theories which have been advanced to account for the growth in student discontent. These stress, particularly, technological determinants which supposedly have made life more difficult, e.g., more population, more pollution, and more noise, or have opened the door to new vicarious experiences and instantaneous communication about events in other parts of the country and world through television.

Much of the literature in the field, of course, emphasizes the role of the educational system as a cause of unrest. Ever since protest erupted on the senior campus of the University of California, Berkeley, numerous interpreters of what is bothering the students have suggested that the large bureaucratic educational institutions have turned them off. Specifically, the large university is seen as inherently impersonal, relying on the large lecture course, the graduate teaching assistant, and a very big student–senior faculty ratio, which frustrates students seeking an educational experience with distinguished scholars. Instead of being treated as a total individual, the student in the megauniversity finds himself a number on an IBM card, registered and graded through use of computers. The presumed decline of close faculty-student relationships has also been blamed by many on the emphasis within the universities on research — on the fact that professors secure prestige and higher salaries through their publications, rather than as a result of the quality of their teaching. The emphasis on research has grown since World War II in response to the enormous increase in funds available through government, industry, and foundations. The teaching loads have declined sharply, and presumably, as Clark Kerr argued in 1963 just before the current wave of unrest began, the undergraduates are shortchanged.

The third approach, that which stresses the role of specific politically relevant historical events as a catalyst which initiated the current wave of protest, points to the recurrent role of student violence and protest since the Middle Ages. Basically, it argues that those revolutionary theorists like Bakunin and Blanqui, who stressed the revolutionary role of intellectuals and students as the inspirers, leaders, and often mass troops of the revolution, were correct. Bringing together evidence of the large-scale student involvement in the revolutionary movements in czarist Russia, nineteenth century France, Germany, and Italy, and various colonial and third world countries more recently, it suggests that the social situation of the students makes them, even more than the proletariat, the revolutionary class par excellence. Elements inherent in the marginal status of youth and students, the lesser commitment to authority demanded of sociological adolescents, freedom to sow "wild oats," the socialization of young people into the idealism of the adult group to which they belong, and the relative ease with which those on campus can be reached and mobilized, all make students more likely than any other stratum to respond to events which undermine a social system. From this perspective, the socially available and idealistic students were activated by two sets of issues which undermined the American polity, first the frustrations endemic in the efforts to secure civil rights and economic equality following the Supreme Court's desegregation decision, and subsequently the immorality or weakness exhibited by the United States in fighting a seemingly weak little nation-enemy in Southeast Asia.

The whole development of student and academic protest had an effect far beyond that which American universities had ever experienced — because of the tremendous increase in the sheer numbers of persons connected with academe. In 1930, there were about a million students and eighty thousand faculty, figures which grew to one million, six hundred seventy-five thousand students and one hundred sixty-five thousand professors by the end of World War II. Twenty-five years later in 1970 there were seven million students and over half a million full-time faculty. These absolute figures mean, among other things, that a relatively small percentage constitutes a large enough critical mass to sustain the demonstrations, organizations, and subscriptions to journals necessary to create a viable social movement. Five percent of the student body now equals over three hundred fifty thousand students. One tenth of the faculty nationally means a body of over fifty thousand people. Faculty and student groups are vocal, mobilizable, and noticeable. Hence, the sheer jump in numbers since 1945, combined with a set of events which activate a minority, can be enough to impress the country that the campus is in revolt.

But politics has not been the only arena which brought tension between students and their elders in the 1960s. Many students exhibited their renunciation of the culture of their parents through innovative forms of dress, hairstyles, use of drugs, obscene language, and more widespread willingness to have a variety of sexual experiences. In this sense, the sixties showed some resemblance to the 1920s, when illegal alcohol, premarital sex, and short skirts also shocked elders into discussions of the generation gap — of the differences between those under and over thirty. And many adults who could accept revolutionary politics as the idealism of young people who would grow more conservative as they grew older, a frequently made observation about student radicals in many countries, found themselves horrified by the new morality of a renunciatory segment of the young.

My involvement in, and concern with, student activism long predated the current wave. While at Townsend Harris High School, then the preparatory school to the City College of New York in the late 1930's, I belonged to the Young People's Socialist League (YPSL), the youth section of the Socialist Party, and to the American Student Union (ASU), an organization whose activities are described in Chapter 5. At the December 1938 convention of the ASU, I was one of very few delegates who opposed the dominant line imposed on the organization by the Communists. I introduced a resolution that condemned Communist, Fascist, and Nazi totalitarianism. Not unexpectedly, it received little support and never came to a vote. Toward the end of my undergraduate career, I served as national chairman of the YPSL, which then had only a few hundred members. The relationship of my student political concerns to my academic career and choice of research topics has been described in detail elsewhere, and I will not repeat it here.[1]

My first research involvement with student politics occurred in 1949–50, when I was an assistant professor at the University of California, Berkeley. The celebrated loyalty oath conflict of that year led me to encourage a course in research methods to study student reaction.[2] Almost a decade later, my interests in the political problems of less developed nations led me to appreciate the need for revolutionary ideology by intellectuals and others concerned with social change in these countries.[3] And further reading about the forces involved in revolutionary change in the history of the West and the present of the third world convinced me that intellectuals and students came close to being the most important force. Some preliminary results of my reading into the comparative literature were reported in a long article written in 1963.[4] Since the empirical literature was quite limited at the time, I undertook to systematically encourage a number of foreign scholars, younger American colleagues, and graduate students, to study the political involvements of universities and students by making research funds available to them from the comparative research programs, first those of the Survey Research Center and Institute of International Studies of the University of California, Berkeley, and later those of the Center for International Affairs at Harvard. Most of these studies have been completed. A description of the background and the nature of these projects may be found in my "Introduction" to the volume on *Latin American Students* by Arthur Liebman, Myron Glazer, and Kenneth

Walker, to be published by Harvard University Press in 1972. The other analyses, which cover North Africa, Yugoslavia, Iran, India, Japan, and other parts of Latin America and Europe, are cited in the Acknowledgments.

I was on the staff of the University of California at Berkeley, the year of the celebrated Berkeley revolt, 1964–1965. Contrary to published gossip, my departure from Berkeley was not a result of my reaction to that event. I had made arrangements in the spring of 1964 to move to Harvard a year later. Ironically, given the contrary rumors, these arrangements were not finalized for another year because of a request from Berkeley administrators that I delay any resignation to avoid the impression that I was leaving because of the turmoil at Berkeley. Previous to the revolt year, and during it, I had been the faculty adviser of the Young People's Socialist League, the same organization I had once chaired nationally, a group which joined the Free Speech Movement. During the Berkeley protests, I also served as faculty adviser to the Cited Students' Organization, an association formed of FSM students who had been charged with violating university rules, which was the only formally recognized campus organization of the FSM. I favored the proposals of the FSM "moderates" (from Students for Goldwater to the YPSL) for liberalization of the university rules which inhibited certain forms of political activity on campus — chiefly fund-raising for political purposes and organizing demonstrations for off-campus protests, particularly civil rights sit-ins — at the same time urging with them that the goals pursued by the FSM and favored from the start by most faculty could and should be pursued without using illegal tactics that might create confrontations with the police. I argued publicly on many occasions that civil disobedience is only justified in the absence of democratic rights.

As in subsequent large-scale student demonstrations elsewhere, the FSM was divided between extremists who openly advocated radicalizing tactics deliberately designed to create a conflict between police and students, and those who saw such tactics as unnecessary to attain the manifest goals of the movement. Few observers, inside or outside of Berkeley, at the time, noted that the plan to occupy Sproul Hall in December 1964 was opposed by some of the groups involved in the movement from its beginning. The Berkeley Revolt was the prototype event of the student movement. The radical wing sought successfully to exacerbate the tactics even after the initial widely supported demands of the movement had almost entirely been met. Most of the faculty supported agreeing to the demands, and backed total amnesty, and assumed that once the issues were settled on the FSM's terms the demonstrations and confrontations would end. But when it became clear that the radical wing of the movement had wider and continuing objectives justifying further civil disobedience, the faculty divided bitterly into distinct factions, divisions which have lasted to the present (1972).

I reacted to the seeming "solution" of the Berkeley crisis in December 1964, when the faculty voted by a large majority to endorse the total position of the FSM *after* the sit-in, with pessimism. In an article Paul Seabury and I wrote during the Christmas vacation, we expressed considerable uneasiness about the consequences for the university of the introduction of tactics of civil disobedience, in terms which we still believe are deserved:

> Most shaken by this sudden crisis . . . has been the human trust that is the ethical basis of any university — or, for that matter, of any community. This delicate though often impersonal confidence between teachers and students, professors and professors, students and students, was severely breached. The wounds left by suspicion and resentment over apparent betrayals of trust will remain for a long time. This is a poignant future problem for the teacher and his students. Once classrooms have been bitterly divided with covert and overt defamation of faculty members as "stooges of the administration" or "tools of the FSM steering committee," the community of scholarship is clearly endangered. . . .
>
> The Berkeley Revolt is not just another California curiosity. This new style of campus political action may affect other campuses, and eventually our national political life. The new student

generation is brilliant and aggressively serious. The number of graduate students who spend years at a university increases steadily. The student leftist movements are growing and probably will continue to grow as they demand totally moral solutions to issues of racial discrimination and foreign policy. The indifference to legality shown by serious students can threaten the foundations of democratic order if it becomes a model for student political action. Extremism in the pursuit of liberty was quite recently a favorite slogan of the radical right. Berkeley has shown that anyone can play this game. The danger now exists that students at other universities will have learned how easily a great university can be brought to its knees if but two or three percent of the student body are willing to engage in actions which may force the police on campus. Universities are probably more vulnerable to civil disobedience tactics than any other institution in the country precisely because those in authority, whether administration or faculty, are liberal. They are reluctant to see force invoked against their students regardless of what the students do. Now that this secret is out, it may be difficult to restrain students from having their way on many university issues, much as occurs on Latin-American campuses.[5]

The concern that deliberate use of the Blanquist tactics of confrontation designed to provoke authority to be repressive would spread through the university world has, of course, been warranted. Given the suspicion against authority which exists among the majority of liberal-to-left-disposed students and faculty, the more extreme groups can rely on mass support if their actions result in a clash between police and demonstrators. Steve Weissman, theoretician of the FSM, openly described to a journalist the discussions among FSM leaders as to how they could force the university to call the police.[6] They regarded an incident in which the police came on campus as necessary for the success of the movement, to further the process of radicalization. The conscious character of this tactic has been attested to by various leaders of the national movement since Berkeley. Thus, two years later in 1967, Stokely Carmichael, former head of the Student Nonviolent Coordinating Committee (SNCC) in a discussion with Carl Oglesby, former president of the Students for a Democratic Society (SDS), published as a lead article in the New Left weekly, the *National Guardian,* described revolutionary strategy:

> People won't fight; they won't fight unless you push — so you push. You create disturbances, you keep pushing the system. You keep drawing up the contradictions until they have to hit back; once your enemy hits back then your revolution starts. If your enemy does not hit back then you do not have a revolution.[7]

A writer in the British *New Left Review* in 1968 also generalized in much the same terms as Weissman and Carmichael. It is necessary, he argued, for student radicals

> to behave as provocatively as necessary and to effectively sanction the University to the extent that they *need* to use force, probably the police. Complete occupation of offices rather than corridors will achieve this. It is at this stage that the administrations commit their ultimate folly, and it is at this stage that the staff [faculty] and less political students will feel encouraged to enter a situation already politically structured.[8]

Perhaps the height of cynicism with respect to boasting about the ability of radicals to manipulate the progressive sympathies of the majority of academia came from Mark Rudd, the leader of the Columbia SDS sit-in demonstration in the spring of 1968. In a speech in the fall of that year, urging Harvard and other Boston area students to launch their own sit-in demonstrations, Rudd advised them not to worry about issues, since the two major Columbia issues were basically non-issues for him.

> Let me tell you. We manufactured the issues. The Institute for Defense Analysis is nothing at Columbia. Just three professors. And the gym issue is bull. It doesn't mean anything to anybody. I had never been to the gym site before the demonstration began. I didn't even know how to get there.[9]

At Harvard in the spring of 1969, the majority of those attending SDS meetings, though hostile to various policies of the university, opposed the demands of the Maoist Worker-Student Alliance faction, to seize University Hall, an administration building,
until SDS could publicize their demands among the students and
give the administration time to refuse them. The Maoist group
wanted a confrontation in the week following the spring vacation
and precipitated it *after being repeatedly turned down at an SDS
meeting.*

> Three times that night SDS had voted against the immediate
> seizure of a building, but the leaders of the Worker-Student Alli-
> ance caucus had no intention of abiding by that action. . . . If
> militant action were delayed, they feared the chance to confront
> the Corporation on the issues would be lost. Before dawn they
> had reached their decision: they would seize University Hall at
> noon that day, April 9, when the first of the New Left's [the dom-
> inant faction in the Harvard SDS] daily rallies was scheduled to
> begin.[10]

Citing these statements is not intended to suggest that the
issues which have been the ostensible causes of various campus
demonstrations from Berkeley to Harvard were not legitimate
concerns about which many students felt deeply before the confrontation. What is in controversy about many of these affairs is
whether the particular problem justified the use of extralegal
methods which sharply divided the campus communities, heightened the antiintellectual right-wing backlash, and ultimately,
according to Sam Brown, the founder of the McCarthy peace
campaign in 1968 and of the antiwar Moratorium movement in
1969, even had a counterproductive effect on the efforts of the
peace movement to influence policy.[11] These issues which have
been argued on many campuses of the nation are essentially the
same as those which divided the Berkeley faculty and student
body through the fateful fall semester of 1964.

Since moving to Harvard in 1965, I have continued my connection with student politics by serving as one of the faculty

advisers for the Harvard chapter of the Young People's Socialist League.[12] In addition, I have edited a number of books, and written many articles dealing with student activism as a social and political phenomenon both in foreign countries and in the United States which seek to integrate the knowledge gathered in various places.[13]

Since I have been involved in considerable writing and lecturing on the subject of academic politics, my views, analyses, and activities have been the subject of frequent comment. Some have attributed a policy-related role to my work in this field. It may, therefore, be worth mentioning that I have never served as advisor or consultant on the subject of student unrest or related topics to any administrative agency, although I have submitted memoranda to both the House Committee on Education and to the President's Commission on Campus Unrest, which presented my views on the university situation. It might also be mentioned, given reports to the contrary, that I have never been personally involved in research on the activities of students in any given overseas country or area other than as an advisor on research and analytic design.

The politicization of academic life, a subject discussed at some length in this book, particularly in Chapters 3 and 6, has greatly affected intellectual judgments and reviews of social science research generally, but particularly in this area. Much of the comment on such research is often closely related to whether the reviewer agrees or disagrees with the political assumptions or conclusions of the author. Thus, beyond those who agree with and praise my writings, I have been sharply criticized by leftists for my "conservative" biases, which allegedly inform my analyses of student unrest, and by right-wingers for my "leftist" or pro-activist orientations.[14] A Mexican paper, *El Universal,* described my writings on student politics as "containing revolutionary directives," and concluded that I was a supporter of the "extreme left in the United States." The right-wing Church League of America in a publication on *Subversion by the Volume,* an attack on publishers for putting out left-wing books, cited me as giving support to "students who rioted," and for being active "among the protesters against the war in Vietnam."[15] The same disparity in evaluation of my general political sociological writings has led some commentators to see me, in the words of the author of an SDS pamphlet, as seeking "to maintain the American celebration," and others as a partisan of social stability, while a variety of political scientists and sociologists have described my work as "reflecting a Marxian frame of reference," or according to two recent works as espousing the same conflict-oriented approach to social analysis followed by C. Wright Mills.[16]

The same variations in judgments about my politics have appeared recently in various journalistic reviews of my book (with Earl Raab) on right-wing movements, *The Politics of Unreason.* Thus a critic in the pro-New Left *New York Review of Books* described the study as reflecting a "conservative" bias; the reviewer for the conservative organ, *The National Review,* was bothered by the "Social-Democratic" orientation of the authors; while the *Bulletin of the John Birch Society* complained about "their ideological bias in favor of totalitarian statism." In sending this analysis of student activism to press, I anticipate similar differences in evaluations.

It is difficult to deal with such disagreements. To speak positively, let me declare again that I place myself politically within the democratic left. Briefly this means supporting efforts to reduce inequality of all kinds as much as is possible within the limits imposed by complex human society. In my judgment, it requires the maintenance and extension of all institutional practices, values, and structural conditions that facilitate opposition by non-elites to those who dominate economically, politically, and socially. Where all three forms of power are monopolized by a tiny elite as they are in authoritarian systems, one party or other, whether legitimated by nominally leftist or rightist ideologies, the great mass will have little or no way of limiting the ability of those who control to dictate the way in which they shall live and work. Hence any movement or social change that undermines institutions facilitating opposition to those in power serves to enhance the potential for authoritarian rule, and for greater inequality. Small minorities command the resources of society, economy, and polity in nations ranging from the Soviet Union, China, Cuba, Greece and Spain, to the United States, Japan, Germany, Britain and Sweden. Unchallenged by organized opposition in the form of political parties, trade unions, criticism in the media, group self-interest organizations, they will always strengthen their power to control, i.e., to exploit the mass. Hence authoritarian systems, even when they call themselves Communist or Socialist, are more reactionary than those in which opposition, however inadequate, exists. Any reader of Chinese or Russian publications can learn the validity of this statement with respect to domestic conditions in that part of the Communist world dominated by, or in alliance with, the other. Each Communist camp documents in elaborate detail the way in which unrestrained power in the other results in mass exploitation. If one assumes that the historical record and sociological analysis support the thesis that, regardless of forms of ownership, powerholders, as a class or stratum, always seek to maintain and enhance their position, it follows that all movements which favor a monopoly of power, or which support states with such social structures, are themselves objectively elitist, opposed to popular sovereignty.

These beliefs have informed my politics, and inevitably my scholarship, since my student days. My interest in the work of Robert Michels, and my first writings as a student about the institutionalized opposition system within the International Typographical Union, which culminated in a book, *Union Democracy*, were dictated by these concerns. As I have frequently stated, I have *never* believed that such a thing as "value-free" scholarship occurs in social science, and certainly not in as highly controversial an area as this one. Each of my earlier books, in fact, contains an introduction or preface in which I seek to give the reader some sense of my own values as they relate to the subject treated in the book, so that the reader may consider these in evaluating the conclusions of the work. Like Max Weber, whose views on these matters are frequently misinterpreted, I believe that there is no such thing as an "ethically neutral" approach. These issues are discussed in some detail in Chapter 6.

And finally, I urge on the impassioned reader, whether supporter or opponent of student activism, that the method of the dialogue, of reasoned discussion and sharp controversy, is necessary both for the advancement of knowledge and for the body politic. Force may end an argument; it can never win it. No one who believes that truth is on his side can honestly object to scholarly investigation, even of himself, his motives, and his actions. And no argument is won by *ad hominem* or guilt-by-association tactics. To accuse a man of being a communist, a fascist, or a tool of the establishment has no bearing on the validity of his statements. It is, of course, quite legitimate to seek to demonstrate that a given course of action or public advocacy will serve the interests of a certain group, or that the methods employed may lead to a result quite contradictory to that advocated by those employing them. But such an argument must be an effort at tracing a logical chain of thought. To state such simple truisms may seem insulting to the reader. Yet it is necessary to make them in this era of heated intellectual controversy, since men on all sides of current issues often forget them.

Rebellion in the University

1

Sources of Student Activism

Any effort to interpret the changing political behavior of American students in recent years is subject to the difficulty that it is dealing with a local aspect of a worldwide phenomenon.[1] Although the events which precipitated student activism vary from country to country, and the targets of student attack differ, there are more common themes than differences in the tactics and ideologies of the movements. Unlike the leftist youth and student movements of the 1930s which were linked to adult political parties, the dominant ones of the 1960s constituted a genuine youth rebellion, one which was almost as much levied against the major parties of the Left, and the Soviet Union, as it was against the moderates and conservatives. The lack of involvement in adult politics gave free rein to the propensity of youth to adhere to absolute principles, to engage in expressive rather than instrumental politics. Relatively unconcerned with the long-term consequences of their actions, the New Left student movements appeared ready to attack all existing structures, including the university, and to use tactics which alienated the majority, in order to make manifest their contempt, their total rejection of the intolerable world created by their elders. This rejection of the ethic of "responsibility" has characterized student groups in Japan, France, Germany, the United States and many other countries.

Most recently, however, this situation has changed somewhat. The American New Left turned during 1969 to an endorsement of Marxism-Leninism.[2] The currently dominant wing of the Students for a Democratic Society (SDS), the Worker-Student Alliance, is in fact the student movement of the Maoist Progressive Labor party. The Young Socialist Alliance, affiliated to the Trotskyist Socialist Workers party, has also achieved an important position within the radical movement, particularly through its major role in the formation of the New Mobilization Committee Against the Vietnam War. Even the old Communist party has begun to regain a position within the student left. And the emergence in strength of the various communist parties within the left-wing student movement has ironically made for a more responsible, less violent and adventuristic, movement. Each of these parties, desirous of winning adult noncampus support, has opposed aggressive confrontationist tactics which antagonize those outside of the movement. Only the so-called Weatherman faction of SDS, which remains unattached to an adult party, continues to advocate confrontationist tactics as a major activity of the student radicals.

The beginning of a new decade has resulted in the usual efforts to predict the future of campus-based activism. Since no one anticipated that the sixties would be characterized by widespread protest, there is no good reason to assume that more recent efforts at prognostication will be more accurate. In any case, these tend to be sharply contradictory. Some fear or hope that the era of unrest and confrontation politics will continue; others venture the conviction that the seventies will produce a new stage in the political cycle, one that sees a return to more scholarly pursuits. The record of the 1969–70 school year would support the first assumption; that of 1970–71 would appear to validate the conclusions of the second.

Certainly those bold enough to proclaim the "end of the

student revolution" during the final year of the sixties had their conclusions severely challenged by events.[3] In spite of extensive effort to "cool" or "repress" campus unrest, the early winter months of 1970 witnessed an increase in the protest wave. The Urban Research Corporation, which has been monitoring student demonstrations, reported more "major incidents" between mid-January and March 23, 1970, than had occurred in a corresponding period of 1969. Reports gathered for the President's Commission on Campus Unrest indicated that there were many more "disruptive" demonstrations in 1969–70, *before* the Cambodian incursion, than in the two previous academic years.[4] The Cambodian events and the killings at Kent State and Jackson State resulted in the first national student strike of long duration.[5] The data from opinion polls, discussed later, indicated that close to half the undergraduate campus population was involved.

Many college administrators and political activists were convinced that the fall semester would witness a continuation of massive political involvement of May and June. Instead, the campuses of the United States probably were less politically involved during 1970–71 than at any time since the beginning of the Vietnam war. Most of the journalistic articles written during this year have been devoted to describing and explaining the reasons for the seeming depolitization of the college community. There were few major demonstrations linked to any given campus. A Harris poll of a national sample of students taken in November 1970, reported that only 7 percent identified their politics as "radical," a drop from the 11 percent who did so during the spring protest wave, a pattern reflected in other surveys. This decline in support for radical politics was the first such reported since 1965.

As the American educational system enters the 1970s, it is clear that two characteristics are present which differ largely from the beginning of the 1960s. There is much less respect for the authority of heads of institutions, whether public, private, or educational; and the large, passive majority of students are much more liberal in their social, economic, and political values. Nevertheless, the bulk of politically active students support "liberal" political activities which basically accept the premises of the American political system. Thus the major student activities of recent years involved participation in the nomination campaigns of Robert Kennedy and Eugene McCarthy, in the 1969 antiwar Moratorium, and in the 1970 strikes — all led by youth still committed to electoral efforts. It would appear that the dominant form of student activism in the 1970s will involve efforts to build reformist political tendencies and pressure group movements, that the resort to civil disobedience which characterized much of the sixties will be less in evidence. This prediction, of course, may go completely awry should American participation in the Vietnam war continue at a high level. As in the case of earlier protest and radical movements, the extent to which such groups accommodate to the rules of the game of a democratic political system will depend on how responsive the system seems to be, or as the radicals would put it, how successful it is in co-opting protest. Co-optation and responsiveness are two words often used to describe the same process. The more responsive the system, the more moderate the leftist and trade-union groups have become in the past; a similar reaction may be anticipated from the current "out" groups, the antiwar students and the black militants.

This prediction, of course, applies largely to the mass of politically concerned students whose political interests have been activated by the major issues of the sixties — racism and war — or who have been drawn into the "counterculture" of youth which has sought to deemphasize materialist goals. Many of them, like Sam Brown, the Harvard Divinity School student who organized the movement which resulted in the McCarthy presidential campaign in 1968, and who also founded the antiwar Moratorium movement which precipitated large demonstrations in the fall of 1969, have concluded that the undifferentiated anti-system attacks of extremist student groups that have gone outside of the regular pressure group and campaign tactics of American politics have been counterproductive. Such efforts have actually reduced rather than increased the efficacy of the antiwar movement in accomplishing its objective of ending the war. In a long analysis to this effect, Brown quotes the statements made by the foreign minister of the Provisional Government of South Vietnam (the Vietcong) , Madame Nguyen Thi Binh. She told a visiting delegation of antiwar leaders from the United States that many American student radicals appeared to be "reluctant to touch political power" and help end the war.[6] By their aggressive tactics and personal life-styles, they have antagonized many older Americans who have been ready to support efforts to force the government to change its war policies.

But while the large majority show signs of returning to ends-oriented politics as distinct from involvement in expressive forms of salvation-oriented styles of life, a small, almost infinitesimal minority has adopted terroristic tactics in frustration against failure to gain any effective base of support either on or off campus. The Weatherman faction is perhaps the best known of a variety of such groups which are prepared to engage in terrorism, assassination, bombing, arson, and kidnapping. Since a few hundred determined terrorists can literally tie up a nation, the changes in the mood of the student population will not serve to moderate the ultramilitant groups. If anything, greater moderation by the mainstream activists may only inflame the terrorists. And the danger exists that such terrorism will give rise to counterterrorism, to the use of repressive tactics by the police and other authorities. A struggle to wipe out urban guerrillas who base themselves in campus communities could, of course, upset the trends pressing the American university to reject confrontation tactics.

The Change from the Fifties

To understand the reasons why the relatively passive postwar generation was replaced by one which contains an activist minority of the "enraged," it is important to note the extent to which some of the conditions that dampened ideological controversy

among intellectuals during the forties and fifties changed in
the sixties. Essentially, the politics of the two earlier decades were
dominated first by the Second World War and then by the cold
war. Given a high degree of support among liberal intellectuals
concerning these events, many who were deeply critical of various
domestic institutions and practices found themselves defending
the fundamental character of their societies as moral and decent
against the totalitarian critics. For a brief period, historically
speaking, Western democratic intellectuals found themselves engaging in actions which belied their role as critics. This period
was broken by changes within Communist society, as well as
increasing awareness of the social conditions existing in the
underdeveloped third world. The breakdown of monolithic
communism, the rise of liberal opposition tendencies in various
Eastern countries, the intensity of the Sino-Soviet split, all served
to undermine the conviction that all men of goodwill and all
non-Communist nations must unite to fight totalitarian expansion. In a real sense, as far as many intellectuals were concerned,
the cold war came to an end.[7]

This change had considerable impact on those members of the
older generation who had remained liberal critics, but had kept
quiet either because they agreed with the assumptions justifying
unity against the Communist threat, or because they feared social
or political sanctions from the supporters of anticommunism.
Many of them had been active when younger in various radical
movements, and though publicly quiescent had continued their
criticisms within private circles. As a group, they were concentrated among college-educated professionals and intellectuals,
including, particularly, university faculties. Jews had been relatively heavily involved in radical activities in the 1930s and 1940s,
a phenomenon which stemmed from continuity with the political
values brought over from the ghettoes of Eastern Europe, from
experience with domestic anti-Semitism which was particularly
strong in the United States until the end of World War II, and
from an identification of Nazism with conservatism and militant
anticommunism.[8] As ideological anticommunism lost strength,

some former radicals and left-liberals returned in some measure to their earlier beliefs. More significant, however, was the emergence among younger intellectuals and students of widespread social criticism, sentiments which were often encouraged by their "liberated" elders. The new generations of liberals who knew not Hitler and Stalin, the 1948 Czech coup or the Hungarian revolution from firsthand experience, found little reason to restrain applying their moral beliefs to politics.

This shift in ideological climate, as well as the rather rapid escalation of protest from words to action, was facilitated by the struggle for Negro rights which emerged in the years following the Supreme Court's school desegregation decision of 1954. This was the perfect issue around which to create a new activist movement, since it engaged the principal aspect of American society, in which the system engaged in actions which were at sharp variance with its manifest creed of equality and democracy. Most Americans, and the university system in toto, recognized that Negro inequality is evil, and in principle approved all actions designed to reduce or eliminate it. Hence race was the easiest issue around which the new political criticism could mobilize. To organize to fight segregation, particularly in the South, was not a radical act. Yet the struggle contributed greatly to radicalizing sections of the young. In this situation, the conservative or traditionalist forces introduced the tactics of civil disobedience, and even of violence; the Southern segregationists refused to accept the law as laid down by the Supreme Court and Congress, and taught the advocates of civil rights, both the black community and the white students, that the regular peaceful methods of democracy would not work. The confrontationist tactics of civil disobedience, which first emerged in the South, were then diffused by the American student movement to other parts of the country and the world, and to other issues both inside and outside of the university.

The aggressive tactics of the civil rights movement were successful, judged by the criteria of actions taken by different agencies of government to outlaw discrimination, and to foster

economic and educational improvements. Whatever the pro-
found limitations of these, the fact remains that more has been
attempted by government to improve the situation of the black
in recent years than in all the preceding years since Reconstruc-
tion. Many of these actions, particularly by the Administration,
Congress and local agencies, can be credited as responses to
political militancy or the fear of ghetto riots. But though these
efforts attest to the value of political action, they have not resulted in any major *visible* change in the position of the bulk of
the Negroes. (Statistical gains are often invisible to all not
directly involved.) They remain preponderantly poor, segregated
and uneducated, securing the leavings of the labor market. To
each group of civil-rights-concerned youth who have come to
political consciousness during this period, the gap between what
ought to be and what actually exists appears to have increased
rather than decreased. They take for granted the existing structure, including the changes which had been made, and react with
outrage against the continued sources of black deprivation.
Older liberals, on the other hand, have often reacted with
pleasure at the considerable progress that has been made within
the past few years. Thus an inevitable age-related split has
occurred.

This division between the generations has been particularly
acute within the Negro community. To younger blacks, the gains
made since the 1950s appear empty, in face of the existing
pattern of Negro social and economic inferiority. And on the
major campuses of the nation, the growing minority of black
students have found themselves in a totally white-dominated
world, facing few, if any, black faculty, and a white student body
whose liberal and radical wing turned increasingly after 1964
from involvement in civil rights protest to activity directed
against the Vietnam war. The concern with black power, with
Negro control over their own communities, and particularly civil
rights organizations, has won growing support among black
college students. Most recently, these students have played a
major role in confronting university administrations with de-

mands for more black students and faculty, and for changes in the curriculum.[9] Black students have been among the major forces initiating sit-ins at schools as diverse and separated as Cornell University, San Francisco State College, Columbia University, Boston University, Northwestern University and many predominantly Negro institutions as well.

The issue of the acceptable pace of reform also has been affected by events abroad, particularly in Cuba and Vietnam. The triumph of the Castro movement, an event dominated by young men, produced an example of a revolution seemingly uncontaminated by Stalinism. Cuban events helped to generate the sense that revolution was both possible and desirable as a way to eliminate social evils. Again generational differences divided the liberal-left communities. The older ones had learned from experience that revolutions could lead to totalitarianism, to new intense forms of exploitation and to cynical betrayals of the popular will. To many youth, raising such matters seemed only to justify inaction against the intolerable aspects of the status quo.

The spread of opposition to the Vietnam war has, of course, become the dominant political issue affecting student activism. To the older generation, including initially most liberals, Vietnam was but the most recent episode in a two-decade-long struggle against Communist imperialist expansion. To the new generations of the children of liberals and former radicals, Vietnam became defined in terms which placed American actions at odds with certain basic American beliefs, those of antiimperialism, and of the right of self-determination of politically weak peoples. Given the existence of a polycentric divided Communism, it simply did not make sense to perceive Vietnamese Communism as an extension of Russian or Chinese power. The very failure of the powerful United States to quickly defeat its small poor Vietnamese opposition has been evidence of the oppressive character of the war, of its being a war in which a foreign power seeks to impose its will by force over another people. The very values which led Americans to be suspicious of, and opposed to, the British, French and Dutch empires, which were called into play to justify World War I and II, and the Korean War, have now been turned against the United States.

To comprehend the reasons for the special confrontationist character of the student antiwar movement, it is necessary to recognize the direct link between it and the tactical lessons learned from the civil rights movement. Sam Brown put it well:

> In the early sixties, young people learned that voting and precinct meetings were not the only effective forms of political activity, that extralegal demonstrations worked in the face of a moral horror, and that American leaders often displayed both cowardice and hypocrisy in race relations. The civil rights movement, with all its implications about American politics, was almost a necessary [prior] condition for antiwar activism on the campus.[10]

It was also important to understand that the passion unleashed by the antiwar movement is strongly related to basic aspects of the American value system. To decry wars, to refuse to go, is at least as American as apple pie. Sol Tax, of the University of Chicago, who has attempted to compare the extent of antiwar activity throughout American history, concluded that the Vietnam war is only our fourth least popular military conflict with a foreign enemy since the Revolutionary War, up to the point negotiations to end it began.[11]

The War of 1812 was intensely unpopular among the merchants and other strata; some New England states threatened to secede on the issue.[12] A vigorous peace movement emerged after the war, whose success among students "was evidenced by the formation of peace societies at Amherst, Dartmouth, and Oberlin and less organized student activities at Harvard, Union, Knox and other colleges".[13] Abraham Lincoln and many Whigs denounced the Mexican War. The abolitionists regarded it as an immoral conflict fought to extend the domain of slavery, and innumerable Catholics objected to fighting a Catholic country. Indeed, the Mexican army was able to form units composed of American deserters.[14] By paying $300, men could and did buy themselves out of the Civil War, which, ironically, since Karl Marx enthusiastically supported it, was the only war regarded popularly as "a rich man's war and a poor man's fight." The antidraft riots of 1863 were the bloodiest of our history.[15] Professors and other intellectuals were vilified in the press and pulpit as traitors for their opposition to the Spanish-American War. Oliver Wendell Holmes expressed his disgust at the "self-righteous" antiimperialist and antiwar talk "which has prevailed to some extent at Harvard College and elsewhere."[16]

In August 1917, the New York *Herald* reported that "in New York City ninety out of the first hundred draftees claimed exemption." The War Department listed 337,649 draft evaders in World War I. The antiwar Socialist party secured its largest vote in history in many cities in the 1917 municipal elections.[17] Our entry into World War II was strongly opposed by an extensive mass movement. Had the United States entered World War II in any way other than through having been attacked, it is clear that a large segment of the country would have continued its opposition to the war after Congress declared it. Opinion surveys taken during the Korean War reported significant majority opposition to it among the population and among college students within two years of its beginning.[18]

The same Protestant propensity for moralistic crusades which has been expressed in various efforts to reform the rest of the world by war also underlies the endeavor of numerous Americans to resist each war as immoral. For many Americans, wars must be moral or immoral; one must do God's work in supporting or opposing them. The United States is the only country in which the majority of the citizens have adhered to what the British called the "dissenting" or "nonconformist" denominations, rather than to groups that are or once were state churches. The values of moralistic dissenters, mainly the Baptists and Methodists, have deeply informed our political history, in terms of a propensity for domestic and international crusades against satanic enemies.[19]

The Sources of Student Unrest: Motivating Factors

A general analysis of the changing political climate as it has encouraged student dissatisfaction, of course, does not explain why students *qua* students have played such an important role in stimulating protest. Here it must be noted that students have almost invariably been more responsive to political trends, to changes in mood, to opportunities for social change, than any other group in the population, except possibly intellectuals. As a result students have played a major role in stimulating unrest and fostering change in many countries. The special role of students has been particularly noted in the revolutions of 1848; in the Russian revolutionary movement, which was largely a student one until 1905; in the various Chinese movements during the first half of the twentieth century; in the different fascist movements in Italy, Germany and Spain before the fascists took power; in a host of colonial and underdeveloped states; and in various communist countries since 1956.[20]

Historically then, one would expect a sharp increase in student activism whenever events call accepted political and social values into question, in times particularly where policy failures seem to question the adequacy of social, economic and political arrangements and institutions. Although it may be argued that student activism is the result rather than the cause of social discontent, it is important to recognize that once activated, student groups have played a major role in mobilizing public opinion behind the causes and ideologies fostered by them. Social unrest causes student unrest, but once they start expressing their disquiet, students and intellectuals have been in many ways the vanguard of political change.

Awareness of the important role of students has led to efforts to detail those aspects of the situation of students generally, as well as in specific times and places, which press them to act politically.

The factors to which attention has been called in the growing literature on the subject may be differentiated between those which *motivate* students to action and those which *facilitate* their participation.

Perhaps the most general hypothesis which has been repeatedly advanced to account for youth protest suggests that it is a result of a process set in motion by rapid rates of social change, by events which create a sharp discrepancy between the formative experiences of parental generations and those of a given generation of youth. Both laymen and experts on youth behavior have agreed with Kingsley Davis's proposition that "rapid social change . . . has crowded historical meaning into the family time-span, has thereby given the offspring a different social content from that which the parent acquired, and consequently has added to the already existent intrinsic differences between parent and youth, a set of extrinsic ones which double the chance of alienation."[21] Or as Norman Birnbaum has put it more recently: "Generational dissidence and revolt are not a perpetual social problem, but assume acute forms only under conditions of extreme dissonance between generational experiences."[22]

As the discussion of the sources of repeated periods of American campus unrest presented in Chapters 4 and 5 should make clear, any wave of discontent can be and has been explained by the concurrent social changes which have upset the normal sources of youthful deference to older generations. While this approach may be valid in the sense that Kingsley Davis presented it, as accounting for greater youthful protest in "modern civilization, in contrast to most societies," it does not explain why certain epochs of rapid change lead to student activism, while others have not. An effort to do so derivative from Freudian analysis suggests that student movements occur whenever "the elder generation, through some presumable historical failure, has become de-authorized in the eyes of the young. . . . They arise wherever social and historical circumstances combine to cause a crisis in loss of generational confidence, which impels the young to resentment and uprising. . . . Rapid social change in and of

itself does not necessarily involve student unrest."[23] The emphasis on the causal role of "de-authorization," however, suffers from
the same methodological problem as the theory of "rapid social
change," in that its advocates seek to demonstrate the congruence of specific events with the presumed presence of the causal
process, and ignore circumstances in which the resultant event—
student unrest — did not take place, though rapid social change
or de-authorization did.

But though various historical sociological theories have been
advanced to account for greater or lesser periods of youth-based
unrest, other hypotheses have been suggested to explain why
youth generally, and students in particular, have shown a more
intense commitment to and greater involvement in movements
favoring radical social change and millenarian hopes, than their
elders. Much of the writings on the subject by psychologists have
been an insistence that youth still resemble Aristotle's portrait of
2,500 years ago that they do "things excessively and vehemently,"
that they "have exalted notions, because they have not yet been
humbled by life or learnt its necessary limitations."[24] Some
contemporary psychologists see a special contemporary disposi-
tion toward excessive anxiety and commitment in the strains of
adolescence, a period which in modern society with its prolonga-
tion of education and career preparation lasts into the twenties
for college students. During this stage of personality development, the individual is faced with the need to establish a
personal identity and select an adult role. The very openness,
freedom to choose alternative paths, characteristic of modern
society, faces the modern adolescent with a more ambiguous, ego-
threatening period than that which confronted his predecessors,
who were much more likely to have an identity and career
handed to them. The reaction of adolescents to this state of
prolonged uncertainty has been well described by Erik Erikson:

> Clearly the adolescent looks most fervently for men and ideas
> to have faith in, which also means men and ideas in whose service
> it would seem worth while to prove oneself trustworthy. . . .

The adolescent now looks for an opportunity to decide with free assent on one of the available or unavoidable avenues of duty and service, and at the same time is mortally afraid of being forced into activities in which he would feel exposed to ridicule or self-doubt.

. . . The adolescent's willingness to put his trust in those peers and leading, or misleading, elders who will give imaginative, if not illusory, scope to his aspirations is only too obvious.[25]

Gordon Allport in analyzing the changes in personality that accompany "maturing" suggested that youth are inherently less able to handle ambiguity, to accept their weaknesses as well as strengths, tend to overreact to stimuli, and lack a high capacity for tolerance.[26]

The sociological analysis has pointed to the same aspects as inherent in the fact that youth, and students in particular, are marginal men. They are in transition between having been dependent on their families for income, status and various forms of security and protection, and taking up their own roles in jobs and families. Studenthood is inherently a tension-creating period. The rapid growth in the number of students, almost eight million today as compared with one and a half million at the end of the 1930s, means both that the composition of the college population, as a group, has come from increasingly less privileged families, and that the value of a college degree for status placement has declined.

The university has become more meritocratic; it is how well you do, rather than who you are that counts. Hence, young people in a society in which education increasingly determines how well they start in the struggle for place, find themselves facing a highly competitive situation. The pressures to conform to the requirements of the education establishment begin for many middle-class and aspiring working-class youth in elementary school and intensify in high school. Hard work and ability at each level only serve to qualify the individual to enter an even more difficult competition at the next rung in the educational ladder. While some succeed, many must show up as mediocre or must rank low.

A number of radical theorists in different countries have suggested that the growing protest movement among students reflects the fact that the student role in capitalist society has essentially become one of an apprentice low-paid member of the new class of professional employees who are essentially workers denied the opportunity for true self-expression in their work role.[27] Society forces increasing numbers of youth to go to university to acquire the skills necessary for the highly specialized jobs which advanced industrial societies must fill. Hence, the student is increasingly a member of an exploited alienated sector of the powerless strata. His protests represent his increased awareness that he is coerced by the elite. As two Canadian Marxists put it:

> [S]tudying has lost any trace of the self-directed activity that it may once have been and has become a form of labor. . . . The ideological mystification of student alienation . . . is the idea that the student is investing in himself. Yet if he asks himself why he is in school, the student must honestly respond with answers that have little or nothing to do with his personal development and growth. . . .
>
> Student labor is alienated in the same sense that the product is for the future employer rather than for the student himself. Since the product is embodied in the skills of the student himself, he becomes alienated from himself. Thus modern education and technology, when continued in the capitalist mode, frequently gives rise to the individual psychological estrangement often confused with the conception of alienation.[28]

This type of analysis, though coming from different roots than that which stresses the adverse consequences on youth of the emphasis on meritocratic competition in the context of sharply increased numbers of students, joins hands with it in specific empirical deductions. Thus, the Belgian Marxist Ernest Mandel stresses the causal impact of the "university explosion," of the fact that a "new social grouping has emerged from the very vitals of capitalism," the millions of university students in America, western Europe, and Japan who are faced with the "insoluble contradictions" of capitalism; that it is impossible to integrate them into "the kinds of jobs they rightly expected when they started their university education."[29] Whether the expansion of the university system is credited to the inherent logic of increasingly egalitarian societies open to merit, whether socialist or capitalist, or is blamed on the need of a more developed industrial capitalism to press an ever growing proportion of youth to continue their education to facilitate the profit system, proponents of each assumption agree that modern university students are increasingly subject to anxieties derivative from the pressures on them to succeed.

There is a variety of evidence which suggests that these tensions affect the emotional stability of many teenagers and college youth, even the most able among them.[30] Such tensions may find varying outlets, of which a rejection of the competitive social system which forces them into a rat race for grades is one. Although such tensions have always been present in the student role, it should be noted that they have intensified considerably in the last decade and a half. The very expansion of the numbers going to universities throughout the world has made the situation worse, more competitive, than before.

The idealism of youth, to which reference is frequently made, is another stimulating factor which is an outgrowth of social expectations. Societies teach youth to adhere to the basic values of the system in absolute terms — equality, honesty, democracy, socialism, and the like. There is a maxim which exists in various forms in many countries: "He who is not a radical at twenty does not have a heart; he who still is one at forty does not have a head." This statement is usually interpreted as a conservative one, assuming radicalism is an unintelligent response to politics. But the first part of the maxim may be even more important than the second, for it denotes a social expectation that young people should be radicals, that the older generation believes that youthful people should be radicals, that the older generation agrees that youthful radicalism is praiseworthy behavior. It is the young conservative, the young "fogie," not the young radical who is out of step with social expectations.[31] The emphasis on youthful reformism is even greater in the United States than in many other countries, for American culture places a premium on being youthful and on the opinions of youth. It tends in general to glorify youth and to deprecate age.

Many American adults are reluctant, even when they consciously disagree sharply, to call students or youth to task. Rather they may encourage youth and students to take independent new positions, rather than emphasize the worth of experience. This ties in with the part of the American self-image which assumes that the United States is a progressive country, one which accepts reform and change.[32] And the truism that the youth will inherit the future is linked with the sense that the youth are the bearers of the progressive ideas which will dominate the future, that youth will contribute to the enduring struggle to make the American creed of equality more meaningful.

The real world, of course, necessarily deviates considerably from the ideal, and part of the process of maturing is to learn to operate in a world of conflicting values, roles, interests, and demands. Such compromises as this requires are viewed by youth as violations of basic morality. They have not established a sense of affinity with adult institutions; experience has not hardened them to imperfections. Their contact with the moral principles of society is abstract and pure; they are not yet tested by personal experience, by contact with reality. Students hang on to idealistic beliefs longer than others. They tend, as Max Weber suggested, to develop an ethic of "absolute ends" rather than of "responsibility."[33] They tend to be committed to ideals rather than institutions. Hence, those events which point up the gap between ideals and reality stimulate them to action.

Many observers of American behavior have pointed to the codification of egalitarian values in the American creed. Americans are taught to believe "that all men are created equal," that they should be given equal opportunity to gain the good things of life, and that all are worthy of equal respect in interpersonal relations. This stress on equality presumably creates an inherent tension with the reality of inequality of income, respect, and power, particularly when it is linked to as obvious a violation of the creed as racial inequality. Yet David Cohen has suggested that the heightened student discontent of recent years has been further stimulated by the fact that an important segment of society, those involved in education, communication, culture creating and diffusing, and the social welfare occupations — and the schools to which this segment of society sends its children — increasingly since World War II have favored an ethos which "resembles nothing so much as that utopia which Marx and subsequent generations of radical critics envisaged." This may be seen most clearly in the elite private schools which "stress spontaneity, creativeness, and a general freedom from rigid constraints in learning. . . . Schooling, in short, is justifiable only when it is playful. . . . This, then, is a situation in which all the tables have been turned: the only acceptable work is that which is play. . . ." And the values and practice of such schools which are "efforts to create utopian enclaves in the midst of capitalist society," enhance for the children of the affluent intelligentsia of America the gap between what is desirable and the need to conform to the class and work ethos of a competitive capitalist society.[34] A similar point has been made by Charles Hampden-Turner, who, in coming to this country from England, was "struck by the strength of developmental and humanist themes in American educational and child rearing philosophers, and the relative weakness of the same themes in commerce and politics. . . . It has long seemed to me only a matter of time before the developmental themes in American life confronted the repressive themes, and before those students nurtured in the better homes and schools came to regard the opportunities offered by business and government as an insult to their achieved levels of psychosocial development."[35]

The strain between the emphases on equality, play, and lack of repression, which characterize many of the private and suburban public schools of the intelligentsia, and the onerous requirements of bureaucratic industrial society, is brought to a head by the requirement that students compete for success through working hard, while remaining sociological adolescents in the university.[36] Their physical maturation which is not paralleled by increased power is another source of frustration for those reared in such families.

Although physiologically mature, and often above the age legally defined as adult, students are expected to refrain from full involvement in the adult world. The very nature of university education is seen as calling for a withdrawal by the institution from the mainstream of society into an ivory tower, free from the constraints of politics and religion. Although living in a society which stresses that adults should establish their own status based on their individual abilities and achievements, students are expected to maintain a status in limbo, or to remain dependent on their family status. Such a situation can be a source of bitterness, especially in a culture like the American, which places so much stress on individual achievement. Thus the student, in addition to the opportunity to acquire an education, also demands the chance both to experiment with adult roles, and to exhibit his ability to achieve a position on his own.[37]

Dependency is, of course, built into the very essence of the university system. Students are dependent, as to the chances of their future placement, on their standing with the faculty. The faculty has the power of certification through its control over grades. This gives them the right to influence what students read, and how they spend much of their time. The American university, in particular, with its stress on frequent examinations and faculty judgments, emphasizes this dependent relationship even more than does the university in most other countries. Hence, the student who leaves home to attend a university finds that he has actually entered a highly controlled situation, while many aspects of the society urge him to become independent.

The constraints imposed on students living in university dormitories have proved to be particularly onerous. By acting in

loco parentis, universities in America took on the role of con-
straining agent over the social life of individuals who increasingly have claimed the right to be autonomous. And in a world
in which eighteen-year olds are eligible for the draft, the effort of
the university to maintain these controls has been inevitably
doomed to failure. With the decline in average age at which
Americans reach sexual maturity from a physical point of view,
and the accompanying changes in the accepted norms concerning
sexual relations, the university has placed itself in the impossible
position of seeking to enforce a status of social dependency —
which even middle-class parents have found difficult to maintain.

The Youth Culture as Motivating Force

It may be argued, however, that student activism in particular,
is among other things, an expression of the need for a distinct
youth culture.[38] The student stratum, as such, tends to create a
whole array of age-group symbols, which sets it apart from others
in society, and from adults in particular. These include unique
patterns of personal appearance, peculiar modes of communication, and special styles of life (relatively low standard of living,
but major expenditures on music or travel, or use of drugs as
compared with adults' consumption of liquor). In their desire to
demonstrate their rejection of the adult world, youth rebels have
repeatedly engaged in forms of expressive behavior which have
been noteworthy for their similarity. Some of those in the American past are presented in Chapters 4 and 5, but it should be
noted that descriptions of such activities in France, Russia, and
Germany in the nineteenth century and the pre–World War I
period read like contemporary accounts of the scene at Telegraph Avenue, Berkeley, or Harvard Square. A report on the
behavior of the young Bohemians in the left bank of Paris, on
the same spot as the May 1968 riots, clearly has this effect.

> [They] held radical-sounding, erratic political ideas which
> somehow were never followed by practical action. According to

Balzac they could be recognized by their off-center cravats, greasy
coats, long beards, and dirty fingernails. The Bohemians of the
1830s and 1840s were young, actually and ideologically; they
claimed that youth itself was the collective expression of genius.
It is exaggerating very little to say that Bohemians hoped to be
seen as a band of intellectual raiders and freebooters, who routed
convention everywhere and kept all contented souls in a state of
dazzled alarm . . . In all accounts of the Bohemia of the
Orleanist years, the first impressions have always to do with its
ingenious techniques of social outrage. When Thackeray first came
on the Paris Bohemia, he was astonished enough to make a careful record of their appearance — their ringlets, straight locks,
toupees, English, Greek and Spanish nets, and the variety of their
beards and jackets.[39]

Similar modes of behavior occurred in czarist Russia:

Among the students of the universities and the higher technical
schools [there appeared] . . . a new and striking original type —
young men and women in slovenly attire, who called in question
and ridiculed the generally received convictions and respectable
conventions of social life, and who talked of reorganizing society
. . . They reversed the traditional order of things even in trivial
matters of external appearance, the males allowing the hair to
grow long and the female adepts cutting it short, and adding
sometimes the additional badge of blue spectacles. Their appearance, manners and conversation were apt to shock ordinary
people, but to this they were profoundly indifferent, for they had
raised themselves above the level of so-called public opinion,
despised Philistine respectability, and rather liked to scandalize
people still under the influence of what they considered
antiquated prejudices. . . .[40]

The activities of the pre–World War I German youth movement have been invidiously described in similar terms:

Turbulent gangs of untidy boys and girls roamed the country.
. . . In bombastic words they announced the gospel of a golden
age. All preceding generations, they emphasized, were simply
idiotic; their incapacity has converted the earth into a hell. . . .

The inflated verbiage of these adolescents was only a poor disguise for their lack of any ideas and of any definite program. They had nothing to say but this: We are young and therefore chosen; we are ingenious because we are young; we are the carriers of the future; we are the deadly foes of the rotten bourgeois and Philistines.[41]

The effort to formulate a specific youth culture which rejected that of the adult world has also repeatedly taken the form of student political groups and ideologies which have little to do with those of the adult political world, often including the revolutionary parties. As the British sociologist Donald MacRae has generalized in his analysis of these cultures:

Adolescent rebellion is older than the universities of the middle ages. It has constantly presented a pattern of temporary bohemianism and a defined and legitimated licence of behavior. Since 1789, it has also involved experiment with radical politics — left and right, nationalist and internationalist. . . .[42]

And these experiments, as S. N. Eisenstadt has indicated, have often taken the form of "various youth and student movements . . . which . . . aim to reform the society in terms of distinct, specific youth values."[43]

The pure youth and student movements have tended toward an ahistorical rejection of a detailed, worked-out, means-ends related form of radical politics. Rather, as one description of Martin Luther's student followers reports, there is "an inclination to primitivism among students. Some of them carried their opposition to Aristotle and scholasticism to the point of rejecting all scholarship, and advocated the innocent simplicity of the Apostles."[44] In the nineteenth century, the chief Marxist leaders, including Karl Marx and Friedrich Engels, themselves, though recognizing that students had, for example, played a major role in all the French revolutions, condemned as irresponsible the expressive politics and personal styles of revolutionary students.[45] The desire of youth to make the revolution at once, without consideration of realistic possibilities, was seen by them and their

successors as "putschism" or "left-wing adventurism," behavior
which they related to the "bourgeois" origins and positions and
aspirations of the radical students, as well as to their youth and
inexperience. Marx and Engels denounced various groups of left-
wing youth for their antiintellectual attitudes and behavior, that
is, an unwillingness to acknowledge that they could learn from
any segment of the adult world. In 1870, Engels wrote to Marx in
harsh terms concerning a rumor that large numbers of Russian
students were planning to emigrate in great numbers to Western
Europe to join the revolutionary movement there. "If there is
anything which might ruin the Western European movement,
then it would be this import of 40,000 more or less educated,
ambitious hungry Russian nihilists."[46] Some indication of what
Engels feared may be seen in a description of the Russian student
movement of that day.

> With the impulsiveness of youth and the recklessness of inex-
> perience, the students went . . . much further than their elders.
> . . . they wanted an immediate, thoroughgoing transformation
> of the existing order of things according to the most advanced
> socialistic principles, and in their youthful, reckless impatience
> they determined to undertake the work themselves.
> . . . some of the Nihilists maintained that things were not yet
> ripe for a rising of the masses, that the pacific propaganda must
> be continued for a considerable time, and that before attempting
> to overthrow the existing social organization some idea should be
> formed as to the order of things which should take its place. The
> majority, however, were too impatient for action to listen to such
> counsels of prudence, and when they encountered opposition on
> the part of the government they urged the necessity of retaliating
> by acts of terrorism. In a brochure issued in 1874 one of the most
> influential leaders (Tkatchev) explained that it was a mistake to
> attach great importance to questions of future social organization
> . . . [T]he reconstruction of society on the *tabula rasa* might
> be left, it was thought, to the spontaneous action of natural
> forces.[47]

The German students were largely supporters of different
forms of right-wing nationalism from the mid-nineteenth century

through their early (1931) majority support in student council elections for the Nazis. The Nazis sought to build on the history of pure antisystem, antiadult youth movements in Germany by alluding to themselves as a youth movement.[48] And the descriptions of the expressive youth culture of the German rightist students closely resemble those of the Russian leftists. Thus the German sociologist, Max Weber, writing about his fellow students in 1885, when he was twenty-one, noted their nationalist and anti-Semitic enthusiasms, and stated that "the most incredible part of the matter is the fantastic ignorance of my age mates about the history of this century. Those from the metropolis are a bit more knowledgeable than the others. But for the rest, there is *tabula rasa.* . . . In their heads domestic politics began less than a decade ago."[49]

Historians of youth movements have noted the similarities in expressive style, in romanticism, in idealism, in commitment to violent actions, which have occurred among groups which have varied considerably in their social and political values. Walter Laqueur, the foremost student of the pre–World War I German movement, has emphasized these common elements:

> The idealism, spirit of sacrifice, devotion to one's people, and revolutionary fervor that marked the *Burschenschaft* [early nineteenth century nationalistic, anti-Semitic, terrorist student groups] have been an inherent part of all youth movements over the last hundred years. It is a mistake to assume the fascist youth movements were an exception to this rule. . . . To be sure, they preached a doctrine of violence, but as Mussolini said, "There is a violence that liberates, and there is a violence that enslaves; there is moral violence and stupid, immoral violence." (Compare Marcuse: "In terms of historical function, there is a difference between revolutionary and reactionary violence, between violence practiced by the oppressed and the oppressors.") . . . .
>
> Youth movements have never been out for personal gain. Whoever describes a youth movement as idealistic only states the obvious. What motivates youth groups is different from what motivates an association for the protection of the interests of small shopkeepers. The fascist experience has shown the immense

potential which inheres in every youth movement can be exploited in the most disastrous way. . . .

Most of the basic beliefs and even the outward fashions of the present world youth movements can be traced back to the period in Europe just before and after the First World War. The German *Neue Schar* of 1919 were the original hippies: long-haired, sandaled, unwashed, they castigated urban civilization, read Hermann Hesse and Indian philosophy, practiced free love, and distributed in their meetings thousands of asters and chrysanthemums. They danced, sang to the music of the guitar, and attended lectures on the "Revolution of the Soul." The modern happening was born in 1910 in Trieste, Parma, Milan, and other Italian cities where the Futurists arranged public meetings to recite their poems, read their manifestos, and exhibit their ultra-modern paintings. No one over thirty, they demanded, should in future be active in politics. . . . The idea of a specific youth culture was first developed in 1913–14 by the German educator Gustav Wyneken. . . .

For the historian of ideas, the back issues of the periodicals of the youth movements, turned yellow with age, make fascinating reading. . . . It is indeed uncanny how despite all the historical differences, the German movement preempted so many of the issues agitating the American movement of today, as well as its literary fashions.[50]

In 1920, Lenin, like Engels before him, expressed serious concern over the expressive behavior of those involved in the radical youth culture.

> The little yellow-beaked birds who have just broken from the egg of bourgeois ideas are always frightfully clever. . . . The youth movement . . . is attacked with the disease of modernity in its attitude towards sexual questions. . . . [T]he so-called "new sexual life" of the youth . . . often seems to me to be . . . an extension of bourgeois brothels. . . . Of course, [the sexual need like] thirst must be satisfied. But will the normal man in normal circumstances lie down in the gutter and drink out of a puddle, or out of a glass with a rim greasy from many lips? . . .
>
> Young people, particularly need the joy and force of life.

Healthy sport, swimming, racing, walking, bodily exercises of every kind, and many-sided intellectual interests. . . . That will give young people more than eternal theories and discussions about sexual problems and the so-called "living to the full." . . .

The revolution . . . cannot tolerate orgiastic conditions. . . . Dissoluteness . . . is bourgeois, is a phenomenon of decay. The proletariat . . . doesn't need intoxication as a narcotic or stimulus. Intoxication as little by sexual exaggeration as by alcohol. . . . I am deeply concerned about the future of our youth.[51]

Most recently, various commentaries on contemporary American student unrest, such as those of John Seeley and Theodore Roszak, which are summarized and accepted in the 1970 *Report of the President's Commission on Campus Unrest,* emphasize in their causal analysis "the formation of a new youth culture that defines itself through a passionate attachment to principle and an opposition to the larger society. At the center of this culture is a romantic celebration of human life, of the unencumbered individual, of the senses, and of nature."[52]

The "counterculture" of youth need not take a political form. Indeed, much of the pre–World War I German youth revolt, as well as lesser similar manifestations in the United States, were not political. The youth culture has often evidenced itself in expressions of cultural renunciation of predominant adult values and behavior with respect to morality, dress, work orientations, achievement norms and the like. Sometimes, it has taken the form of youth-based new varieties of religious expression. Various forms of "deviance" from the point of view of the adult world have served as anchorage points to bring large numbers of young people together in a solidaristic relationship. As Walter Laqueur has noted: "Whether a certain movement became political or unpolitical, whether it opted for the Left or the Right, depended on the historical context: it hardly needs to be explained in detail why youth movements were preponderantly right-wing after the First World War, while more recently most have tended to the left. But beyond the particular political

orientation there are underlying motives which have remained
remarkably consistent throughout."

> Youth movements have always been extreme, emotional,
> enthusiastic; they have never been moderate or rational. . . .
> Underlying their beliefs has always been a common anti-capital-
> ist, anti-bourgeois denominator, a conviction that the established
> order is corrupt to the bones and beyond redemption by par-
> liamentary means of reform. The ideologies of democracy and
> liberalism have always been seen as an irretrievable part of the
> whole rotten system; all politicians, of course, are crooks. Equally
> common to all youth groups is a profound pessimism about the
> future of present-day culture and an assumption that traditional
> enlightened concepts like tolerance are out of date. The older
> generation has landed the world in a mess, and a radical new
> beginning, a revolution, is needed. Youth movements have never
> been willing to accept the lessons of the past; each generation is
> always regarded as the first (and the last) in history. And the
> young have always found admiring adults to confirm them in
> their beliefs.[53]

The University and Faculty as Sources of Unrest

In the modern developed world, particularly in the United
States, the conditions of university life make politics a particularly critical source of self-expression. Students are given ample
opportunity to discuss and study political matters. The university, itself, in spite of its emphasis on academic freedom and on
being nonpartisan, is increasingly involved in politics, as professors fulfill ever-growing roles as party activists, intellectual
commentators on political events, advisers, consultants, and researchers on policy-relevant matters. Many students are thus in
centers of great political significance, but have little or no share
in the political status of the university. If it is to express a sense
of separate identity, student politics as part of the student culture must be outside of and in opposition to that of most of the
adults.

Although the student protest is directed against much of the adult world, including the faculty, any analysis of the sources of student activism, per se, must recognize that student values and political concerns are often closely related to those of the faculty. Certainly in the United States, faculties have shown by their reaction to student protest, from the Berkeley events of 1964–65 to the demonstrations against the Cambodian incursion in May and June 1970, that large segments of the professoriate and student bodies stand closer to each other in political reactions than either do to the rest of the American body politic.[54]

Intellectuals, that is, those concerned with the creation of art, culture, literature, science, and knowledge, whether academics or not, are involved with creation and innovation and are ideally partisans of the abstract and the ideal. Their occupational activities require them to value new discoveries and ideas. Originality, departure from what is established and officially accepted, is a central value in the outlook of the modern intellectual. More generally, in the tradition of the intellectual classes of Western society, there are important currents of long duration and great intellectual value which have set the intellectuals against established authority. These include scientism, romanticism, revolutionary apocalypticism, and populism. These traditions largely form the characteristic outlook of the intellectuals outside universities. Universities have been institutions established by or supported by the authoritative center of society — political and ecclesiastical — and they have been integrated into the tasks of training young persons for careers connected with the central functions of society and culture. But they, too, by their stress on scientific discipline, on creativity, and on detachment from the idols of the marketplace, have nurtured a critical attitude. Especially in the social sciences has there been a tension between society's need to affirm the dominant systems of practices and belief and the intellectual's critical attitude toward all systems.

The American university increasingly has become a major occupational outlet for many of the brightest people who seek to be innovative and free of the ideological restrictions and materialistic commitments which they believe are inherent in the corporate and professional worlds. Once liberal faculty become overtly political, their influence has tended to be self-accelerating. Evidence drawn from a variety of surveys of student attitudes indicates that colleges have a liberalizing effect on young people, particularly in areas linked to universalistic principles, racial equality, internationalism, peace, class relationships, as well as in more personal beliefs such as religion and sexual behavior.[55] Samuel Stouffer pointed out over fifteen years ago that the conservatives who attack the universities for "corrupting" young people are right from their political and moral standpoints.

But if faculty help to create a climate of opinion which presses students to the left, ironically, at least some of the sources of student malaise stem from the fact that changes in the role of the faculty have contributed to making the situation of being a student less attractive than it once was. With increasing size and greater pressures on faculty to do research, publish, and take part in extramural activities, inherently one should expect to find poorer instruction, more faculty aloofness, and administrative indifference to students. The research-oriented faculty increasingly give a larger proportion of their limited teaching time to graduate students. These activities are, of course, not new; as noted later, students and administrators have complained about faculty neglect of teaching and of students since the last century. Yet the research-consulting culture clearly spread far beyond its earlier boundaries in the "golden" age of academe which began during World War II.[56]

The very increase in the importance of the university as a center of influence and power, and as the major accrediting institution of the society, has reduced the informal influence of students within the university. The higher estates of the university, administrators and faculty, however, have sought to maintain their traditional authority and prerogatives, while reducing their own "responsibility" for the quality of the personal and intellectual lives of their students. This development is not simply or even principally a function of the growth of the university; it reflects even more the increased "professionaliza-tion" of the faculty, the extent to which "teaching" as such has continued to decline as the main identification of the role of being a professor.[57]

The changes in the roles of the faculty, their increased involve-ment in a national prestige system, based on evaluations of their scholarly achievements or extramural activities, the sharp in-crease in their income, derivative in large part from the fact that many schools are in competition for those who have or promise to attain general reputations, and the concomitant decline in fac-ulty teaching obligations have not necessarily made for a "hap-pier" professoriate. Faculty, like students, are in an increasingly competitive situation, one in which men see themselves being judged as to their position in national and local pecking orders. With the depreciation of the teaching function as a local source of economic reward and status, many faculty become deeply dissatisfied and anxious. Ironically, the better universities and colleges, which are increasingly competitive with each other in efforts at stockpiling distinguished scholars, are more likely to encourage such feelings among both their older and younger faculty by invidiously rewarding, often in a very public fashion, those men who are most valuable in this race for institutional prestige. Such sentiments reinforce faculty propensities to oppose the administrations of these schools, as well as the dominant values and institutions of the large society. Hence, many distin-guished professors find solace in student militancy directed against the forces they hold responsible for their felt sense of status insecurity. The same faculty members who demand and secure lower teaching loads (especially after student revolts which further reduce the "bargaining strength" of the univer-sity) often tell their students that they are neglected and misused by the administration and trustees.

It may be argued that American students, as students, are subject to greater strains and fewer rewards than those of previ-ous generations, with the exception of the Depression generation. Although the demand for "student power," for increased influence by students over the decision-making process in the university, tends on the whole to be raised by the left-wing activist group, the receptivity which this demand secures in wider circles of students may reflect an increased sense of grievance, because the more distinguished universities in terms of scholarly quality of faculty and students demand more, yet give less in the form of personal relations (informal influence) among students, faculty and administration. Thus, as in the case of workers and employees in bureaucratized industry, a sort of syndicalism has been in the offing for many decades which seeks to regain symbolically for students as a group the influence which they think they have lost individually as a result of changes in the organization of universities. Subjectively, of course, students as the "inferior" class in power and status terms would appear to have always complained bitterly about "unfair" treatment from the faculty. This has been the substance of complaint and often violent protest literally for centuries in American colleges. As Lawrence Vesey argues, there is much in the professor-student relationship which produces "class" ideology and resentment, almost without regard to variation in objective condition.[58]

One analyst of student protest, the Berkeley sociologist David Matza, has suggested that the repeated appeal of populism, of "the belief in the creativity and in the superior worth of the ordinary people, of the uneducated and the unintellectual," which has appeared in various student movements from nineteenth century Russia to the contemporary American glorification of the poorest blacks, is in part, at least, a way of attacking the moral position of their teachers.

> Among students, the appeal of populism is not simply an outgrowth of traditional radical propensities. Just as the apocalyptic mentality has a special appeal to youth, so, too, does populism. Students have a special liking for populism because it is a vehicle for an effective attack on the professional authority and a way of defending against unflattering assessment of themselves. For the radical and the bohemian, too, a belief in populism allows

pol- activity ✓ job

students who perceive themselves as avant-garde to deflect the contrary judgments of academic elders.[59]

The unconceptualized sense of grievance with their situation, a sense which in many cases is often directed against the university, also may make many students, particularly those with a politically critical background, more receptive to political action directed against trends in the larger society. The two sources of activism thus reinforce one another; the more directly political uses campus discontent to create a set of issues around which to build a movement, while campus discontent may express itself in wider political issues. These are general aspects of student motivation to activism. There are many aspects in the situation of the group which *facilitate* mass activity, which make it easier to recruit for such action.

Facilitating Factors

Young people are more available for new political movements than adults. As new citizens, as people entering the political arena, they are less committed to existing ideologies, they have few or no explicit political commitments, they have no previous personal positions to defend, they are less identified with people and institutions which are responsible for the status quo. Inherently, they know less recent history than adults. For this current generation, as noted earlier, the key formative events in foreign policy terms have been the Vietnam war, and domestically, in the United States, heightened awareness of the oppressed position of the American Negroes.

Students are also more available because of the lesser commitments they have to their "occupational" role as compared to adults. Max Weber, many years ago, pointed out that political activity is to a considerable extent a function of the extent to which job requirements are *dispensable*. In his terms, those who could take time off from work without suffering economic consequences are much more likely to be active than those who have to punch a time clock.[60] Students (and professors) have perhaps the most dispensable job requirements of all. Students may drop out of school, may put off their studies for short or long periods, without paying a great price. They may often delay taking examinations. The numbers who dropped their books to take part in the McCarthy primary campaigns are a recent illustration of this.

Linked with this is the factor of "responsibility." As compared to other groups, students simply have fewer responsibilities in the form of commitments to families and jobs. Thus, the existence of punitive sanctions against extremist activism is less likely to affect students than those with greater responsibilities to others, or to a career ladder. Moreover, as noted earlier, students remain adolescents or juveniles sociologically, and they are often implicitly treated as such legally, particularly when they violate the law. In many societies, a number of the students involved in politically or otherwise motivated infractions are literally the children of the elite, a fact which serves to reduce the will to punish them. In addition, universities are generally run by liberal individuals who are not inclined to invoke severe sanctions against students. Students, as Daniel Cohn-Bendit has pointed out, are under less pressure to conform than other strata.[61]

Another factor which facilitates student political involvement is the physical situation of the university which makes it relatively easy to mobilize students who are disposed to act politically. The campus is the ideal place in which to find large numbers of people in a common situation. Many universities have over thirty thousand students concentrated in a small area. New ideas which arise as a response to a given issue may move readily among the students, and find their maximum base of support. Only a small percentage of these massive bodies can often make large demonstrations. Thus, from 1965 to 1967, although opinion polls indicated that the great majority of American students supported the Vietnam war — that antiwar sentiment within the group was no greater than in the population as a whole — the campus opposition was able to have a great impact because it could be mobilized. The antiwar student minority could and did man impressive antiwar demonstrations.

Although there can be little doubt that the current period of student unrest has had more impact on the body politic than any previous epoch in American history, the evidence is not conclusive, apart from the demonstrations of May and June 1970 against the Cambodian incursion, that a greater *percentage* of students have shown antagonism to the society or the university than in some earlier periods of unrest. The sheer magnitude of the educational establishment, the greater ease of communication across distances, and the presence of certain common issues, have made it possible to mobilize large-scale demonstrations. Beyond this, the introduction of the tactics of civil disobedience and confrontation, stemming in large part from the civil rights movement, has given protesters a weapon through which a small percentage of the student body can bring entire universities to their knees. And the inability of universities to handle such situations except by relying on outside force (with rare exceptions) often brought to the support of the demonstrators the majority of the campus population, both student and faculty, who were outraged by the violation of the historic norms of university autonomy, and by the sight of student-police clashes which almost never occurred without some blood being spilled.

The larger explanation for the rise of activism during the past half decade or so must lie primarily in political events: the emergence of the civil rights and Vietnam issues in a particular post-Stalinist political epoch. These gave to the more radically disposed students the issues; their social situation gave them the stimulus; and the campus situation furnished them with the means to build a movement.

Any effort, therefore, to understand the weight and impact of the activist groups must be placed within the context of an analysis of the opinions of the student population as a whole. Fortunately, a variety of surveys conducted between 1965 and 1971 permits this to be done. The next chapter reports on them.

2

Polls and Protest

Much of the discussion of the wave of protest which emerged in the late 1960s has presented it as a "youth revolt." It is important to recognize that the increasing opposition of American college students towards the war and the concomitant growth in radical-left sentiments among them does not represent an age-group phenomenon. There are other generation-units, to use Karl Mannheim's term, among American youth who have highly disparate sentiments. Idealism among a large segment of noncollege youth has been reflected heavily in a show of patriotic feelings, support for the war, and even disproportionate involvement in backing George Wallace's presidential candidacy in 1968.[1] Opinion surveys dealing with the relationship of age as such to opinion towards the Vietnam war indicate that from 1965 to 1971, those in the lowest adult age group, twenty-one to twenty-nine years old, were consistently *less likely* to oppose the war than their elders though the gap narrowed in recent years. In fact, those fifty and older were most likely to think participation in the war a mistake. This report, of course, includes both students and nonstudents, who are quite different in their views.

There is no question that young people turned against the war

TABLE 1

Percent in Different Age Groups Who Consider American Intervention
in the Vietnam War a Mistake 1965–1971

		PERCENT CONSIDERING THE VIETNAM WAR A MISTAKE		
NATIONWIDE GALLUP POLL RESULTS		21–29 YEARS	30–49 YEARS	50 YEARS AND OVER
1965:	August	14	22	29
1966:	March	21	23	30
	May	29	32	42
	September	37	28	40
	November	21	30	36
1967:	May	31	34	42
	July	32	37	50
	October	43	43	53
1968:	February	40	46	48
	March	46	47	52
	April	38	46	54
	August	48	48	61
	October	44	49	64
1969:	February	49	49	57
	October	58	54	63
1971:	May	59	60	63

Source: Hazel Erskine, "The Polls: Is War A Mistake?" *Public Opinion Quarterly* 34 (Spring 1970), p. 134; and Gallup Poll release, June 6, 1971.

as the conflict continued, but so did older ones. And those fifty and over remained the most antiwar age group through to 1971. This "is even more surprising in view of the propensity of older people not to express opinions. Those under thirty averaged only about 8 percent with no opinion on the question over the years, as compared with an average of 15 percent without opinions among the fifty-and-over. This leaves positive war backing among youth even stronger than the preceding table would indicate. . . ."[2] These conclusions are based on a review of the data collected by the Gallup Poll. Two senior researchers of the Survey Research Center of the University of Michigan report that the results of their national surveys point in the same direction. "This 'generation gap' that one would have expected wherein the young oppose the war and the old support it, simply failed to appear. . . ."[3]

Student Opinion on Vietnam

The many national inquiries of student opinion since campus activities secured national attention in the fall of 1964 have documented a gradual shift to the left in the thinking of the student population, constant increases in opposition to the war, and growing expressions of criticism of the content of teaching and the internal organization of the academic establishment. The results of these surveys have also shown the increased activism of the black students, their resentments, and the heightened sympathy for their goals among the large majority of whites.

The survey data permit comparisons with dominant attitudes among noncollege youth, and with the adult population. In general, the noncollege youth have been much more conservative on domestic, foreign policy, and cultural issues than the students. There is clearly a gap in opinions and behavior between the average reaction of college students and others, but the gap is *not* a generational one; rather it is between those on and off campus regardless of age. Faculty, who have also been surveyed in some detail, are clearly much more opposed than students to militant activism and campus politicization. Yet on substantive political policy issues, Vietnam, civil rights, domestic social policy, as a group, they are fairly close to their students. Both tend to espouse as their dominant political ideology what might be described as Kennedy-McCarthy liberalism, the program of the left-liberal antiwar wing of the Democratic party. Self-identified conservatives among the students are between 15 and 20 percent; among the faculty about a quarter. Left-wing radicals run to between five and ten percent; the faculty resembles the students in this respect (see Tables 5 and 6).

The noncollege population, on the other hand, has gradually moved in a more conservative direction over the past half-decade. Increasing numbers of them identify themselves as conservatives rather than liberals, so that by 1970 many more citizens described themselves as conservatives (52 percent), than as liberals (34 percent).[4] Noncollege youth, whether over or under twenty-one, have also differed consistently from the college students. On a number of issues, not only on Vietnam, the noncollege youth have been more conservative than their campus peers and their elders. Three surveys, taken within a few months of each other, of national samples of students, faculty, and the U.S. adult population as a whole, point up the considerable differences between opinion on and off the campuses of America (Table 6).

Although massive demonstrations against the Vietnam war began in 1965 in some large high-quality schools such as Berkeley (Vietnam Day), Ann Arbor (teach-ins on the war), and Madison, the survey data, as noted earlier, indicate that the majority of students supported the war until 1968. In 1965, for example, the Harris Survey reported that only 24 percent of those with opinions on the war favored negotiations and American withdrawal from Vietnam.[5] Samuel Lubell concluded in the spring of 1966 that "two thirds of the students interviewed continue to back our Vietnam policy which is about the same proportion of support one finds in the country as a whole."[6] Another national survey of students taken by the Gallup Poll in May and June 1966, indicated that 47 percent of college youth endorsed the way "Johnson is handling the situation in Vietnam," while 23 percent disagreed because they thought the U.S. should be more aggressive, and another 16 percent opposed the President's policies for being "indecisive" or "inconsistent."[7] A Gallup survey of student opinion on Vietnam taken a year later in 1967 "showed 49 percent of students in favor of a policy of escalation compared to 35 percent who wanted military activity to be reduced."[8] Not until the spring of 1968 did the proportion of students who thought that the United States had made a mistake in getting involved in Vietnam reach 50 percent.[9] At the time, 48 percent of the public, but only 38 percent of the entire twenty-one- to thirty-year-old age group, gave the same response, suggesting the existence of a rather large opinion gap on the war between college and noncollege youth. This difference has continued in succeeding years.

Lubell, who interviewed students through the 1967–68 school year, essentially agreed with the Gallup findings that that was the year in which the campus turned against the war. Lubell credited the shift to concern over the draft spurred on by the fact that "Congress had changed the law [dropping deferments for graduate students] so that graduate students and seniors, on graduation, would be taken first." He concluded at the start of the 1968–69 school year that the unrest would grow, that "real stability is not likely to be regained until the unresolved crisis outside of the universities is broken."[10] Yet despite the increasing opposition to the war, only 7 percent of a 1968 Gallup sample of students stated that they would refuse to serve if drafted.[11]

Opposition to the Vietnam war, the perception that it was a mistake, continued to grow following the dramatic Communist Tet offensive in February, the cessation of the bombing of North Vietnam in April and the beginning of negotiations in Paris. In effect, once the U.S. government gave up the goal of defeating the Communists on the battlefield, it became impossible to prevent a steady erosion of support for the war, particularly, though obviously far from exclusively, on campus. Two Gallup samples of students taken two and a half years apart dramatically point up the change in opinion (Table 2).

Other survey organizations which compared views over shorter periods after the President's announcement about negotiations found a continuing growth in "dovish" or withdrawal sentiments. In reviewing changes in attitudes which had occurred between his two student surveys, one conducted in October 1968 and the other six months later in March and April 1969, Daniel Yankelovich concluded: "On college campuses, pacifist sentiments have spread from the more liberal students to the

TABLE 2

Proportion of Students Identifying Themselves as
"Hawks"* or "Doves," 1967 and 1969 (Percent)

	SPRING 1967	FALL 1969
Dove	35	69
Hawk	49	20
No Opinion	16	11

* In response to the question: "People are called 'hawks' if they want to step up our military effort in Vietnam. They are called 'doves' if they want to reduce our military effort in Vietnam. How would you describe yourself — as a 'hawk' or as a 'dove'?"

Source: Gallup Poll release, December 21, 1969.

more moderate and conservative students."[12] Harris found that the proportion of students who, when asked whether a man's refusal to be drafted because of opposition to the Vietnam war, led them to respect him more or less, indicated "more respect," had jumped from 29 percent in spring 1968 to 48 percent in spring 1969.[13] Comparing attitudes in the fall of 1969, between late September and the end of November, during which time the two massive Moratorium and Mobilization protests occurred, the Gilbert Youth Poll reported "an increase, from 28 percent in the first poll to 43 percent in the second, among those who feel the only proper action would be 'complete and prompt withdrawal of American troops.'" A similar indication of a dramatic jump in strong opposition to the war was recorded in two polls taken by the Yankelovich survey organization. The proportion strongly agreeing with the statement "The war in Vietnam is pure imperialism" increased from 16 percent in the spring of 1969 to 41 percent in 1970, just before the Cambodian events. Those strongly disagreeing dropped from 44 to 21 percent.[14]

Yet though most students opposed the war, the survey data would suggest that a majority accepted the new Nixon administration's policy of Vietnamization as a means of getting out. The administration was able to co-opt some of the campus opposition.

Thus a Gallup survey of college students taken in May 1969 reported that when asked: "Do you approve or disapprove of the way Nixon is handling his job as President?" 57 percent approved, 27 percent disapproved and 16 percent had no opinion.[15] A second 1969 Gallup national student poll taken in the fall found that students were seemingly losing interest in the protest, though they remained heavily against the war. *Newsweek,* in reporting the survey, concluded that "the mood of the American campus is apparently undergoing a striking change: militancy and violence are in good measure giving way to passivity and personal introspection, and the revolutionary impulse seems — for a while, at least — to have largely spent itself."[16] When asked specifically what they thought "of the way President Nixon is handling the situation in Vietnam," more students (50 percent) approved than objected (44 percent).[17] The interviewing for this survey was done in October, at a time when organized efforts to mobilize campus opposition to the war were at a height — between the October 15 Moratorium demonstration and the November 15 Mobilization which culminated in a massive Washington march, the goals of which were heavily supported by the same students (69 percent).[18]

The reaction against the May 1970 Cambodian incursion, of course, produced the largest and most extensive student protest movement the United States has ever experienced. It involved more students at more campuses than in earlier years. And the survey data document the extent of participation, as well as the fact that the attitudes of students in general moved to the left, not only with respect to the war itself, but on other issues as well. Two national surveys taken during the Cambodian protest caught the full flush of this discontent. The largest one, a poll of the attitudes of 7300 students on nearly 200 campuses taken for *Playboy* by a major national opinion organization, reported that 36 percent favored pulling out "now"; 29 percent supported speeding up withdrawal; 26 percent would have continued "the administration's timetable for honorable withdrawal," while only 9 percent were still in favor of fighting for "total victory."

The Harris Poll, though presenting respondents with somewhat different alternatives, secured almost identical results. With respect to the war, Harris found that 54 percent now favored stopping the fighting and bringing the boys back home, as compared with 34 percent for a phased withdrawal, and 9 percent who wanted to expand the war.[19] This finding may be contrasted with the results of a 1965 survey of students conducted for *Playboy*, which reported that 6 percent were for immediate withdrawal, 35 percent supported continued fighting in South Vietnam, and 56 percent wanted to escalate by invading North Vietnam.[20] The antagonism to the Cambodian events naturally led to a drastic decline in student opinion of the way President Nixon was handling the war. Fifty-nine percent gave him a rating of "poor," 17 percent said fair, and only 22 percent would say pretty good or excellent.[21] Only 27 percent of the students interviewed thought the President was right in ordering troops into Cambodia.[22] And 60 percent said the action had increased their opposition to American policy in Indo-China.[23]

The increased participation in protest activities has been documented by the Harris Survey. The data presented in Table 3 clearly indicate a considerable escalation in the numbers who took part in demonstrations over a five-year period.

The same pattern of escalation of campus protest has been reported in a survey of the presidents of colleges and universities conducted during the summer of 1970 for the President's Com-

TABLE 3

Student Participation in Activism (Percent)

	1965	1969	1970
Signed Petition	72	84	87
Demonstrated	29	40	60
Picketed	18	18	29

Sources: "The Harris Survey," The Washington *Post*, March 25, 1965; "The Harris Survey," June 30, 1969; "Report of the May 1970 Harris Survey of Students," pp. 155, 157.

mission on Campus Unrest. As indicated in Table 4, the percent of schools with significant incidents more than doubled
from the academic year 1967–1968 to the pre-Cambodian part of
the school year 1969–1970. Strikingly, the proportion again increased by more than twofold for the protests against the Cambodian incursion. The results of this survey underestimated the
extent of the protest since administrators were asked to only
report on "incidents which resulted in the disruption of the
normal functioning of the institution." A similar questionnaire
sent to administrators by the Carnegie Commission on Higher
Education concerning the May–June 1970 events inquired as to
all forms of protest, including nondisruptive "essentially peaceful demonstrations," and reported that there "was some form of
organized dissent on 57 percent of the campuses."[24]

One of the most striking aspects of these antiwar protests is the
extent to which they reached into relatively moderate political
sectors among students. Thus a nationwide study of five thousand students by two psychologists, Kenneth and Mary Gergen,
taken in 1969–70, before the Cambodian incursion (sample

TABLE 4

Number and Percent of Incidents of Campus Unrest Reported by
Administrators During Three Years (Number of Administrators Reporting: 1,569)

	YEAR			
INCIDENTS OF UNREST	1967–1968	1968–1969	1969 TO APRIL 30, 1970	MAY 1, 1970 TO JUNE 30, 1970
Number of Incidents	136	272	388	508
Number of Schools with Incidents	96	171	220	508
Percent of Schools with Incidents	6.1	10.8	14.0	32.4

Source: Garth Buchanan and Joan Brackett, *Summary Results of the Survey for the President's Commission on Campus Unrest* (Washington, D.C.: The Urban Institute, September 1970), Chart 1, p. 9.

somewhat overweighted to schools towards the middle and higher levels of academe) reports that "over 42 percent . . . had demonstrated against the war. . . . The data indicate that in an average group of 100 antiwar demonstrators, one might find 13 Republicans, 20 Democrats, 62 Independents, and only 5 persons who identify themselves as Radicals. The overwhelming majority of the demonstrators place a high value on traditional American ideals."[25]

The 1970 post-Cambodian incursion Harris Survey reported a heterogeneous mix as well. Thus, though almost all self-described far leftists (91 percent), and most liberals (74 percent) took part, over one third (37 percent) of the middle-of-the-road students did as well.[26]

The Spread of Political Discontent

Although antiwar protest has been the most striking feature of student activism in recent years, the survey data document the extent to which the campus has moved to the left politically over the years. From 1968 to 1970 the proportion describing their politics as radical or extreme left increased from 4 to 11 percent. More striking perhaps is the fact that in June 1970, the proportion of students who identified in this way was not much smaller than those who looked upon themselves as conservatives.

The Gergens' 1969–70 survey of five thousand students in thirty-nine schools also reported a significant shift in student general political sentiment which they linked to opposition to the war. "Over 40 percent of the sample indicate that the war has altered their political affiliation, and of these, only 7 percent have increased their commitment to one of the two major parties. The remaining 93 percent of this group [or 37 percent of the total sample] became more 'liberal,' 'radical,' 'disillusioned with party politics,' and otherwise alienated from party politics."[27]

But though there is no question of the shift to the left among the students, it is curious that the various attempts to estimate the proportion of students who are alienated or supportive of radical activism, have agreed from 1968 to the fall of 1970 on a figure of about 10 percent, of whom perhaps one third are reported to have revolutionary views. Thus in 1968, Samuel Lubell classified students on the basis of their responses to ten items and concluded that with "only one in every ten students interviewed did these ten items link up to a pattern of general revolt or 'alienation.' "[28] A Roper study in the winter of 1968–69 asked students to evaluate four basic institutions: politics, administration of justice, business and industry, and higher education. It found that "9 percent of the seniors are *very* critical of our basic institutions generally; 18 percent are *very* favorable," and while large majorities thought all four were "basically sound," the same majorities thought they "need improvement."[29]

The most comprehensive effort to specify types of responses, the Yankelovich-CBS study based on spring 1969 data, established five types: "Revolutionaries," who held all of a five-belief index affirming that the American social system is "too rotten for repair," that destroying property and assaulting police are justifiable tactics, etc.; "Radical Dissidents," who held one or more of these beliefs, but not all of them; "Moderate Reformers," who agreed with six or more statements about the need for specific reforms; "Moderates," who agreed with less than six of these statements; and "Conservatives," who held a coherent set of beliefs about the need for more law and order, the American Way of Life being superior to all others, and so forth. Among the college students, 3 percent were identified as "Revolutionaries," 10 percent were grouped as "Radical Dissidents," 39 percent were classified as "Reformers," 37 percent were described as "Moderates," and only 11 percent were defined as "Conservatives." Conversely, however, among the noncollege youth interviewed by Yankelovich, 50 percent were located in the "Moderate" category, and 21 percent were "Conservative" as defined by attitude responses.[30]

The Gilbert Youth Poll interviewed a national sample in the spring of 1970, but did not ask as explicit questions as the others, thus not permitting a direct comparison. Its results also suggested, however, that the "alienated" were still a minority, since when faced with a choice between agreeing that the U.S. form of government "needs considerable change" or that it is "just about right," 60 percent chose the latter statement.[31]

In examining the results of various national surveys of students from 1965 to 1970, it is difficult to come to any definitive conclusions concerning the depth of and enduring quality of the grievances felt by American students and their portent for continued tension between a significant portion of them and the government. The approximately 10 percent who show up as "radicals," "alienated," or "dissidents," in the surveys completed during 1969–70 may be contrasted with those who identified "socialism" (24 percent), or "communism" (6 percent) as positive terms in a 1936 Roper-Fortune national student survey. Those who advocate fundamental changes in the American system today (75 percent in a post-Cambodia Harris poll) compare with the 68 percent who favored "a revision in our attitude about property rights" in the 1936 report.[32] At the other end of the spectrum, Harris reported that in 1969 and 1970 the percentages of students who identified their politics as "conservative" were 16 and 15, (Table 5) figures which are identical with the

TABLE 5

Political Self-Identification of American College Students (Percent)

	SPRING 1968	SPRING 1969	SPRING 1970	FALL 1970
Radical or Far Left	4	8	11	7
Liberal	39	44	43	35
Middle-of-Road	33	32	26	34
Conservative and Far Right	24	16	15	19

Source: "The Harris Survey," June 30, 1969; Report of the May 1970, Harris Survey of Students, p. 3; Louis Harris and Associates, *Youth Attitudes for Life Magazine Year End Issue* (New York: November 1970), p. 65.

15 percent who told Roper in a 1936 national student survey that they felt positive about the term "conservatism."

The survey of students conducted by Harris during the "quiet" fall semester of 1970 clearly suggested that the increase in support for radical politics which accompanied the escalation in antiwar protest in 1969 and 1970 may be reversing, that the 1970s may witness a new, less radical political cycle. It is also possible that the various surveys reported on here have overestimated the move to the left which occurred during the sixties. Each of the various national polls, Gallup, Harris, Roper, the College Poll, and others have generally been based on national samples running from 1,000 to 2,000 students. There is some reason to believe that these organizations have oversampled the more selective or higher quality schools, or that their respondents on given campuses were selected using quota sample rather than probability (randomly from list of students registered) procedures. These "biases" may have resulted in an overestimation of the more radical or alienated segment. Evidence that this is so may be seen in the fact that some of the polls have greatly overestimated the membership of the Students for a Democratic Society (SDS). The largest single effort to sample American student opinion conducted by the Carnegie Commission on Higher Education with the cooperation of the research staff of the American Council on Education in December 1969 reported a more conservative student body than the other surveys did. Its weighted national sample of 70,000 undergraduates and 30,000 graduate students and 60,000 faculty members at 300 institutions found fewer on the "left" and more self-identified "conservatives" among the students than the smaller surveys (see Table 6).

A second large survey of almost 8,000 undergraduates conducted a few months later by Peter Rossi also reported a relatively moderate student population. "Politically, 40 percent of the students called themselves moderate, 32 percent liberal, 14 percent conservative, 5 percent radical, and 2 percent very conservative. . . . The students also were asked to predict things that would be im-

TABLE 6

Political Self-Identification of Undergraduates, Graduates and Faculty
Compared to U.S. Population (1969) (Percent)

	UNDER-GRADUATES	GRADUATE STUDENTS	FACULTY	U.S. POPULATION	
Left	5	5	5		
Liberal	40	37	41	Liberal	15
Middle-of-Road	36	27	27	Moderately Liberal	18
Conservative	19	30	28	Total Liberal	33
				Moderately Conservative	28
				Conservative	23
				Total Conservative	51
				No Opinion	16

Source: Philip W. Semas, "Students 'Satisfied' with Education, Most of Them and Teachers Agree," *The Chronicle of Higher Education* 5 (January 18, 1971), p. 2. U.S. population figures from a Gallup survey taken in July 1969 as reported in *Gallup Opinion Index*, Report No. 50, (August 1969), p. 9.

portant to them ten years hence. Out of six choices, family life was listed as being of first or second importance by 87 percent of the students, and a career was listed first or second by 64 percent. Only 9 percent of the students listed 'community involvement' first or second among the six choices."[33]

The conclusion that only a small minority of American students have ever been alienated from the body politic is iterated in the findings of a variety of polls conducted between 1965 and 1971 which indicated considerable support for diverse aspects of American society other than those linked to foreign policy, the war, and racism. During the spring of 1965, in the first year of large-scale protest, a national sample expressed confidence in the policies of dominant American domestic institutions, particularly those linked to economic and professional elites. The majority voiced a "great deal" of confidence in the medical profession, banks and financial institutions, higher education, and big corporations. Students as a group were much less favorable to the arts, the United Nations, the civil rights movement, religion, and the labor movement, as indicated in Table 7.

Perhaps more significant than the positive responses reported in the above table in indicating how little alienation from American institutions existed among students in general in 1964–65, the academic year of the Berkeley revolt and the emergence of mass demonstrations against the war, is the very small

TABLE 7

How Students View the World Around Them; Responses to the Question "How Much Confidence Do You Have in These Institutions?" (Percent)

	GREAT DEAL	ONLY SOME	HARDLY ANY	NOT SURE
Scientific Community	76	20	2	2
Medical Profession	73	22	5	—
Banks & Financial Inst.	66	29	3	2
U.S. Supreme Court	65	28	6	1
Higher Education	64	32	4	—
Big Corporations	52	40	7	1
Executive Branch of Federal Government	49	42	9	—
The Arts	46	43	5	6
Psychiatric Field	44	44	7	5
Congress	39	52	8	1
The Military	38	43	17	2
The United Nations	35	49	14	2
Organized Religion	34	46	18	2
Civil Rights Movement	33	47	19	1
The Democratic Party	22	63	10	5
The Press	20	57	21	2
Advertising	16	38	44	2
Organized Labor	13	55	29	3
Television	13	46	39	2
The Republican Party	12	53	29	6

Source: "Campus '65," *Newsweek* (March 22, 1965), p. 45, from The Harris Survey.

percentage who indicated "hardly any confidence" in the dominant economic organizations. A year later in the spring of 1966,
Samuel Lubell found that 60 percent of the students he interviewed praised the role of business, while only 15 percent were
critical. Lubell also reported that an unspecified majority were
for "a stronger federal government but against a guaranteed
annual income," and for "a more rapid extension of civil rights
but against radical intermarriage." He concluded his analysis by
commenting that in "their political thinking, far from being
'alienated,' the students remain basically like the rest of the
country. . . ."[34]

Two surveys of student opinion in the winter and spring of the
1968–69 academic year also point up the limitations on any
judgment that American college students as a stratum had become alienated from dominant institutions or the body politic.
The relevant findings from a Roper survey of freshmen and
seniors are contained in Table 8.

The results of the Roper survey clearly do not suggest that the
bulk of American students were hostile to American institutions
in the winter of 1968–69, although they had turned decisively
against the Vietnam war. A somewhat similar picture of the
sentiments of the national student stratum was presented in a
subsequent poll completed for *Psychology Today* in the spring of
1969. This survey found that 65 percent disapproved of U.S.
involvement in Vietnam, 39 percent indicating strong feelings
and 26 percent mild ones.[35] On most other questions, however,
they were much less critical of American institutions and policies.

The *Psychology Today* survey reaffirmed the findings of the
Roper poll that the large majority of American students were not
antagonistic to American institutions. The Yankelovich-CBS survey of four thousand youth, half of them in college, taken in
March and April 1969, supplied further evidence that college
students, though more alienated and radical than the sample of
noncollege youth aged seventeen to twenty-three, still favored
working within the democratic system. Though the large majority of white students agreed that America is to some degree a

TABLE 8

Attitudes Toward Four Institutions of a National Sample of Freshmen and Seniors (Winter 1968–69) (Percent)

	BASICALLY SOUND: ESSENTIALLY GOOD	BASICALLY SOUND: NEEDS SOME ASSISTANCE	NOT TOO SOUND: NEEDS MANY IMPROVE-MENTS	BASICALLY UNSOUND: NEEDS FUNDA-MENTAL OVER-HAULING
Business				
Seniors	39	48	7	3
Freshmen	48	37	9	1
Political System				
Seniors	10	72	15	2
Freshmen	11	70	16	3
Administrative Justice				
Seniors	20	54	21	3
Freshmen	23	50	21	4
Higher Education				
Seniors	19	56	19	4
Freshmen	32	49	15	2

Source: Roper Research Associates, *A Study of the Beliefs and Attitudes of Male College Seniors, Freshmen, and Alumni,* May 1969, pp. 56, 60.

"racist nation," only 21 percent said they would welcome "more vigorous protests by blacks," 59 percent said they would disapprove of such protests. Eighty-eight percent of the white students believed that the "American system can respond effectively" to the need for change. Eighty-nine percent agreed that the radical left is as much a threat as the radical right. Close to three quarters of the entire student sample (72 percent) "believe that competition encourages excellence," and that "the right to private property is sacred," (75 percent) .[36]

A fourth national survey organization, the College Poll, which

TABLE 9

Attitudes Toward a Variety of American Institutions — Spring 1969
(Percent)

	SA*	MA	DK	MD	SD
Universities:					
1. On the whole, college has been a deep disappointment to me.	4	4	2	26	56
2. The university environment has helped me find out about myself.	43	42	5	7	3
3. I don't feel I am learning very much in college.	4	13	1	28	53
4. American universities have largely abdicated their responsibility to deal with vital moral issues.	9	30	18	33	9
Social Issues:					
1. Negroes would be better off if they took advantage of the opportunities available to them rather than spending so much time protesting.	20	35	7	23	15
2. Those who knock free enterprise misunderstand what made this a great nation.	26	41	11	15	7
3. The events of 1968 prove that it is futile to work within existing political structures.	8	25	11	34	23
4. There is no point in trying to change existing political structures; if one is interested in change he must work outside these structures.	3	11	7	42	35

* SA = Strongly Agree; MA = Mildly Agree; DK = Do Not Know;
MD = Mildly Disagree; SD = Strongly Disagree

Source: "A Study of the Inward Generation," Special Report published by *Psychology Today,* October 1969.

regularly queries samples of students for newspapers and NBC, also reported that the dominant mood on campus during 1968–69 was liberal, sympathetic to civil rights demands, and antiwar. Its results also portrayed a student population which was far from extremism in its views. Thus 63 percent said they believed that "the ROTC belongs on campus" during the year in which ROTC was under sharp attack from SDS and antiwar groups. When the concept of a voluntary ROTC was introduced, the proportion approving of ROTC on campus rose to almost 80 percent![37] When asked "Do you object to your university or college participating in general projects to aid the national defense" only 23 percent said "Yes," they disapproved; 76 percent indicated they had no objection.[38] Although 78 percent favored "Afro-American" courses being offered at their school, 68 percent were opposed to black student control over the selection of the faculty in these courses.[39] The College Poll also reported that over three fifths (62 percent) said they are "getting tired of all the campus unrest," 80 percent felt "that students who break the law in campus fights should be arrested and expelled."[40]

A number of national surveys taken in the spring 1970 semester before the Cambodian incursion revealed a strongly critical, reform oriented, but still preponderantly nonalienated, student population. Accompanying its increased opposition to the Vietnam war was growing support for "fundamental reform" of various major institutions. The proportions favoring such changes in institutions such as big business and the military had risen from about one third to close to half, between 1969 and 1970 in Yankelovich surveys. Yet relatively few students agreed with doing away with specific establishment institutions. Only 12 percent, for example, would have done away with the FBI, another 19 percent favored fundamental reform of the institution, while 28 would have changed it moderately, and the largest single group, 40 percent, were against any "substantial change." Only 14 percent advocated fundamental reform of the Constitution; another 2 percent would have "done away with" it; the overwhelming majority favored "moderate change" (37 percent) or "no substantial change" (47 percent). The greatest hostility was dedicated against foreign policy and racial discrimination. Thus 48 percent strongly agreed that "our foreign policy is based on our own narrow economic and power interests," and 53 percent held the same view about the statement: "Basically, we are a racist nation." In spite of these specific criticisms, only 8 percent agreed in the same antagonistic terms with the comment: "The whole social system ought to be replaced by an entirely new one; the existing structures are too rotten for repair."[41] A second national survey, the Gilbert Youth Poll found that only 16 percent stated that they thought equal rights for minority groups could not be achieved under our present form of government. Two thirds were opposed to control over business profits; about the same proportion rejected paying for medical bills through public taxation; 60 percent were against a government-guaranteed minimum income.[42] The Rossi survey found strong support for protest, since 47 percent disagreed that "laws that are unjust should be obeyed until they are changed." Conversely, a much larger percentage, 72, disagreed with the statement: "To do anything rewarding one must work outside the regular institutions of our society."[43] A study completed by Gallup just before the Cambodian incursion in late April unfortunately asked few questions which bore in any way on degree of alienation from American values. One did inquire as to whether "you think people who are successful get ahead largely because of their luck or largely because of their ability?" Only 9 percent of the students said "luck"; fully 88 percent thought that success is a result of "ability." And in spite of the widespread endorsements of the legalization of marijuana, only half the students interviewed thought that the "use of marijuana should be made legal."[44]

The obvious question arises to what extent the events surrounding the Cambodian incursion, the killings at Kent State and Jackson State, and the mass involvement in the various forms of protest during May and June of 1970 increased the alienation from the American political system. Clearly, no study made during those events could answer this question. In the heat of the reaction to these occurrences, students and others made judgments about the President and the operation of the national political system, some of which were explicitly challenged by events after the school year ended. A Harris Survey conducted in late May reported that the confidence expressed in the President's Vietnam policy or in his general activities had almost totally vanished among students as a result of these events. Thus, as noted earlier, 59 percent said his handling of the war was "poor" in their judgment; 67 percent said they thought he had not "been frank and straightforward about the Vietnam war"; more believed the military operation in Cambodia would lengthen the war (37 percent) than thought it would shorten it (21 percent); and only 19 percent accepted the President's statement that our troops would stay in Cambodia less than eight weeks. Over half (52 percent) thought United States troops would remain in Cambodia for six months or more.

Much larger proportions of students polled during this period than in earlier surveys endorsed the need for fundamental changes (75 percent), believed that demonstrations are an effective form of protest (58 percent), and felt that social progress is more likely to come about through radical pressures (44 percent), as many as thought through institutional reforms (45 percent). And while more students said that the May events had brought students and faculty closer together (54 percent) than those who said they separated them (20 percent), more of them were also inclined as seeing these events separating students and university administrations (42 percent) than bringing them together (28 percent). Most students (67 percent) believed that student protest would speed up needed changes, although close to four fifths of them (79 percent) thought that radical pressures would have their greatest impact through institutional changes rather than through efforts to overthrow the system (10 percent).[45]

Yet if the responses to these questions point up the extensive academic reaction to the Cambodian events, some other replies suggest that even at the height of the protests, student reaction expressed less than total alienation. In spite of the increased hostility to the military and the war, only 25 percent of the Harris respondents were in favor of not having ROTC on campus. Thirty-seven percent favored continuing it as a credit course, while another 33 percent supported an on-campus non-credit ROTC.[46] Only 30 percent said that individual professors should not "be allowed to undertake research projects for the military," as contrasted with 62 percent who supported their right to do so.[47] Demonstrations against companies doing defense business recruiting on campus were frequent from 1968 on. Yet even in late May 1970, only 22 percent opposed such activities, while almost three quarters (72 percent) said that companies engaged in defense work should be "permitted to recruit at college."[48] When asked by Harris *after* the Kent State killings who has been more responsible for the violence at college protests, the demonstrators or the authorities, only 17 percent replied the "authorities," an equal proportion blamed the "demonstrators," while 64 percent said "both." The survey completed about the same time for *Playboy* also inquired about responsibility for the Kent State killings, but offered respondents somewhat different alternatives. The largest group, 43 percent, agreed that the deaths were "attributable to the Nixon Administration's hostile attitude toward dissent," 38 percent thought they were an accident, "no one's fault," while 19 percent blamed the students.[49] Speaking more generally, the large majority of the Harris Survey students (69 percent) thought that "school authorities are right to ask the police for help when students threaten violence," as compared with but 21 percent who considered them wrong to do so.[50] While most of the students (52 percent) believed that it was wrong to seek help from the National Guard in such situations, almost as many (42 percent) said that the "National Guard has acted responsibly in most cases" as thought they were irresponsible (46 percent).

The most extensive investigation of a variety of student attitudes completed in the peaceful fall of 1970 by Louis Harris found, as noted earlier (see Table 5), fewer self-identified radicals and more conservatives than during the Cambodian protests in May. Unfortunately, the other questions asked by Harris were not comparable with those in his earlier study. Nevertheless, they add up to a picture of a relatively moderate and unalienated studenthood. Less than one quarter, 24 percent, had "hardly any confidence" in the ability of the "government to solve the problems of the 70s"; only one fifth, 20 percent, favored changes

"to the point of socialism"; 59 percent opposed "a guaranteed annual income," 65 percent disapproved of efforts to secure "enforced racial balance through school busing"; and only 33
percent would not be willing to "work for a company that
handles defense contracts." The vast majority reported "happy"
family experiences. Over 80 percent said that their parents'
married life had been happy, that their family had had enough
money, and that their fathers had been happy in their work. Less
than a third, 30 percent, indicated that they had trouble com-
municating with their parents.[51]

Other national surveys of student opinion taken during the
1970–71 academic year also suggest a less radical campus population. A Gallup Poll taken close to the end of 1970 reported that
the "size of what is termed the 'radical left' is somewhat smaller
than is sometimes believed" since only 4 percent "considered
themselves to be members of the 'radical left.' " In commenting on
other aspects of this same survey, *Newsweek* noted that "the
vast majority of college students appears to be firmly wedded to
the traditional American values. . . . Fully seven out of ten
students believe there is too little emphasis today on family life. . . .
the overwhelming majority of the college population still en-
dorses the Puritan ethic as the best way to the good life. Asked
whether 'hard work and effort are necessary for you to achieve
personal fulfillment and satisfaction,' a stunning 85 percent
answered 'yes.' "[52] The College Poll found that the proportion who
said they "would marry a person regardless of race, color or creed"
had declined from 71 percent in 1969 to 58 in late 1970. The objectors were mainly concerned about interracial marriages. The
same organization reported that 78 percent were opposed to
"forced integration of the suburbs . . . [to] help alleviate the
slums of our cities." Ninety percent were against giving any special
preference to black students in admission to college. In April 1971
the College Poll reported that the percentage agreeing that this is
a "racist country" had declined from 58 percent in 1969 to 41 percent. In May, it indicated that 70 percent rated the FBI as "Ex-

cellent or Good." Only 10 percent gave it a "Poor" rating. A different survey group, the Campus Poll, found that 67 percent of the
students thought that the leaders of the women's liberation
movement were "too extreme in demands." Curiously, female
students were less likely to favor the movement and more prone
to think its leaders too extreme than male ones. The same poll
indicated that 82 percent of students interviewed thought it
"important" that the "U.S. maintain an effective military defense" (44 percent highly important). But though these responses suggest a relatively conservative studenthood, the
Campus Poll also found in the fall that 24 percent agreed that
"revolutionary tactics are necessary to effect significant social and
political change in the U.S." It suggested that such attitudes declined steadily through the year. Thus, it reported in March
1971 that only 9.5 percent felt that "a person's disagreement
with a particular law justifies his disobedience to it." In a survey
conducted two months earlier, almost twice as many, 18.5 percent,
had approved of civil disobedience.[53]

The findings that the great majority of American students
were not alienated or sympathetic to radical causes even at the
height of major, well-publicized nationwide demonstrations have
also been reported for other countries characterized by major
student protests. Surveys of French youth and students after the
May 1968 events, perhaps the most potent student protest wave
in a Western country, indicated that the great majority were opposed to a "radical transformation of society" in September 1968,
four months after the great strike. Only 12 percent of a representative sample of students indicated that they agreed with this
objective, as contrasted with 54 percent who said their personal
concerns with reforms were limited to education, and 31 percent
who were only interested in passing their exams. Subsequent
French surveys provided an impression of "reasonable youth";
almost 90 percent said they were personally "happy." More recently, a survey of student opinion in the spring of 1970 at
Nanterre, the suburban Parisian university at which the 1968

revolt started, which is generally recognized as the most radical school in France, found one quarter (24 percent) in favor of revolution.[54] In Italy, second only to France in the extent of the 1968 strikes, and which had the most potent and widespread pattern of student strikes and violence in Europe during 1969 and 1970, a national student survey completed in 1969 also points up the minority status of militant student activism. As one report of this survey indicates, its results lend "weight to the hypothesis of the so-called 'silent majority.'" Only 9 percent of the student sample approved of the methods of the activists; 16 percent supported "revolution"; but when asked to state their favorite country only 4 percent listed a Communist or Third World one — the great majority gave western democratic countries with England in the lead (20 percent) and the United States second (15.5 percent).[55] The results of a 1966 national survey of Japanese students, who have had the longest history of militant, often violent, student protest since World War II, coincide with the American and European findings concerning the relative moderateness of the views of the large majority. Only 22 percent of a national sample of 1769 Japanese students disagreed with the statement "Students should not strike for political matters" (6 percent strongly); and even fewer, 15 percent, rejected the conservative interpretation that "student movements are run only by a few activists" (4 percent strongly).[56]

Attitudes to the University

The information about student attitudes towards the university also presents a mixed picture as to the extent to which structural characteristics or academic policies are a source of student unrest. A leading historian of education, Lawrence Veysey, has indicated that student complaints about the policies of faculty and administration have *always* been widespread in American academe, that they are rooted in a kind of "class tension," in the reactions of the students to being the inferior social class in the system.[57] A prominent British sociologist, Bryan

Wilson, has also suggested that "student unrest has, thus, been
. . . inherent in the student situation. . . . [M]odern universities are institutions almost inviting disruption. . . . Discipline
in universities was less exacting than that expected of citizens in
city streets. And yet, these were large institutions, bringing
together large numbers of energetic young people who experienced a relatively common circumstance that might, by a Marxist, readily be defined as 'dependent' and 'underprivileged,'
imposed by an identifiable 'opposing' class of dons. Had not
younger members been socialized to academic values and university allegiance, universities would long ago, have been places
almost ready-made for a class struggle. . . ."[58]

The first major eruption of the current wave of student protest, that in Berkeley in 1964–1965, has been intensively studied
by various social scientists. One of the earliest analyses based on
interviews with Berkeley students concluded that the "data do
not suggest that dissatisfaction with the education process played
any role at all." Robert Somers found large majorities agreeing
with statements that the administration and faculty were doing a
very good educational job. For example, when asked "how well
satisfied they were with 'courses, examinations, professors, etc.,'
. . . only 17 percent expressed any degree of dissatisfaction." But
as Somers noted, more important than the fact that the large
majority were "satisfied" was the finding "that the minority of
students who *are* dissatisfied with the courses, examinations, or
professors are little more likely to be found among the militants
than those who are satisfied."[59] A second survey of Berkeley
students taken in the spring of 1965 also reported that unhappi-
ness with the university as an educational institution ". . . was
on the whole unrelated to support for the FSM."[60] The campus
militants did differ considerably from those not involved in the
Free Speech Movement (FSM) protest in their political ideologies. That is, what distinguished student reaction to this supposedly first great revolt against the multiversity — impersonal
treatment, faculty neglect of students, and the like — was not
feelings about the quality of education at the University of

California, but political ideology. The more liberal or radical a student was on general social issues, the more likely he was to support or participate in the FSM. The bulk of those who were directly involved in actual demonstrations had been active in earlier political or civil rights protests.[61] The evidence would appear to be clear that the Berkeley revolt was a politically motivated event, not an effort to change the structure of academe or its educational policies.

Robert Somers repeated much of his 1964 study four years later, after Berkeley had been the scene of continued political protest, of a growing radical student movement, and of repeated confrontations with authority, both the police and the university administration. As a result of the original protest movement and the various interpretations crediting student unrest to inadequate educational programs, the Berkeley campus had also been engaged in considerable education experimentation designed to involve students in the planning of courses, to heighten the social "relevance" of their education, and to increase personal relationships between faculty and students. The educational experience of Berkeley students should have clearly improved as judged by the criteria raised by movement-oriented critics, both faculty and students. Yet Somers found a decline over the years in the proportion satisfied with courses, etc., from 83 percent in the fall of 1964 to 69 percent in 1968. Seemingly, if answers to the surveys are taken as reflections of objective quality, teaching and other aspects of education had worsened somewhat as a result of the reforms.[62]

The trends reflected in the data from national surveys bearing on student attitudes towards the university and educational reform tend to resemble those from Berkeley. A Harris Survey conducted in the spring of 1965 during the first year of large-scale student demonstrations, which inquired into "confidence in various institutions," (Table 7), found the two institutions with lowest negative percentages (4 percent) were "higher education," and the "scientific community." As at Berkeley, the heightened national student discontent generally produced increased complaint about specific institutions, including particularly higher education. The Roper student poll conducted in winter 1968–1969, reported that 23 percent of the seniors and 17 percent of the freshmen stated that higher education was "not too sound," or "basically unsound," while only 19 percent of the seniors and 32 percent of the freshmen thought it was "basically sound and essentially good." These answers represented a considerable decline in support for higher education as compared to the Harris 1965 findings, but it should be noted that comparable changes occurred with respect to student views towards the political system, business and industry, and the system of administering justice (see Tables 7 and 8). The Gergens' 1969–1970 survey results also indicate that the increased criticism of the university is part of a general antiestablishment syndrome dictated by concern about the war. There is some indication in their analysis that draft policies and the general disruptive effects of the war on personal plans continued to play the causal role Lubell attributed to them in 1967–1968 in stimulating antiwar sentiment.

> Approximately one out of every three students has altered his career plans as a result of the war. The modal student is seeking a draft-exempt occupation, while many others indicate extreme confusion over their future. . . . In some schools, over a third of the students have altered their course of study as a result of the war. . . . More than one of every five students traces his dissatisfaction with his curriculum and rules governing student life to the war. . . . Emotional upheaval is particularly prevalent. Between 60 and 70 percent of the students have experienced increased anger, worry, and depression as a result of the war.[63]

Different studies suggest, however, that higher education has remained in better esteem among students than other institutions. The results of Roper's inquiries as to how much confidence they had in various categories of "leaders" indicated much more trust in "leaders in education" than in those in politics or other institutions.[64] Only 7 percent of the seniors replied "not much confidence" in education leaders. In another study conducted

early in 1969, Yankelovich differentiated students between "prac-
tical-minded," those going to college to earn more money, who
comprised 57 percent of his sample, and "forerunners," generally
from more affluent backgrounds in better schools and studying
liberal arts subjects, for whom college means something more
intangible, including "the opportunity to change things."[65] The
latter were naturally more reform-minded than the former, but
both groups placed the university lowest on their list of six "areas
which need fundamental reform," with the one exception that
more forerunners favored reforming the universities than favored
reforming trade unions.[66] A Gallup student poll taken in the
fall of 1969, while reiterating the comparative findings of Roper's
1969 and Harris's 1965 results that students had less confidence
in universities than had been true for four years earlier, also
reported, similar to Yankelovich, that universities received the
largest vote of approval among nine institutions rated by the
students. The percent "favorable" to universities was 68, as
compared to 56 for business and Congress, 46 for the courts, 37
for high schools, and 33 for organized religion.[67]

In spite of the growing evidence of student dissatisfaction with
various aspects of the university, the largest single, statistically
most sophisticated survey of American students — that conducted by the Carnegie Commission on Higher Education in
December 1969 — found that "undergraduates are generally
satisfied with their education." Only 13 percent "said that they
were dissatisfied. . . . Specifically, more than two thirds of the
undergraduates said that they were satisfied with student-faculty
relations, their relations with other students, the quality of classroom instruction, the intellectual environment of the campus,
and the college administration."[68] One year later, a very much
smaller sample of students interviewed by Harris gave similar
responses. Again only 13 percent said that they were "dissatisfied
with their own education, thus far."[69]

Any increase in specific complaint about higher education
between 1965 and 1970 may be linked, in large part, to the fact
that the educationally dissatisfied were increasingly to be found

among the politically discontented as the years of protest went on. That is, political ideology became more closely linked to educational ideology. Those students who are disposed to the left now describe the university as a bad place; more conservative students are much less hostile. This is shown conclusively both in Yankelovich and Gallup 1969 national student surveys. Demonstrators are much more disposed to think that students should have "a greater say concerning the academic side of colleges," than others.[70] The more liberal-to-left students are more likely to say that universities need fundamental reform than the more moderate or conservative ones.

These findings, of course, do not indicate anything about the predominant direction of the relationship; that is, it is possible that growing discontent with education led many students to become political protesters. While this undoubtedly occurred in many cases, a large number of studies of the social background of student activists, and of the campus population generally, indicate that there is strong intergenerational continuity in political orientations. These researches, to be discussed in the following chapter, agree with Kenneth Keniston's insightful descriptive phrase that many of the early student radicals of the 1960s were "red-diaper babies," the offspring of leftists of an earlier generation. The liberals also tended to come from liberal backgrounds. Given such evidence, it seems highly probable that the correlations between political and educational discontent reported in the various surveys are largely a result of political criticism producing a generalized antisystem point of view which includes the university. Hence, the increase in negative responses about the university over the short period 1965–1970, the growth in demands for major structural changes, have reflected the escalation of political protest, the growing radicalization of the student body, more than the worsening of the educational experience in these years.

These conclusions are reinforced by the findings of three studies of student attitudes and behavior at the three institutions which experienced the most dramatic confrontations in 1968

(Columbia), 1969 (Harvard) and 1970 (the University of California at Santa Barbara). The sit-in demonstrations and strikes at the first two, and the repeated conflicts with the police and violence at the latter, were explained in various reports as stemming from assorted educational inadequacies, or failings of the university as a "community." Yet in each instance, elaborate efforts to determine the factors which led students to participate in or support the protests indicated that as in Berkeley during 1964–65, the best predictor of reaction to the confrontations was the general political ideology of the students, while their attitude towards the university had relatively little effect. The nature of this relationship may be seen in a table drawn from the survey of Columbia students in May 1968.

TABLE 10

Relationship Between Political Beliefs and School Dissatisfaction in Affecting Support for the Goals of the Demonstration — Columbia Students, May 1968
(Figures Refer to Percent Supporting Goals)

SCHOOL DISSATIS- FACTION INDEX*	LEFT-RIGHT POLITICAL INDEX*			
	RIGHT	MEDIUM RIGHT	MEDIUM LEFT	LEFT
Low	5	22	59	72
Medium low	7	27	68	88
Medium high	18	36	65	92
High	10	41	79	95

* The Political Index is composed of a number of items including attitude toward the Vietnam war, black power, the Poor People's March, presidential candidates, and party support. The School Dissatisfaction Scale is formed from six items taken from Somers' studies of Berkeley students such as attitudes towards courses, impersonality as a result of size, concern for the educational welfare of the students.

Source: From a survey based on a random sample of 2,000 Columbia students completed by the Bureau of Applied Social Research. I am very grateful to Alan Barton for permission to use these and other unpublished data from his study.

It is clear from Table 10 that political orientations were much more important than educational grievances in determining the reactions of Columbia students toward the 1968 protests. In analyzing the factors related to *participation* in the sit-ins, Alan Barton found that, as in Berkeley in 1964, previous involvement in protest groups was most important. The overwhelming majority of those who took part (83 percent) had been active in earlier forms of antiwar or civil rights work. The combination of a record of activism and leftist attitudes made for a much greater likelihood of involvement in the sit-ins, than did either factor alone. Thus, the Columbia demonstrations of 1968 were clearly a result of the prior existence of activist political groups, and the fact that they occurred had relatively little to do with the assets or liabilities of Columbia as an educational institution.

Similar conclusions are suggested about the sit-in in the Harvard University administration building and the consequent student strike which occurred in April 1969. An analysis of the reactions of a sample of Harvard students conducted by Marshall Meyer concluded that the main source of support for the demonstrations, and of antagonism to Harvard, was an underlying commitment to a leftist ideology. Student respondents were classified on a nine point attitude scale from left to right. When interviewed, almost two thirds (65 percent) of those who were grouped in the two most leftist categories thought that "the takeover of the building was justified," a proportion which declined to one third (33 percent) for the next category (moderate left), and to *two* percent for those who were in the three most conservative groupings. Meyer explicitly addressed himself to evaluating the thesis that radical protest is a consequence of the failings of the Harvard faculty.

Some critics and a committee of Harvard's overseers have concluded that loss of intimacy between students and faculty is the major source of tension. Were this the case, our data would reveal the absence of student-faculty contact and a correlation between leftism and the absence of contact. In fact they do not. Seventy-eight percent of Harvard students say they are friendly with one or more faculty members; three quarters talk with an instructor outside of class at least once a week; and a quarter have these interchanges more than three times a week. Moreover, there is no relationship between a student's acquaintance with faculty members and his political position. . . . This evidence [means] that attempts to promote closer relationships between students and faculty will not diminish the level of unrest though they may have other salutary effects.[71]

The same pattern is indicated by the results of an elaborate study of the factors related to the sharp escalation of protest on the Santa Barbara campus of the University of California (UCSB), which rivaled Berkeley in 1969–70 in propensity to sustain demonstrations that end in violence. Although many of the demonstrations at UCSB pressed for institutional changes, Robert Smith concluded that "the findings here indicate that dissatisfaction from the war is a major determinant of student militancy even in protests that are unrelated to the war."

The frequency of campus protests is closely related to disaffection from the Vietnam war. When disaffection is high, campus protests are frequent. This is true even when the protests are not manifestly about the war or war-related issues. These aggregate relationships between disaffection and protest also hold true for individual students. Students who are disaffected are considerably more militant [on other issues]. This relationship is true even when a range of other test variables that independently affect militancy are simultaneously controlled. . . .

At UCSB disaffection from the war provides the most powerful explanation for the change in student militancy and campus protests. This is true because the level of disaffection has increased tremendously over the last three academic years, while the levels of the test variables and the political and social characteristics of the faculty and students have remained constant. . . . It is the change in the level of disaffection that has caused the change in the frequency of campus protests and the decline in the quality of intellectual life.[72]

The fact remains, of course, that the number of protests, sit-ins, and other demonstrations dedicated to changing the university steadily increased from 1965 to 1970. This has been documented in various surveys of the issues raised in different situations.[73] University administrations and faculties have been forced to react to demands to change the curriculum, modify the forms of academic governance, reform methods of teaching, and the like. Since the groups which press for such changes usually accompany them with charges that the existing policies are a major source of student discontent, many involved with universities not unnaturally conclude that this is so, that students are being treated badly, and that if various changes are made, the discontent will disappear. But if it is true that much of the increase in complaint about the university has been a *consequence* of the growth in political unrest, then *educational reform can not be expected to reduce student unrest,* in particular those related to extramural issues. And in fact, a recent survey of over twelve hundred institutions reports that those which have made major educational adjustments, including increased student participation in governance, have *not* reduced their proneness to unrest as a result. But this is not the whole story since there is also good statistical evidence derived from aggregate data (characteristics of institutions) that the propensities of schools to experience demonstrations is related to various indicators of bureaucratic (impersonal) treatment of students. (See discussion of these and other relevant studies in Chapter 3, pp. 96–100.) It is true, however, that the university is in many ways considered the best institution by all sectors of student opinion, even though the growth in political discontent results in more disruption on campus than within any other environment. Whatever discontented students think of the relative merits and sins of the university, there is no other establishment target which can be so easily attacked and affected, giving considerable publicity, and at a minimum risk of arrest and severe punishment. This was Daniel Cohn-Bendit's message, when he stated that as compared to other strata, students had no real excuse to avoid joining in militant actions.[74]

The Overestimation of the Dramatic

The evidence presented here from the various national opinion surveys, while documenting the increased opposition to the Vietnam war and the concomitant growth in radical and critical sentiments toward social institutions (at least up to the summer of 1970), generally indicates that the alienated include a relatively small proportion of the student population (10 percent). The state of opinion on campus cannot be gauged from observing demonstrations, or even through securing estimates of such opinion from campus leaders, whether these be university administrators, student body officers, or any other set of authorities. Informants have a strong tendency to overestimate the extent of support for highly visible forms of behavior.

The general point may be demonstrated with respect to the proportions involved in drug taking on American campuses. A Gilbert national survey of youth (February 1970), asked respondents to estimate the percent of their own age group who have tried drugs. Among college students in the sample (1005), close to two thirds (65 percent) guessed 50 percent or more have tried drugs, 34 percent thought 70 percent or more have done so. The same survey found that only one third of the college student respondents reported that they had ever had any experience with a drug, marijuana or other. The proportion who were involved with regular use of drugs at the time was, of course, much smaller, just under 10 percent.[75]

This study illustrates the extent to which students, themselves, overestimate the extent to which their fellows have engaged in a form of well-publicized illicit behavior, much as students and others have exaggerated the propensity of *others* to violate middle-class sexual morality. Although there can be little doubt that the norms of the "counterculture," particularly with respect to use of drugs, have steadily gained adherents on campus from

1965 down to the present (1971), the mass media and those directly involved in or professionally working with such students have invariably overestimated the spread of drugs and other aspects of the new styles of personal expression. In a 1968 review of the literature on drug use, Kenneth Keniston concluded that such behavior was limited to a small minority of the campus population. Extensive use of drugs was to be found primarily in a small group of schools, generally the elite colleges and universities which admit the brightest students, many from liberal intellectual family backgrounds.[76] Different national surveys completed in 1969 yielded results in line with Keniston and Gilbert. Roper reported that 76 percent of the college seniors said that they had never tried marijuana, and that 96 percent had never used LSD. Only 2 percent said they use it occasionally.[77] The Gallup survey of students in all classes in November found results very comparable to those of Roper. In response to an anonymous secret ballot, 68 percent stated they had never tried marijuana, 88 percent had not taken barbiturates, and 92 percent had never used LSD.[78] The College Poll found that 62 percent denied ever taking "drugs such as marijuana or LSD."[79] The Spring 1970 Yankelovich survey reported that only 30 percent rejected outright "the prohibition against marijuana." Almost half, 48 percent, said they accepted it easily, while 22 percent stated that they accepted it reluctantly.[80] By the time of the Cambodian protests in May–June 1970, the proportion of students who told interviewers in the *Playboy* survey that they had ever used marijuana had gone over 40 percent for the first time. Yet only 13 percent said they used it "frequently."[81] A report of a poll taken by Gallup in December 1970 stressed that the percentage of students who reported having taken marijuana at least *once* had doubled between the spring of 1969 and winter 1970 — from 22 percent to 42 percent. About one student in six (17 percent) used the drug an average of once a week. But the Gallup results agree with those reported to *Playboy* that a majority were still "virgin" with respect to use of pot.[82] The Fall 1970 Harris Survey did not ask about personal use of drugs, but did inquire

concerning attitudes toward the law. Only 53 percent of the college students interviewed thought that marijuana should be
legalized.[83]

Although many in the older generation have an image of
college students as slovenly, bearded, and long-haired, this
stereotype does not jibe with the impression which Gallup interviewers formed of the national sample they interviewed in April
1969. Only 6 percent of the men had beards, and 10 percent were
reported to be dressed in sloppy clothes. The interviewers judged
that 81 percent of the male students and 94 percent of the
females had "generally neat appearances." In the late fall of 1970,
Gallup interviewers reported that close to half the students (45
percent) still had "short hair," another 23 percent had long hair
which did not come over the ear. Thus, the proportion with hair
that went below the ear was about one quarter of the college
population, with only 7 percent among them wearing it down to
the shoulder.[84] The Yankelovich survey reported that only 38
percent in spring 1969 and 30 percent in 1970 of the college youth
verbally "reject the idea of conforming in dress and grooming."
A majority (59 percent) "would welcome more emphasis on respect for authority."[85]

Since the results of these surveys are so much at variance with
the conceptions of student attitudes and behavior presented by
the media, and held by many students, particularly the more
activist among them, and by college administrators, some may
question their accuracy. The best argument for their reliability
and validity is that twelve different national survey organizations
varying in their method (anonymous questionnaire using different questions, or personal interview), and necessarily dealing
with different samples of institutions, produce a high degree of
consensus. It may be argued that the more left-disposed students
are underrepresented, since in the last year or so SDS and other
extreme left groups and publications have attacked survey
studies of student attitudes as "pig research," serving the interests of the academic establishment. It is curious, therefore, as
noted earlier, that some of these surveys would seem to overestimate the membership of SDS. For example, the Yankelovich

study suggests that close to 4 percent of the student sample claimed membership in SDS.[86] Given a total student population of over seven million in 1968–1969, this would have meant an SDS membership of around 280,000. SDS, before its split at its 1969 convention, only claimed a national dues-paying membership of some 7,000, with another 30,000 involved in local chapter activities. It would seem that either the sample was drawn from institutions in which SDS is disproportionately strong, or that some sympathetic nonmembers claim membership. The argument that some who have engaged in formally illicit behavior such as smoking marijuana will not admit it to interviewers, thus resulting in an underestimation of those involved, may have some validity, but the findings of studies using anonymous questionnaires are not very different from those based on personal interviews.

The opinion surveys of American students indicate that the large majority are not sympathetic with radical doctrines and tactics; most of them seemingly are conventional with respect to appearance, use of drugs, and dedication to academic achievement and a "straight" career. Many more still fill the stadiums to cheer on their varsity eleven on fall Saturdays than take part in political rallies or demonstrations of any kind. Yet the fact remains that the anti-Establishment Youth Culture grew constantly year by year during the 1960s. Though but a small minority are radical, increasing proportions, often majorities, are discontented with the way the country is run. Perhaps no other issue has done as much to alienate American students from American society and polity as the Vietnam war. Continued participation in it convinces many that they can have no confidence in the nation's rulers, in the elites of the older generation which permit it to continue. Obviously, many factors other than the war have pointed up to the young the seeming contradiction between the potential of an affluent society and the reality of social evils such as racial discrimination and poverty. Most students took a liberal-to-left critical posture as America entered the 1970s.

The fact of predominant campus liberalism, commitment to

egalitarianism in class and racial relations, and opposition to
war, explains the ability of the extreme left to set the tone in
many colleges. For most students support the overt goals of most
demonstrations. The majority is against the war, and, therefore,
looks with some sympathy on efforts to symbolically oppose it
through confrontations directed against ROTC, defense-related
research, and recruiters for defense-involved corporations. The
vast majority views black inequality as a crime and consequently
supports to some extent sit-ins or other demonstrations dedicated
to improve the position of the blacks. The majority, though not
participant in the drug culture, supports the rights of others to
do so. Thus, efforts to restrict the use of marijuana, and university cooperation with the police in enforcing narcotics laws are
met with hostility.

Efforts to mobilize the "moderates" against the extremists
usually fail because authority is seen as defending social evils or
outmoded forms of authority. This is particularly true when
outside force is brought to a campus to suppress a demonstration
or maintain order. The resistance by the noninvolved students to
such efforts is not simply a manifestation of "generational solidarity" or the affirmation of the principle of university autonomy, it is also motivated by the sympathy of the campus majority
for the "objectives," if not the "tactics," of the demonstrators. To
stress the minority status of the radicals or the habitual drug
users does not mean that the majority has been opposed to
them. The student vanguard has been powerful from 1965 to
1970 precisely because the majority of students has been politicized in a left direction by the events of the 1960s, particularly
the opposition to the war.

The decline in manifest campus radicalism as reported in the
polls in the academic year 1970–71 and in the use of confrontationist tactics during this period may reflect the fall-off in
American involvement in Vietnam. The fact that the United
States pulled out all its ground troops from Cambodia, an act
unanticipated by the majority of students polled by Harris in
May 1970, the continued withdrawal of American troops from Viet-

nam, and the sharp decline in casualties and battle news from that country, all would seem to have reduced student concern about American military policy. A report by the Urban Research Institute of campus protests in the fall 1970 term indicates that not only did protest drop off, but that it was much less likely to have involved use of violent tactics, and "that the focus of campus protest switched . . . from antiwar demonstrations to demands for minority recognition." Presumably many of these were run by black students and did not involve the white radicals.[87]

The promise of the Cambodia demonstrators to campaign vigorously in the fall elections in 1970 for antiwar candidates was not honored by the vast majority. Rather, some conservative candidates like James Buckley in New York were astonished by the turnout of conservative student activists.[88] Similar reports concerning the decline of left-wing activism stemming from the campus came in from Britain, France, Germany, Japan, and other countries.[89] It is difficult to understand what factors, the reduced war effort apart, are operating. The one common feature present in Britain, parts of western Europe, and the United States, is the end of a high level of prosperity for university graduates. Radical sociologists Milton Mankoff and Richard Flacks have noted the possibility that economic uncertainty may weaken certain forms of student protest. "The collapse of the counter-culture of the 1920s in the face of economic depression suggests that one must eschew any linear theory of societal change. The cultural revolt of the present period presupposes economic stability and affluence, conditions which, given the cyclical behavior of capitalist economics, should not be taken for granted."[90]

To some degree the change in the student mood and behavior may be a consequence of developments among the organized radical groups. In the United States and other countries as well the various extremist groups have followed a pattern of splitting and turning viciously on each other. The German SDS dissolved in the spring of 1970. The various factions of the Zengakuren in Japan spend much more energy denouncing each other than the policies they oppose. They have also used violence in such internecine struggles. In France, the assorted *groupiscules* also see those who spread false doctrine on the left as the main enemy. In the United States, SDS first divided among a number of factions, and then split into two major ones, one of which became an underground terrorist organization, the Weathermen, while the other became the student section of the dogmatic Maoist Progressive Labor Party. Fratricidal conflict in all countries meant a smaller and smaller membership, which reinforced the propensity to engage in violence, e.g., bombings, assaults, kidnappings. Whatever effect such behavior has on the policies of the political elite, it is clear that resort to such tactics discourages the more moderate elements who are sympathetic to the movement's general objectives. When each group seeks to demonstrate that it is more truly revolutionary and even violent than the other, it contributes to the growth of moral revulsion against activism among the mass. When extremist groups fling mud at each other, some of it sticks to each, and they lose what claim they had to moral leadership. Thus, in an ironic yet logical fashion, the very same factors which contributed to the increased radicalization of the student movement, to the greater influence of the extremists, have also served to undermine the political involvement of the majority. A kind of Gresham's law of extreme politics operates in which the more aggressive constantly drive out the more moderate, which means that they also press the sympathetic periphery to withdraw from politics. Kenneth Keniston has given eloquent expression to the feelings of those involved in the recent American student movement to exposure to a process that has occurred often with rightist as well as leftist extremists.

> The violent rhetoric that came to pervade the student movement could be passed off as mere talk. But when that rhetoric culminated in murder, then the members of the student movement had to face for the first time their own complicity with the very violence against which they struggled.
> The agony of the counterculture then, involves above all its

confrontation, at an individual and a collective level, with its own destructiveness. In explaining the silence of this year, the sense of discouragement and despair, the feeling of embarrassment and shame are indeed important. . . . The members of the student movement gradually came to realize that if they allowed themselves to be led by their most rigid factions, dogmatism and death lay at the end of their road.[91]

To explain the changes in the predominant student mood as a consequence of specific historical events which have provided them with a different formative set of generational experiences than earlier generations does not account for the intragenerational variations. We have already seen that there is an enormous intragenerational gap between the political and social attitudes of university students and their less privileged age-mates at work in factories and offices. The statistical data presenting the distribution of attitudes and behavior among students conceals other variations which differentiate undergraduates. The eight million not only include a radical minority, they contain millions of conservatives; there are still many students who take the Protestant ethic seriously; most female undergraduates are still virgins;[92] as noted, the majority have never experimented with drugs; three quarters of the men do not wear their hair long below their ears. The many discussions of students written in recent years ignore the culture of the "squares." But a detailed examination of the factors contributing to activism should help our understanding of the general phenomenon of student protest. The following chapter deals with research on these issues.

3

Who Are the Activists?

Social Background

The major conclusions to be drawn from the large number of studies of student activism (particularly those of Kenneth Keniston and Richard Flacks) in the United States and other countries is that leftist students are largely the children of leftist or liberal parents. The activists, particularly, are more radical or activist than their parents, but both parents and children are located on the same side of the spectrum.[1] In the United States, where left-wing radical parties or consistently liberal orientations with respect to race relations, foreign policy, and socioeconomic egalitarianism have relatively little support among the less educated and poorer strata, such orientations have found the bulk of their backing among a well-educated segment of the affluent engaged in intellectual and welfare occupations, and among members of traditionally progressively disposed religious groups, particularly the liberal Protestant denominations and the Jews.[2] In other countries, in which leftist socialist and communist parties have heavy backing from workers, leftist students are more likely to come from less privileged families.

In countries as diverse as Japan, the Netherlands, Sweden, Brazil, Germany, and Britain, the available evidence would suggest that leftist tendencies secure disproportionate backing from the less well-to-do among the university student population.[3] And it seems clear, that the variation between the pattern in the United States and these other countries is related to generational political continuity. As Klaus Allerbeck puts it, these results suggest "that the affluence-radicalism correlation in the U.S. is no causal relation, but a by-product of the relations of political ideology and social stratification which are not the same in the U.S. and in Germany." What emerges from the studies of student political behavior in various countries "is the importance of the political orientations of parents for the political behavior of their children."[4] In the United States, the members of Young Americans for Freedom and other conservative and right-wing youth groups come from conservative family backgrounds.[5] Students are more idealistic and committed than their parents, but generally in the same direction.

Studies of earlier movements, both leftist ones in the United States before World War I and in the 1930s, and fascist groups in Europe, suggest a similar pattern of generational continuity. Bruno Bettelheim, who has observed the growth of student support for Nazism in Germany before 1933, and for the New Left in the United States, has commented on these similarities:

> It is mainly the children of leftist parents who become . . . student revolutionaries in our society, just as in other places and other times the children of conservative parents, under similar emotional conditions, spearheaded right wing radicalism. It was the children of conservative German parents, for example, who . . . felt a need to lay their bodies on the line for ideas their parents had only lukewarmly held . . . They felt, too, that this was a means of rebirth, a way to revitalize an ossified society, to create a new society; with little patience for the voice of reason, they asked for authenticity and confrontation. All these were the main tenets of Hitler's academic youth, as they are now those of our own student left.
>
> Thus, while the emotional constellations which make for very different student revolts are strangely similar, the specific political

content of a student revolt depends to a large degree on the
beliefs of the students' parents. For in many ways rebellion repre-
sents a desperate wish by youth to do better than their parents in
exactly those beliefs in which parents seem weakest.[6]

In the United States, intellectuals, academics, writers, and so
forth tend disproportionately to support the Left for reasons
which are discussed elsewhere. They are predominantly liberal
Democrats, or supporters of left-wing minor parties.[7] And various
surveys indicate that students who are intellectually oriented,
who identify themselves as "intellectuals," or who aspire to
intellectual pursuits after graduation, are also much more prone
to be on the left and favorable to activism than those inclined to
business and professional occupations.[8]

Among both faculty and students, there are clear-cut correlations between disciplines and political orientations. On the
whole, those involved in the social sciences and humanities, or in
the more pure theoretical fields of science, in that order, are more
likely to be on the left than those in the more practical, applied,
or experimental fields.[9] Such variations, however, would appear
to be more a product of selective entrance into different disciplines than of the effects of the content of the fields on those
pursuing them as students or practitioners. Thus studies of
entering freshmen have reported similar relationships between
intended college major and political attitudes as found among
seniors, graduate students and faculty.[10] Morris Rosenberg, who
conducted a panel study (repeat interviews with the same people
two years apart) of students, reported that political orientation
proved to be a major determinant of shifts in undergraduate
major.[11] A large proportion of the minority of conservatives who
chose liberal (in political terms) majors as freshmen changed to
subjects studied by most conservatives, while many liberals who
had selected conservative majors tended to shift to fields which
were presumably more congenial with their political outlook.

The relationships between academic fields and political sympathies are also linked to the finding that the leftist activists

within American universities tend to come from relatively well-to-do backgrounds as compared to the student population generally. A comparison by Westby and Braungart of the delegates to conventions of SDS and YAF also indicated that the left-wingers come from somewhat more affluent backgrounds than the rightists. The majority of the latter were the children of conservative businessmen and professionals, but they included a significant proportion, one fifth, from working-class origins, a group almost unrepresented among the SDS delegates.[12] In a follow-up study which included samples of students from a number of universities, Braungart found that 39 percent of the YAF members and 17 percent of those belonging to SDS were of working-class backgrounds. Comparing members of these two groups with those belonging to the Young Democrats and Young Republicans indicated that a larger proportion of SDS members came from upper-middle-class families (55 percent) than was true of the other three groups, or of a control group of students who did not belong to political groupings.[13]

The continued validity of these relationships, as radical student protest has spread out through the campuses of the country, and has enrolled in places and strata not reached in early years, should be expected to decline. Studies of the pattern of growth of new social movements generally have suggested that the earliest recruits tend to come from different strata and political backgrounds than those who form its modal groups when it is a mass movement. In the case of the American student movement, it almost necessarily began with the scions of the relatively well-to-do, liberal-to-left, disproportionately Jewish intelligentsia — the largest pool of those ideologically disposed to sympathize with radical student action in the population. But as student activism permeated beyond its initial support group, it necessarily would have had to recruit from the less-well-to-do coming from less politicized family backgrounds and from more diverse religious orientations. The initial relationships should persist, of course, but in a weakened form.

An opportunity to test these assumptions was provided by

access to the results of a national survey of American students by the Harris poll in May 1970 during the massive protest strikes against the Cambodian incursion. Harris asked respondents whether they had taken part in demonstrations, and also to classify themselves among five political positions ranging from "far left" to "far right." The students also reported on the political stance of their parents in similar terms. Since the students described themselves as considerably more liberal than their parents, inherently most of those on the left must have shifted sharply from the political views of their parents. Thus, ten times as many students described their own politics as "far left," as used that term for their fathers' political views. Conversely, conservatives were three times as numerous among fathers as among their offspring. As the data in Table 11 indicate, most children of liberals are still liberals; many of the conservatives have moved to the left. The reports for the offspring of the far right and far left are unfortunately based on far too few cases to permit reliable estimates.

The persistence of a relationship between middle-class status and support for the far left among college students as recently as May 1970 may be seen in the results from the Harris poll presented in Table 12. The children of professionals and of white collar workers were more likely to identify themselves as far leftists than the offspring of manual workers. Those involved in business ownership or managerial tasks, whether urban or rural, however, were least likely to produce left-wingers. The differences in ideology were only loosely linked to family incomes. Nevertheless, the more well-to-do were somewhat more likely to have far left children than the very poor, while student conservatives were disproportionately to be found among those from less affluent families. Religious identification remained more closely correlated to political identification. Those who reported being Jewish or having no religious orientation were much more likely to identify with the far left than students with a Christian religious affiliation.

Though the Harris Survey suggests that the factors reported in

TABLE 11

Relationship Between Political Opinions of Parents and Students — May 1970 (Percent)

STUDENTS' POLITICAL STANCE

	FAR RIGHT	CONSERV-ATIVE	MIDDLE OF THE ROAD	LIBERAL	FAR LEFT	NOT SURE	TOTAL
MOTHER'S STAND ON MOST ISSUES							
Far Right	13	15	33	28	9	3	100
Conservative	1	27	29	34	6	3	100
Middle-of-Road	1	8	33	45	10	2	99
Liberal	1	2	9	60	24	4	100
Far Left		17		17	67		101
Not Sure	3	12	44	16	6	19	100
Total	2	15	27	41	11	4	100
FATHER'S STAND ON MOST ISSUES							
Far Right	2	11	24	40	21	1	99
Conservative	1	24	27	38	7	2	99
Middle-of-Road	2	10	34	42	9	3	100
Liberal		1	7	64	24	4	100
Far Left	16		32	10	42		100
Not Sure	2	8	26	30	6	28	100
Total	2	15	26	42	11	4	100

Source: Report of Harris Survey of Students, May 20–28, 1970, pp. 383–384.

TABLE 12

Relationship of Family Socioeconomic and Religious Background to
Political Identification — May 1970 (Percent)

CHARACTERISTICS	FAR RIGHT & CON- SERVATIVE	MIDDLE- OF-ROAD	LIBERAL	FAR LEFT	TOTAL
Father's Occupation:					
Professional, Technical	15	26	42	17	100
Manager, Official,					
Proprietor	19	25	50	6	100
Clerical, Sales	15	27	40	18	100
Manual	15	27	46	12	100
Farmer, Farm					
Laborer	53	26	22	—	101
Family Income:					
$20,000 and over	14	24	48	14	100
$15,000 to $19,999	18	28	41	12	99
$10,000 to $14,999	17	25	49	10	101
$7,000 to $9,999	22	34	34	10	100
Less than $7,000	20	28	42	11	101
Religious Preference:					
Protestant	26	36	35	2	99
Catholic	20	34	41	4	99
Jewish	5	28	44	23	100
Other	13	15	54	18	100
None	4	12	55	29	100

Source: Report of Harris Survey of Students, May 20–28, pp. 389, 393, 395.

early studies of SDS and other activist groups as correlates of left-
wing ideology among college were still important in 1970, the
fact remains that as the movement grew it did broaden its base
somewhat. The relationship between income and left-wing
identification, for example, was fairly weak by 1970. Some indication of a process of change in the characteristics of student
activists is indicated in the results of a study of University of
Wisconsin students by Mankoff and Flacks. They contrasted the

backgrounds of those students who had been "active politically . . . for three or more years prior to May 1968, when the questionnaires were distributed," and those who became involved subsequently. Their findings suggested that a change in the social class character and political family background of left student activists accompanies growth. As the movement penetrated into new segments of the student body, it recruited from less well-to-do students from less politicized families. In the Wisconsin case, the newer breed of radical supporters tended to come increasingly from those from smaller cities and apostate Catholic religious backgrounds as well.[14]

These findings jibe with what we know about the growth of new social movements generally in the body politic. Most radical movements, when new and small, tend to find their first recruits and supporters among the relatively more well-to-do and better educated, even though their program may be oriented to the manifest interests of the less privileged, and undereducated. The latter lack the psychic security and ability to work towards long-term goals which the former possess to a greater degree. When such movements grow, however, they usually secure the backing of population groups who are quite different from their early members.[15] It may, therefore, be argued that what is unusual about the growth of the American student movement is not that it has spread into diverse and less privileged student strata, but that it has done it so slowly — that the original associations between relatively privileged backgrounds and leftist commitment persist for so long.

The continuation of the "Movement's" somewhat greater appeal to the more well-to-do may be related to the consistent findings concerning the academic orientations of the left students. As noted earlier, they are disproportionately involved in liberal arts subjects (social science, humanities, and natural science in that order), and are more prone to be interested in abstract rather than practical subjects than the less politicized and more conservative students. Many studies of students in different disciplines suggest that those who major in the liberal arts subjects and have an intellectual or scholarly bent have well-educated parents, while first-generation college students of working-class origins tend to be vocationally oriented in a narrow sense.[16] They are more likely to be found among those preparing to become engineers, businessmen, and the like. They come disproportionately from that segment of the less well-to-do which is strongly oriented towards upward mobility and the values of the privileged. Their strong concentration on professional objectives, plus the need of many of them to hold a job during school term, also results in these students being less available for political activities than those from more affluent families. These findings may help to explain the fact that colleges attended by large numbers of less well-to-do students, apart from blacks, were less likely to be strongholds of left-wing groups during the 1960s and 1970 than those which educated the scions of the upper-middle class.

Not surprisingly, the black student activists do not resemble the white militants in their social background and aspirations. As suggested earlier, their principal objectives are not to change the fundamental character of the society or to engage in expressive personal protest, but rather to improve the position of the blacks within the larger society generally, and inside the university in particular. Although to achieve their objectives they often find it necessary to engage in militant, sometimes violent forms of protest, their goals are similar to the instrumental ones of the less privileged, sometimes racist, white youth. They want a better life, more money, a job with higher status, social dignity. The black student activists are less aspiring for personal advantages than other black youth, seeing themselves as leaders of their people, but they clearly differ from the white activists. A study of 264 black student activists in fifteen colleges and universities in 1969 indicated that the blacks came from much poorer families than the whites. Only 11 percent had college graduate parents. While most white activists are undecided about future careers, 76 percent of the black militants "said they were fairly certain!"[17]

The political reputation of certain schools, therefore, may be linked to sources of selective recruitment and the resultant political orientation of their students. Those with a large number of well-to-do Jewish students, or currently, with the rise of Negro militancy, of black students, have tended to be centers of activism. High-level liberal arts institutions with an intellectual aura attract students oriented to becoming intellectuals. Thus we may account for the pattern of student protest at schools like Reed, Swarthmore, Antioch and others. The best state universities, as judged in terms of faculty scholarly prominence, e.g., California, Michigan, and Wisconsin, are also schools which have become the most important centers of confrontationist politics. These schools attract a disproportionate number of intellectually oriented students, including many Jews. The same finding occurs among predominantly black colleges and universities in studies of factors related to protest participation among their students.[18]

Generally, the greater the proportion of students from high socioeconomic status (SES) homes, the greater has been the rate of participation. The association may be explained by other variables that are related to the proportion of high SES students. For instance, schools of high quality generally have a higher proportion of students from high SES backgrounds and also have higher rates of student participation.

Participation in the 1970 Strike Wave

Two surveys of student participation in antiwar protests in the spring of 1970, one by Mary and Kenneth Gergen and the other by the Harris Survey, reinforce the conclusion that the general set of correlates associated with activism had not basically changed. The Gergens secured data from a national sample of 5,000 students, both before and during the Cambodian protests. The demonstrators were predominantly "from a prosperous home . . . ; their parents have in the main, gone to college, and most frequently their fathers are either professional men or are in the higher echelons of business." They were disproportionately Jewish, or of no church affiliation. "The bulk of the protestors attend nonsectarian colleges which are rated as 'moderately selective' to 'very selective' in admissions policies. . . . The major field of interest for the protestor is the social sciences, where 40 percent concentrate. One fourth are in the humanities, and only 15 percent major in natural science."[19]

The Harris poll of student behavior and opinion during the protest wave against the Cambodian incursion also differentiated among respondents with respect to many of the factors which had been investigated in earlier studies of activism. It distinguished the kinds of academic backgrounds which were more or less likely to have led students to participate in the demonstrations. Eighty-five percent of those interviewed reported that demonstrations had taken place at their schools. Fifty-eight percent of the students at schools which had demonstrations indicated that they had taken part. This means that about half the college population in the United States (49 percent) actually were involved in protests during the Cambodian incursion. The relevant characteristics of those so engaged at schools with protest are reported in Table 13.

The findings of the Harris poll conducted during the 1970 national strike wave on the whole are surprisingly comparable to the results of studies dealing with characteristics of left-wing ideologists and activists. They do not permit, of course, any statistical specification of the relative effect of the different factors in a multivariate context, since all that is available is the percentage distributions.

The very low rate of participation of the self-described Protestants is quite difficult to explain. In part, it is linked to the low involvements of those at denominationally controlled schools, and of Southerners. Other data in this survey indicate that the children of farmers are far more conservative than those from other occupational backgrounds, and almost all of them are Protestants. The low rate may also reflect the fact that many birthright Protestants who become radicals report their religion as "none." Family political background (mother's stand "on most issues") clearly has a considerable impact on the availability of students for protest activities. What is perhaps more impressive than the variations among the different background traits is the extent to which protest had spread during May and June of 1970 into environments which had previously been unreceptive, such as relatively low-quality schools, or those controlled by religious denominations. Southern students remained resistant, but even among them, 38 percent of those in schools that had protests, report personal involvement in them.

Perhaps the most interesting finding included in Table 13 is the difference in the behavior of white and black students. Fewer of the latter were at schools which had protests — presumably these were largely segregated black colleges in the South. But even among students who were at demonstrating institutions, black students were less likely to have taken part in these actions than whites. This discrepancy in racial behavior was not a function of greater support for the war among the blacks. If anything, the Harris data indicate that the black students were more hostile to the conflict than the whites. Fully 72 percent of the blacks thought President Nixon was doing a "poor" job in handling the war as compared with 58 percent among the whites; 65 percent of the blacks would bring the soldiers home as soon as possible, while only 52 percent of the whites had the same opinion. The black students also reported a greater propensity than whites to having engaged in protest activities *before* Cambodia. Thus 41 percent of the former and 29 of the latter had been on a picket line; and 31 percent of the blacks and 24 percent of the whites had visited a public official.[20] The Yankelovich-CBS survey completed in the spring of 1969 pointed to similar racial differences. Black students in general were much more critical of the war and the social system, and more supportive of demonstrations and of militancy than whites. (Parenthetically it should be noted that noncollege working youth, including the blacks among them, were *much less militant* or critical of various policies and institutions than the white college students. The black working youth, who of course comprise the large

TABLE 13

Background Characteristics Related to Participation in Protests or Demonstrations During the Cambodian Incursion — May 1970

	PERCENT PARTICIPATED IF SCHOOL HAD PROTESTS	PERCENT AT SCHOOLS WITH PROTESTS
Region		
East	71	90
Midwest	54	88
South	38	63
West	67	99
Size School		
10,000 and over	67	94
3,000–9,999	47	82
Under 3,000	57	69
Type School		
Public	58	85
Private, Nondenom.	69	83
Denominational	44	79
Admissions Standards		
Above Average	69	94
Average	60	94
Below Average	49	72
School Class		
Freshmen	61	85
Sophomores	62	83
Juniors	56	82
Seniors	54	84
Major Subject		
Humanities and Social Sciences	68	85
Natural and Physical Sciences	59	} 82
Other (Professional Schools)	45	
Race		
Black	51	64
White	59	85

TABLE 13 *(continued)*

	PERCENT PARTICIPATED IF SCHOOL HAD PROTESTS	PERCENT AT SCHOOLS WITH PROTESTS
Sex		
Male	61	83
Female	55	84
Father's Occupation		
Professional and Technical	64	87
Manager or Proprietor or Official	58	80
Clerical, Sales	64	90
Manual	60	79
Farmer, Farm Laborer	20	39
Family Income		
$20,000 and over	63	86
$15,000 to $19,999	60	82
$10,000 to $14,999	77	66
$7,000 to $9,999	54	77
Less than $7,000	51	69
Religion		
None	80	94
Other	66	92
Jews	73	90
Catholics	60	82
Protestants	36	71
Ideology		
Far Left	91	97
Liberal	74	88
Middle-of-Road	37	79
Conservative and Far Right	14	69
Mother's Ideology		
Far Left	80	86
Liberal	69	87
Middle-of-Road	62	84
Conservative	51	80
Far Right	49	78

Source: Report of Harris Survey of Students, May 20–28, 1970.

majority of black young people, repeatedly rejected the use of aggressive protest tactics, often by large majorities, while the black college students were the most militant of the four youth groups, i.e., white college, white noncollege, black college, black noncollege) .[21]

The indications that black college youth are militantly anti-war, but were relatively low in participation in the anti-Cambodian incursion demonstrations, can probably be explained as a consequence of the growing gap which exists between black and white students. The black students tend to abstain from protests led by white radicals or liberals. They keep their distance even when they agree. But the fact that they are visibly non-present at white-run antiwar rallies clearly does not imply a lack of opposition. The evidence from a variety of investigations definitely indicates that black college students are much more discontented than whites.[22] And they are much more likely to continue to press for major changes when the Vietnam war ends. Since the far left as well as the more liberal white students are disposed to back race-related demonstrations, the probabilities are great that the major campus issues once the war ends will be linked to civil rights.

Determinants of Protest-Proneness

The evidence available differs as to whether the propensity of a given institution to sustain protest is largely a consequence of the type of students who are attracted to it, or is also a function of the treatment which students receive from the faculty and institution in terms of values and personal relations. Faculty surveys strongly indicate that the more intellectually prestigious a school in the United States, the more liberal-to-left the political outlook of its faculty.[23] Seemingly, therefore, students from more intellectual cultural and political backgrounds — liberal to left — attend schools where such orientations and values are reinforced by their teachers. Thus, it has been argued by some that a sufficiently large enrollment to provide a critical mass for impressive demonstrations and the appropriate type of student body should result in a politicized campus under present conditions, almost without regard to the administrative policies pursued. The case for this thesis has been supported in a number of research publications. It was initially sustained statistically by Alexander Astin in a study based on a sample of thirty-five thousand students in 246 schools in the 1967–68 school year. His analyses were designed to estimate the relative importance of student and institutional variables. He concluded:

> The proportion of students who participate in demonstrations against either the war in Vietnam or racial discrimination can be predicted with substantial accuracy solely from a knowledge of the characteristics of the students who enter the institution. . . . Environmental factors seem to be somewhat more important with respect to protests against the administrative policies of the college, although student input characteristics still appear to carry much more weight than environmental characteristics in determining whether or not such protests will occur.[24]

A number of subsequent studies dealing with questionnaire data and incidents of protest from later school years have all agreed that sympathy for student activism, involvement in demonstrations, and propensity of institutions to sustain protests, have been correlated with size and quality of institution, plus various student characteristics, particularly those associated with a liberal-to-left family political orientation. For example, in dealing with protests which occurred during 1968–1969, Astin and Bayer reported that given the same type of student body, large universities are more likely to have demonstrations than smaller ones.[25] Hodgkinson analyzed reports for 1230 institutions secured in 1968–1969, which dealt with whether they "had experienced an *increase* in student protest and demonstrations during the last ten years."[26] He also found that the more scholarly committed schools, as indicated by the highest degree awarded and research involvements of faculty, were most inclined to have had an increase. Size also was closely associated with tendency to sustain protests. The range of difference ran from 88 percent for those with more than twenty-five thousand students to 14 percent for schools with less than one thousand enrolled.[27]

Two independent surveys of the characteristics of institutions involved in the May 1970 protests against the Cambodian incursion also reiterated the results of the earlier studies. The Carnegie Commission on Higher Education and the President's Commission on Campus Unrest, each sent out questionnaires to the presidents of all colleges and universities (the government one also wrote to the chairmen of faculty senates and of student governments) inquiring as to the nature, extent, and "causes" of demonstrations. The Carnegie study found that the more selective the student body and the larger the institution, the more likely it had been to have had a significant protest activity. Identical results were reported by the staff of the President's Commission.[28]

Many of the respondents to the President's Commission questionnaire, particularly the student body presidents, suggested that increased involvement of students in university governance would reduce the likelihood of major outbreaks in the future. These assumptions were challenged by Hodgkinson's findings that "an increase in student control in institutional policy making" did not appear to reduce the rate of protests; if anything, the "reverse would seem to be more likely." He reached the conclusion "that tinkering with structures may not be any long-term solution to problems of student protest . . . [since] There are quite clearly protest-prone students and protest-prone faculty."[29]

Many of these results, of course, can be interpreted to reinforce the argument that the basic factor accounting for more activism at larger schools is not impersonality, bureaucracy, but the presence of a "critical mass." Kenneth Keniston and Michael Lerner in defending this thesis at length pointed out that actually "there are *fewer* protests per 10,000 students at large universities than at small ones." Using American Council on Education data for 1968–69, they indicated that in four year colleges, there were

2.63 protests *per* 10,000 students in schools with less than 1,000 enrolled as compared with but .69 *per* 10,000 in schools with more than 5,000 students on the campus. And they concluded that the reason for the relationship between size of institution and demonstrations is that "there is more of everything at larger institutions. Larger campuses are also more likely to have chapters of Young Americans for Freedom (a right-wing group), literary magazines, science clubs, fraternities, and massive football rallies. The obvious explanation is that, compared to small colleges, large universities have more students available for almost everything. Not surprisingly, they have more and bigger protests as well." They deduced, therefore, that "the main reason some campuses experience more and bigger protests than others is that these campuses admit more of the kinds of students who appear 'protest-prone.' "[30]

There is a growing body of evidence, however, that schools play a role as centers of activism beyond what may be explained by the characteristics of their students. It may be suggested that the political traditions and images of certain institutions help to determine the orientation of their students and faculty, and, more generally, that protest-proneness is related to the way colleges treat their students.

In the United States, Madison and Berkeley have maintained a record as centers of radicalism. The University of Wisconsin image goes back to before World War I — the strength of progressive and socialist politics in the state contributed to its political aura. Berkeley is a particularly interesting case in point. The San Francisco Bay Area has a history dating back to the turn of the century as being among the most liberal-left communities in the nation. Various data pertaining to the Berkeley campus since the end of World War II point up the continuity of that university as a center of leftism. Berkeley was the only major institution in the country to sustain a major faculty revolt against restrictive anti-Communist personnel policies in the form of the loyalty oath controversy of 1949–50.[31] The data collected by Paul Lazarsfeld in a national opinion survey of the attitudes of social scientists, conducted in 1954 to evaluate the effect of McCarthy-ism on universities, indicated in an unpublished analysis that the Berkeley faculty members were the most liberal of any of the schools sampled in this study, a pattern which subsequent events suggest continued into the sixties.

In 1963–64, the year before the celebrated Berkeley student revolt, San Francisco Bay Area students received national pub-licity for a series of massive successful sit-in demonstrations at various business firms — designed to secure jobs for Negroes. Prior to the emergence of the FSM protest, the Berkeley campus probably had more different left-wing and activist groups with more members than any other school in the country. The vigor and effectiveness of the Free Speech Movement must in some part be credited to the prior existence of a well-organized and politi-cally experienced group of activist students. A study of the six hundred students who held a police car captive in the first major confrontation of the affair in October 1964, reported that over half of them had taken part in at least one previous demonstra-tion, and that 17 percent indicated they had taken part in *seven or more*.[32] Since the Berkeley revolt, Bay Area activists have continued their leading role, by major efforts to disrupt the operation of the Selective Service, by conducting two of the four most publicized student demonstrations of 1967–68, and in six major confrontations during 1968–69. During the protests against the Cambodian incursion in 1970, large segments of the Berkeley faculty and students again took the lead in efforts to "reconsti-tute" the university in classroom-based efforts to end the war and "the social conditions which made the war possible," which involved giving regular grade credit for participation in election campaigns and other political activities.

It is interesting to note that in analyzing the factors which explain why the Free University of Berlin "is the Berkeley of West Germany," that is, the leading center of militant student activism, Jürgen Habermas, a leading sociologist who also hap-pens to be a strong supporter of left-wing politics, points to causal factors in the background of Berlin, which strongly resemble those present in Berkeley in 1964. First, the Free University has been the most liberal one in the country, that is students have had more "extensive rights and powers" than elsewhere. "Second, the composition of the student body, as shown by empirical studies, favors politicization owing to selective immigration from West Germany." Those students who seek to escape West German conscription, more likely on that score to be leftist, can do so by moving to West Berlin. "Third, the proportion of politically conscious and liberal-minded professors at some of the Berlin faculties is, in my estimation, considerably higher than at universities in the Federal Republic. Hence, students in Berlin have always been able to count on the solidarity of a group of their professors."[33] Thus, Professor Habermas argued that the basic reasons for a heightened level of political disturbances and violence at the Free University were clearly not a consequence of its relative educational deficiencies, but rather that, as at Berkeley, it attracted many more radically disposed students and professors than other universities.

The efforts to argue or demonstrate that the protest-proneness of institutions of higher education are solely a function of the presence of a critical mass of left-oriented students would seem, however, to exaggerate the case. In a more recent detailed analysis of data on campus unrest for the 1968–69 academic year, Astin and Bayer reported, that holding other factors constant, those institutions with fewer protests "have environments characterized by a high degree of concern for the individual student." The protest-prone schools were those in which "students and faculty had little involvement in class, [and] students were not on warm, friendly terms with the instructor," and had "an environment which lacks cohesiveness (measured primarily by number of close friendships among the students). . . ." Astin also reported using 1969–70 data that "the size of an institution and its emphasis on graduate work seem to be causally related to the emergence of protests, even after adjustments are made for differences in student characteristics."[34] Blau and Slaughter, in a survey of the relationship between propensity to sustain demonstrations and various characteristics of over a thousand schools, came to similar conclusions relying on 1967–68 data. They found that school size, indicators of student intellectual ability, impersonality (as reflected in the extent to which a school uses computers for administrative purposes), capacity for intellectual innovation as indicated by the presence of new fields of learning, and willingness to give the students the right to evaluate teacher performance, were each *independently* associated with student protest.[35]

The various studies of the institutional correlates of student activism in the 1960s thus suggest the importance of three sets of factors: (1) size, insofar as it may be regarded as a source of the critical mass, the number necessary to sustain a protest movement and demonstrations; (2) bureaucratization, or degree of impersonal treatment of students; and (3) the politically relevant or predisposing characteristics which students (and faculty) bring with them to university. These findings, though as yet incomplete and tentative, and varying considerably for different types of political protest, do offer some solace to those who would seek to reduce the severity of demonstrations by following a policy of "counter-bureaucratization." It should be noted, however, that the extant research would still indicate that greater administrative flexibility has less of an effect on propensity for activism than factors linked to size or student characteristics. Whether or not a student is a radical, or demonstrates against racism or the Vietnam war, would appear to result much more from his social background and orientations than from the way he is treated by his university.

In stressing that involvement in leftist student activism is to a considerable degree a function of the general political orientation which students bring to the university, it is not being argued that major changes in attitude do not occur, or even that conversions rarely take place. Universities clearly do have an important liberalizing effect so that there has been a significant shift to the left. This even occurred during the "silent fifties." A considerable number of students in the late 1960s have been much more radical in their actions and opinions than earlier postwar generations of American students, or than their parents. The larger events which created a basis for a renewed visible radical movement have influenced many students to the left of the orientation in which they were reared. Many students of liberal parents have felt impelled to act out the moral imperatives implicit in the seemingly "academic" liberalism of the older generation. Political events, combined with various elements in the situation of students, pressed a number of liberal students to become active radicals.

Kenneth Keniston and William Cowdry conclude from a survey of Yale that the students "most likely to hold radical beliefs *and* act on them" are those whose fathers have similar social and political values to their own. Those who hold radical beliefs, but are not active politically, are more likely to report that their fathers are unlike themselves.[36] The principal predisposing factors which determined who among the students would become activists, therefore, existed before they entered the university.

However, if we hold pre-university orientation constant, it obviously will make a difference which university a student attends, what major he chooses, who his friends are on the campus, what his relations are with his teachers of varying political persuasions, what particular extracurricular activities he happens to get involved in, and the like. The relationships between the orientations which students form before university and the choices they make after entering which help maintain their general political stances are only correlations; many students necessarily behave differently from the way these relationships would predict.

Clearly, conversions, drastic changes in belief, in political identity, do occur among university students, as among other groups. During a period in which events shift the larger political climate to the left or right, young people, with fewer ties to the past, are undoubtedly more likely to change than older ones. There is also a special aspect of university life which enhances the chances that certain groups of students will be more likely to find satisfaction in intense political experience. Various studies suggest that mobility, particularly geographic mobility, where one becomes a stranger in an unfamiliar social context, is conducive to making individuals available for causes which invoke intense commitment.

Thus new students, or recent transfers, are more likely to be politically active than those who have been in the social system for longer periods.[37] Local students, or those relatively close to home, are less likely to be active than those who are a considerable distance from their home communities. In Berkeley, Madison and other university centers, the activists have come disproportionately from the ranks of the migrants, and of recently arrived new students.

Psychological Research

Some of the research by psychologists seeks to go beyond the analysis of factors which seem to have a direct impact on political choice. Psychologists have also sought to account for varying orientations and degrees of involvement by personality traits. Thus they have looked at such factors as variations in the way different groups of students have been reared by their parents, i.e., in a permissive or authoritarian atmosphere, as well as investigating family relationships, student intelligence, sociability and the like. Such studies have reported interesting and relatively consistent differences between the minority of student activists and the rest of the student population. These widely heralded findings are unconvincing, in large part because few of the extant studies hold constant the sociological and politically relevant factors in the backgrounds of the students. For example, Richard Flacks, and Westby and Braungart, report that leftist activists tend to be the offspring of permissive families as judged by child-rearing practices, and of families characterized by a strong mother who dominates family life and decisions.[38] Conversely, conservative activists tend to come from families with more strict relationships between parents and children, and in which the father plays a dominant controlling role. To a con siderable extent these differences correspond to the variations reported in studies of Jewish and Protestant families. Childhood rearing practices tend to be linked to sociocultural political outlooks. To prove that such factors play an independent role in determining the political choices of students, it would first be necessary to compare students *within* similar ethnic, religious and political cultural environments. Efforts to do this by Lamar Thomas, dealing with the children of politically active parents from both ends of the political spectrum, found no relationship between activism and permissiveness among students, when parental "cause-orientation" was held constant.[39] Jeanne Block and Norma Haan, while agreeing that the extent of parental permissiveness is not associated with activism, did find that activists are likely to come from families in which parents stressed training for independence. Block and Haan attempted to control for the effect of religion, to test a suggestion of mine that some of the differences in child-rearing backgrounds between activists and conservatives may reflect ethnic-cultural variations. Although Block and her colleagues concluded that their results "undermined" this hypothesis, they appear very inconclusive since they report on extremely small percentage differences between a group of thirty-eight "conventionals" and thirty-five "activists," who are non-Jewish.[40] It is, therefore, still difficult to conclude that socialization experiences, as such, have an independent causal effect, that is independent of family values which bore relatively directly on politics. Thus Kenneth Keniston, in summing up the recent evidence bearing on the earlier critique of mine which raised this question, concluded:

> . . . the issue cannot be settled with only the evidence at hand. In all probability, several interacting factors are involved. On the one hand, it seems clear that *if* children are brought up in upper-middle-class professional families with humanitarian, expressive and intellectual values, and *if* the techniques of discipline emphasize independence and reasoning, and *if* the parents are themselves politically liberal and politically active, then the chances of the child's being an activist are greatly increased, regardless of

factors like religion. But it is also clear that these conditions are
fulfilled most often in Jewish families. And there may be still
other factors associated with social class and religion that independently promote activism; for example, being in a Jewish
minority group that has preserved its culture in the face of opposing community pressures for centuries may in some way prepare
or permit the individual to take controversial positions as a
student.[41]

Thus far student protestors have been discussed as if they were
a relatively coherent group of activists who, though varying in
their ideas as to how to reconstruct society, agree in rejecting the
polity and culture. They should, however, be differentiated into
two groups, the radicals and the renouncers, segments which are
often confused with each other because, on the surface, their
behavior, their antiestablishment beliefs, their total rejection of
the system, often seem the same. Yet in a real sense, the radicals
are closer to other protestors such as the Wallacite white youth or
the black militants, since all three are basically concerned with
owning Western industrial society. The renouncers are essentially interested in *disowning* Western society. The terms "re-
nouncer" or "renunciation tendency" are clearly inadequate, yet
they are useful, for it would be a definite mistake to describe this
tendency as "radical" or "revolutionary." In fact, in its rejection
of much of the modern world, including the use of, and products
of, large-scale technology and urbanization, it is much closer in
outlook to many classic conservative or reactionary doctrines.
One reason why it has been difficult to analyze the renunciatory
tendency apart from the other forms of militant student protest
is that there is, in fact, considerable overlap between the radicals
and the renouncers. Many students move back and forth between them. Many radicals engage in renunciatory styles of dress
and personal behavior. Most renouncers agree with the specific
antisystem activities of the radicals.

The distinction between the radical and renunciatory tendencies among youth, or in society generally, is, of course, related
to comparable distinctions drawn in other analyses. The sociolo-

gist David Matza has suggested that deviant behavior among youth may take one of three forms, delinquent, bohemian, or radical. All three are "specifically antibourgeois," i.e., reject private property relations. Delinquency, however, "seems most pronounced among that section of youth which terminates its education during or at the end of high school. Radicalism and bohemianism, particularly in the United States, are apparently enmeshed within the system of higher education." The bohemians, as Matza uses the term, those who are "opposed to the mechanized, organized, centralized, and increasingly collectivized nature of modern capitalism," come close to the concept of the renouncers.[42] The psychologist Kenneth Keniston has similarly differentiated student deviants between the "alienated," who are apolitical, romantic and aesthetic in their orientation, and the "activists," who are political, humanitarian and universalistic.[43]

More recently, another sociologist, Alvin Gouldner, has pointed to the emergence within the protest movement of the "psychedelic culture," which "differs profoundly from the protest movements and 'causes' of the 1930s, however politically radical, for psychedelic culture rejects the central values to which *all* variants of industrial society are committed. . . . [It] resists . . . routine economic roles whether high or low, inhibition of expression, repression of impulse, and all the other personal and social requisites of a society organized around the optimization of utility. Psychedelic culture rejects the value of conforming usefulness, counterposing to it, as a standard, that each must 'do his thing.' In short, many, particularly among the young, are now orienting themselves increasingly to expressive rather than utilitarian standards, to expressive rather than instrumental politics. . . ."[44]

The distinction between the politically radical and the culturally renunciatory protestors suggested here has not been made in most of the sociological research literature on student activism. Some psychologists, however, have attempted to isolate differences between "hippies," "nihilists," habitual drug users, and political radicals, analyses which come close to differentiating between the renunciatory and radical tendencies. These indicate that the renunciatory group is involved in some sort of generational conflict, of rejection of traditional or conservative views of their parents, while the political radicals come from the liberal-left family backgrounds. Both groups, of course, share a radical rejection of the conventional society. As Kenneth Keniston has described the difference:

> [the political radical tends to follow] the pathway of identification. Both father and son are described as expressive, humanitarian, and idealistic. The son identifies with his father, although the son is usually more radical. Such sons are very likely to be radicals in action as well as in beliefs. . . . There is, however, clearly a second pathway to radical beliefs, though less often to radical actions: the pathway of rejection of identification. Such students describe themselves as expressive, idealistic, and humanitarian, but describe their fathers as distinctly *not* any of these things. They are rather less likely to be politically active, more likely to adopt an apolitical or "hippie" style of dissent, and, if they become involved in political action, more likely to fall within the "nihilist" group.[45]

Jeanne Block and her colleagues have pursued similar differentiations between "activists" — those disillusioned with the status quo, involved in antiestablishment protest *and* supporting programs and policies designed to do something about "pain and poverty and injustice" — and those "dissenters" who are also involved in antiestablishment protests, but who do not seek to change the policies and institutions they object to through positive action. Activists differ from dissenters in evaluating their relationships with their parents more positively. The dissenters tend to describe a "conflicted, unsatisfying parental relationship," one which presumably precipitated or justified a break with family social values.[46]

Studies of committed drug users among students also indicate that they differ from those who express their antagonisms to society more through organized political activities than through expressive forms of personal deviance in similar ways to those reported above. Richard Blum concluded that "families with greater divergency of opinion, more distant relationships to the children, and more unresolved parent-child interpersonal crises seem to be those which generate the drug explorers."[47]

But if the psychological research does suggest that those engaged in renunciatory activities are disproportionately recruited from the ranks of individuals with histories of family conflict and personal difficulties, a number of analysts of left-wing political activists have reported that "the findings on activists are reasonably consistent in showing that on the average, they are good students and are psychologically 'healthy'. . . . They can also be close to their families rather than rebellious and can reflect intellectual, humanistic, and democratic ideals fostered in the home."[48] As one study summed up its findings, "few college students in general can match the positive development of these personality characteristics that distinguish student activists from their college contemporaries."[49] Many writers and researchers dealing with the background and values of student activists have continued — up until 1971, at least — to elaborate on these supposedly positive traits of the active protesters.

These reports on the psychological "health" of left-wing militants pose an interesting problem in the sociology of knowledge, for a number of other studies and evaluations of the research literature have pointed for many years to the fact that almost all the analyses of student activism which conclude that the left-wing militants exhibit "superior" attributes are based on comparisons with the student body as a whole, rather than with activists of other ideological persuasions. A 1966 review of the extant studies pointed to the evidence that conservative activists, as well as those involved in student government affairs, possessed some of the psychologically healthy traits assigned to the campus militants.[50]

More recent efforts to systematically compare various groups of involved students refute the thesis that leftist activists are the noblemen of the campus. The psychologist Larry Kerpelman explicitly set out to analyze the psychological traits of different groups of students on a number of campuses: "left activists, middle-of-the-road activists, right activists, left nonactivists, middle-of-the-road nonactivists, and right nonactivists." He concluded that "characteristics that have been identified with left activists . . . characterize the involved generally . . . All student activists, no matter what their ideology, are less needful of support and nurturance, value leadership more, are more socially ascendant and assertive, and are more sociable than students who are not politically active."[51]

Similar conclusions with respect to consistency of political action and ideology were reported by Cowdry and Keniston in their study of a random sample of 1968 Yale seniors. They found when comparing the characteristics of students who were for or against the Vietnam war that those whose actions (signing or refusing to sign an antiwar petition) were consistent with their beliefs about the war were more like each other than either resembled the "inconsistent" antiwar group.[52]

A somewhat different study designed to test the assumption that "militant radicals" were psychologically healthier than moderates and nonmilitant conservatives, also found it necessary to reject the assumption that radical students are psychologically "healthier."

> There were statistically significant differences between the student types on four of the six personality measures: Authoritarianism, Dogmatism, Paranoia and Personal Efficacy. Militant radicals were the least authoritarian and the least dogmatic while nonmilitant conservatives were the most authoritarian and the most dogmatic. These findings supported the view of student radicals as "healthy" personalities. On the other hand, militant radicals were most paranoid and least efficacious. Clearly, if one assumes that it is more desirable to be lower on paranoia and higher on efficacy, these findings do not fit the "healthy" personality thesis.[53]

Various early surveys suggested that left-wing activists were superior academically to other students. This finding has also been challenged since a comparison of various analyses indicate that the alleged superiority of the leftists is based on *"self-reported* grade-point averages," but that surveys which compare the *"actual"* grades reveal no differences.[54] Left activists seemingly have a propensity to "perceive themselves as ranking higher . . . than they are in reality."[55] These findings that left-wing activists, such as members of SDS or participants in sit-ins, do not have higher grades than other students may seem at first hand to contradict the previously reported relationship between school academic quality and propensity to sustain demonstrations. In fact, it does not. The latter linkage is derived from the relationship in America between intellectuality, as reflected in cultural tastes and occupational preferences, and political liberalism. Schools which are strong in the liberal arts, the nonprofessional subjects generally, attract students from relatively well-to-do, high culture-oriented and politically liberal families. They tend also to be better qualified for admission to the more selective colleges. The more prestigious a school, therefore, the more likely it is to have a significant segment of its student body predisposed to sympathetically support militant protests. But *within* such institutions, the available data clearly indicate that those who are deeply involved in radical activity resemble those active in other groupings in terms of scholarly achievements. In general, those who have the psychic energy to be active, whether as conservatives, moderates, or leftists, tend to be somewhat more qualified academically, than passive students.

Reports on the as yet scanty research on the characteristics of activists, as distinct from opinion survey results concerning the supporters of leftist activism in the student population as a whole, suggest in other countries also that the small group of committed militants may differ considerably from the population which sympathizes with their general political orientation. Thus, although leftist students and sympathizers with militant radical groups tend on the average to be of lower socio-economic status than the student body as a whole in various countries in Europe and Japan, reports from France, Germany and Japan indicate that the activist core group tends to resemble those in the United

States, in being disproportionately composed of the children of men engaged in intellectually linked high status professions, particularly academe itself. Presumably being of a high status, intellectually oriented, left-leaning background provides the political predisposition, the family support, and the psychic security, in a university environment, to engage in radical protest. The less privileged supporters of radical ideas in these countries remain close to their family values but, like their more conservative status compeers in America, are too involved in trying to secure vocational benefits from their university experience to be active in politics.

The reports that American left activists have more "democratic values" than other students have also been challenged by the results of a study which attempted to test a hypothesis of mine regarding the source of the reported positive traits. It appeared that "their ideologies rather than their true sentiments . . . are dictating the answers . . . [that] leftists who have demonstrated intolerance and authoritarian behavior traits in practice may still give voice or pencil to liberal values in principle."[56] Miller and Everson report that their findings show "a remarkable fit with the Lipset thesis (and understandably somewhat disconcerting to the authors of this paper). We cannot reject the Lipset model. In fact, it provides the best fit of any model tested."[57]

Many scholars in this field have generally ignored the contradictory evidence and methodological inadequacies of studies purporting to demonstrate the greater academic success and healthier personalities of left-wing activists. Given the sharp discrepancies in research data, it becomes obvious that we must ask why. Curiously, the most insightful explanation for the bias has been suggested by an investigator, Richard Blum, who himself has given expression to the positive stereotype. Blum points out that there is a correspondence of interests and values between the intellectual community and the protesting students.

> The importance of adjustment, of curiosity, of social criticism, and of "progressive" sociopolitical doctrine, as well as an

emphasis on . . . spontaneity in relationships, and on being antagonistic toward traditional authority, are likely to be found in the social sciences and mind-studying trades, or espoused by their members, as well as by the liberal students. Consequently, when these students and clinicians undertake to evaluate today's left and/or drug-using students, they are often looking at people much like themselves . . . [Their] "liking" reactions [for these students] probably reflect preferences for people acting more as . . . [they] thought people ought to act . . . The danger is that the evaluation may be positive only because of the charm of the young people without the investigators' recognizing the grounds for their reactions and without coming to grips with either fundaments or implications of student behavior. We are posing the problem of investigator indentification with his subjects, of "countertransference," in which it may be — as some of the students contend — that the young are admired because they act out the fantasies of their frustrated elders. The corollary danger is also acute and is commonplace. When conservative people offer their more negative evaluations . . . many university and professionally based people reject outright what the "reactionaries" have to say.[58]

As the 1960s drew to a close, a second factor entered overtly to affect the selection of research topics and the way in which research results are presented. With increasing polarization on campus, many of the more radical activists concluded that no useful function could be served by their cooperating with social science inquiries concerning student activism. Empirical research was defined as "pig research," as inherently a form of counterinsurgency, regardless of the political values of the scholars involved. Two major national studies of student behavior, one conducted by the American Council on Education and the other by the Carnegie Commission on Higher Education, were frequently attacked in the left-wing student press, and students were urged not to cooperate, not to permit themselves to be interviewed. At least one major analyst of student protest, the Santa Barbara sociologist Richard Flacks, who had been active in SDS as a student and who has remained an active radical as a

faculty member, announced at the 1969 session of the American
Sociological Association on student activism, that he no longer
would do empirical studies of student activists, since his experience had convinced him that establishment forces made use of his
work in spite of his intentions. Another equally creative sympathetic student of student radicalism, Kenneth Keniston, raised
the issue of the unhappy political consequences of reporting
unpalatable facts about radical students in the context of a
review of a book on the Harvard demonstrations of 1969 written
by Steven Kelman, the national chairman of the Young People's
Socialist League, which was strongly hostile to SDS and the
Harvard militants. Keniston was sharply criticized by sociologist
Dennis Wrong, for this position.

> Reviewing Steven Kelman's account of student politics at Har-
> vard, *Push Comes to Shove,* Kenneth Keniston concedes the
> validity of Kelman's charge that the SDS radicals "are undemo-
> cratic, manipulative, and self-righteous to the point of snobbery
> and elitism," but then observes that although "Kelman's angry
> book is written almost entirely to those on his Left . . . his book
> will mostly be read by those far to his Right, and it will be used
> (much against his wishes) to provide further ammunition for the
> Reagans, Mitchells, and Agnews in their politically profitable war
> against the alienated and radical young". . . .
>
> [O]ne finds Keniston clucking his tongue over Kelman's
> "exposé of the dirty linen of cultural revolutionaries and political
> revolutionaries in Harvard SDS," as if the only important con-
> sideration was what the right-wing neighbors will say.[59]

The political values and concerns of scholarly researchers are
not the only element which may produce variations in research
results. Studies concentrating primarily on activists which attempt to distinguish the social and psychological traits of students of different persuasions are also confronted by special
analytical problems. Whether or not students direct their extracurricular energies into politics is strongly linked to political
orientations. Studies of student bodies in different countries

indicate that those on the left generally (and the small group on the extreme right) view politics as an appropriate and even necessary university activity.[60] Committed morally to the need for major social changes, leftists feel that the university should be an agency for social change; that both they and their professors should devote a considerable portion of their activities to politics.

Conversely, however, the less leftist students are, the more likely they are to disagree with this view, the more prone they will be to feel that the university should be an apolitical "house of study." Liberals and leftists, therefore, are much more likely to be politically active than moderates and conservatives. A relatively strong conservative stance will not be reflected in membership or activity in a conservative political club. This means that on any given campus or in any country, the visible forms of student politics will suggest that the student population as a whole is more liberal or radical leftist than it actually is. Since conservative academic ideology fosters campus political passivity, one should not expect to find much conservative activity.

Presumably it takes a lower threshold of political interest or concern to activate a liberal or leftist than a conservative. One would deduce, therefore, that the average conservative student activist should be more of an extremist within his ideological tendency than the average liberal. Hence a comparison of campus activists of different persuasions should find a greater share of extremists among the conservatives than among the liberals.

The Conflict Continues

Students, as the discussion in the next two chapters suggests, have more often than not contained an unruly minority, ready to protest whatever offends them, within or outside the university. It can be strongly argued that the circumstances of their being a "privileged" group which give them the psychic security to act are also among the factors which make their activism possible. It can be argued on the same grounds that a politically inactive student population is a cause for greater misgivings than an active one. The fact remains, however, that a large part of the group of self-identified "radicals" in the American movement which began in the mid-sixties have been close to total alienation from the rational and the political world. The overwhelming majority of them do *not* belong to any of the numerous "small c" communist groups which dominate the organized New Left and maintain some links (though often very nebulous) to philosophical and tactical doctrines of Marxism-Leninism. They belong, in fact, to the renunciatory rather than the radical tendency. The anarchist Paul Goodman, whose writings were a basic text for many of the Berkeley activists of 1964–65, and who was invited to teach at San Francisco State, with the students voluntarily paying the bill, wrote at the end of the decade with troubled concern about the future of the movement with which he once almost totally identified. As he points out, many students had isolated themselves from any ability to communicate about reality.

> There was no knowledge, but only the sociology of knowledge. They had so well learned that physical and sociological research is subsidized and conducted for the benefit of the ruling class that they did not believe there was such a thing as simple truth. To be required to learn something was a trap by which the young were put down and co-opted. . . .
>
> Inevitably, the alienated seem to be inconsistent in how they take the present world. Hippies attack technology and are scornful of rationality, but they buy up electronic equipment and motorcycles, and with them the whole infra-structure. Activists say that civil liberties are bourgeois and they shout down their opponents. But they clamor in court for their civil liberties. Those who say that the university is an agent of the powers that be, do not mean thereby to reassert the ideal role of the university, but to use the university for their own propaganda.
>
> Though each one is doing his thing, there is not much idiosyncracy in the spontaneous variety. The political radicals are, as if mesmerized, repeating the power plays, factionalism, random abuse, and tactical lies that aborted the movement in the thirties. And I have learned, to my disgust, that a major reason why the

young don't trust people over thirty is that they don't understand them, and are too conceited to try. Having grown up in a world too meaningless to learn anything, they know very little and are quick to resent it.[61]

Others on the left have noted the strong similarities between the action-oriented segments of their movement and the extreme right. The national New Left weekly, *The Guardian,* in reporting on a meeting of the National Youth Alliance, an overtly racist advocate of Right Power violence and an offshoot of "Youth for Wallace," commented: "Contemporary commentators often lump the extremes of right and left together. Indeed, despite obvious differences there were striking similarities exhibited . . ."[62] Some sections of the movement have gone even further to point up the close resemblances between some groups on the New Left and the original youth-oriented Fascist party of Benito Mussolini. An editorial in *The Campaigner,* published by the New York and Philadelphia Regional SDS Labor Committees, stated : "There is a near identity between the arguments of anarchists (around the Columbia strike movement, e.g.) [that is, Mark Rudd and his followers who became the Weathermen faction] and Mussolini's polemics for action against theory, against program."[63]

An article in the same magazine argued:

> It is an irony of history that certain New Leftists today would be quite at home with Mussolini's radical polemics . . . We must look to historical precedent in order to reveal the dangers inherent in certain New Left rhetoric today. . . . [Mussolini] fought for the idea that the revolution would be decided in the streets. . . . Similarly, fascism celebrated youth as a class. "Giovenezza" was the official Italian hymn to youth; similar examples are found in Nazi propaganda. The image of youth was extended to attack on the "older" capitalist nations, the "old," effete parliamentary bureaucrats.

The authors of this article go on to point to other similarities, including the evolution of the ideas of Georges Sorel, the French syndicalist theoretician, "the spiritual leader of those Italian syndicalists who produced the fascist movement. 'Purgative violence,' so recently repopularized by the writings of Frantz Fanon, played a central role in the revised [fascist] syndicalist theory."[64]

Perhaps more significant than this criticism by one SDS faction of another is the fact that a detailed analysis of the ideology and behavior generally of the current wave of new radicalism by Irving Louis Horowitz, the literary executor of C. Wright Mills and radical authority on revolutionary thought, came independently to similar conclusions.

> This is the first generation in American society, at least in this century, to combine political radicalism with irrationalism. . . .
>
> The current style of radicalism is abrasive, physical, impatient and eclectic. . . . This moralistic style is a ready handmaiden to the "totalitarian democracy" that the historian Jacob Talmon spoke of. It is a fanatic attempt to impose a new social order upon the world, rather than to await the verdict of consensus-building formulas among disparate individuals as well as the historical muses.
>
> [T]he modern Left movement . . . is not so much an attack on the world of ideas as it is an attack on the idea that reason is the only modex of knowing. The suspicion is that reason is an ideology that teaches us to stand between two extremes, unable to act. This identification of liberalism with the spirit of judiciousness and prudence is precisely why liberalism, at the psychological level, continues to be the main target for radical jibes. . . .
>
> *Fascism returns to the United States not as a right-wing ideology, but almost as a quasi-leftist ideology,* an ironic outcome that Sorel anticipated in his own writings when he celebrated Mussolini and Lenin as if they were really two peas in one pod.[65]

The sociologist Peter Berger, who has been active in the peace organization SANE as well as in various antiwar protests, also reports that as a European emigré, "observing the [American] radicals in action, I was repeatedly reminded of the storm troopers that marched through my childhood in Europe." Trying to understand this emotional reaction, he found that Old Left (Communist) activists did not produce this feeling in him, although he was opposed to them. He was forced to conclude that the New Left has strong similarities to facism which is lacking in the Old Left.

What is specifically fascist about this ideology?

A movement characterized by its negations rather than by a positive vision of the future: The new radicals take it as *ipso facto* evidence of counterrevolutionary intellectualism if one asks specific questions about their design for the future . . . The basic counter-position is between "the movement" (*die Bewegung*, as the Nazis called themselves) and "the system" (*das System* . . .) — the one absolutely noble and embodying the wave of the future, the other absolutely corrupt and representing nothing but decaying stasis. . . . Liberal democracy is a sham and, indeed, is the principal enemy. . . . Rationality is nothing but manipulation on behalf of "the system. . . ."

The clearest symptom of the continuity of . . . themes is the mystique of the street. I recall a recent scene I watched on television, a group of students chanting rhythmically, "The streets belong to the people" — and the almost physical shock, as I remembered, at this moment, the opening lines of the second verse of the "Horst Wessel Lied," the anthem of the Nazi movement: "Die Strasse frei den brauen Bataillonen . . ." — "Clear the streets for the Brown battalions. . . ."

The political cult of youth: How, in the midst of all the glorification of youth that surrounds us today, could one forget that the anthem of Mussolini's Italy began with the invocation "Giovinezza, giovinezza, primavera di bellezza . . ." — "Youth, youth, springtime of beauty. . . ."?

The totalization of friend and foe, and the concomitant dehumanization of the latter: Again, linguistic usage is highly instructive here. Anyone who remembers the Nazi use of *Saujuden* (Jewish pigs) should stop to reflect about the human implication of the current usage of the term "pigs."

Finally, the assurance of the radicals that they represent a mystical "general will," even though it is undiscoverable by empirical means. . . . This elitism is particularly repulsive in view of the democratic rhetoric. . . . In fact, the new radicals are not only contemptuous of the mechanisms of liberal parliamentary democracy; they are fundamentally contemptuous of *any* procedures designed to find out what the people want for themselves. . . .

If one adds up these themes, one is confronted by an ideological constellation that strikingly resembles the common core of Italian and German fascism. Indeed, one is drawn to the conclusion that the concepts and interpretations drawn by many contemporary radicals from Marxism are grafted upon a body of motives and perspectives on the world that have nothing to do with Marxism.[66]

Similar parallelisms have been drawn by foreign leftist intellectuals, such as the Anglo-Canadian anarchist, George Woodcock, and Jurgen Habermas, Germany's most prominent radical sociologist. But the question must be raised to what extent this common ideology and tactics have comparable roots. As Berger notes, the Italian fascist party glorified "youth." Before the seizure of power it was, in fact, largely an antisystem youth party. Few leaders other than Mussolini were over thirty. Many of its activists were students. The German Nazi movement was somewhat different, but again, it should be noted that its earliest centers of strength were the universities. The Nazis captured control of the national German student organization and of the student councils in the bulk of the universities by 1931, before they had anything like comparable strength in any other stratum. As in Italy, their activists were young men.[67] Where youth is unrestrained by being part of an adult party or organization, it is probable that youth's variant of radicalism, whether rightist or leftist, will take on the violence-prone elitist orientations noted by Berger and the others.

Writing close to sixty years ago, the young undergraduate socialist Randolph Bourne, perhaps the most impressive young radical intellectual the United States ever produced, discussed at length the characteristics of youth in politics. Much of his analyses and descriptions of the collegiate youth before World War I are prescient of Berger's harsh descriptions, although Bourne himself was largely positive.

> Youth can never think of itself as anything but the master of things. . . . Its enthusiasm for a noble cause is apt to be all mixed up with a picture of itself leading the cohorts to victory. The youth never sees himself as a soldier in the ranks, but as the leader, bringing in some long-awaited change by a brilliant *coup d'etat.* . . .
>
> The youth of today are willful, selfish, heartless, in their rebellion. They are changing the system blindly and blunderingly. They feel the pressure, and without stopping to ask questions or analyze the situation, they burst the doors and flee away. Their seeming initiative is more animal spirits than anything else. . . .
>
> It is a fallacy of radical youth to demand all or nothing, and to view every partial activity as compromise. Either engage in something that will bring revolution and transformation all at one blow, or do nothing, it seems to say. . . .
>
> Radical youth is apt to long for some supreme sacrifice and feels that a lesser surrender is worth nothing. But better than sacrifice is efficiency! It is absurd to stand perplexedly waiting for the great occasion, unwilling to make the little efforts and to test the little occasions, and unwilling to work at developing the power that would make those occasions great.[68]

But Randolph Bourne's complaints about some of the traits of the radical youth of his day were only reiterating ancient descriptions of the tension between youth and authority. Much of this was known, at least as early as Aristotle, who said:

> [Youth] have exalted notions, because they have not yet been humbled by life or learnt its necessary limitations; moreover their hopeful disposition makes them think themselves equal to great things — and that means having exalted notions. They would always rather do noble deeds than useful ones: their lives are regulated more by moral feeling than by reasoning. . . . All their mistakes are in the direction of doing things excessively and vehemently. . . .
>
> [T]hey love too much, hate too much, and the same with

everything else. They think they know everything, and are always
quite sure about it; this, in fact, is why they overdo everything.[69]

In essence what Aristotle and more recent commentators on the
values and attitudes of youth have said is that youth lacks restraint. If political behavior can be seen as a combination of
impulse and restraint, then young people are much more likely
to press for the attainment of seemingly positive ends, and to
ignore the extent to which the means used shape the ends which
are achieved. Restraint, in essence, involves curbs on the means
one uses to secure what one wants. And as Earl Raab and I have
noted in our analysis of right-wing extremism, "Democratic
commitment can be seen essentially as a matter of restraint." The
Bill of Rights is couched in the language of restraint: "Congress
shall make no law . . ." It is the essence of extremism in politics
to eliminate restraint, to conceptualize the struggle as one between absolute good versus absolute evil, thereby justifying the
use of any tactics.[70] Political socialization in democracy involves
learning about restraints, about means-ends relationships, as well
as about how to secure objectives. It must develop a political
superego, which limits the uninhibited desire to destroy those in
the way. And the greater propensity of youth for the "ethic of
absolute ends" as distinct from the "ethic of responsibility" discussed earlier is another way of saying that youth politics are
more likely to reflect impulse than restraint. It also is another
way of indicating that youth are more prone to favor change,
reform, radicalism of all varieties, than older people. Youth-
based movements, therefore, whether of the left or right, should
have major elements in common.

This point may again be illustrated by reference to extreme
right-wing movements. In 1968, many in the noncollege segment
of American youth showed their propensity to go to political
extremes in defense of their values by disproportionately backing
George Wallace. All opinion polls agreed that in various stages
of his campaign up to and including Election Day, Wallace
secured more votes from the twenty-one- to twenty-nine-year-old

group than from older age cohorts. He was also heavily backed according to opinion surveys among high school youth, particularly those of less well-to-do parentage who had no plans for a college education. Postelection surveys continue to point up Wallace's youth appeal. A Gallup Poll taken in March 1971 found that 20 percent of the new eighteen-to-twenty-one-year-old voter group preferred Wallace to Nixon or Muskie and Humphrey. Among the over-twenty-one electorate, Wallace's support was much less, 13 percent.[71] Since relatively few college students prefer the Alabaman, this means that his following among the under-twenty-one-year-old noncollege electorate is more than 25 percent.

Within the Wallace movement itself, the youth segment, which formed the independent group, the National Youth Alliance, after the election, turned out to be much more overtly racist, pro-violence, and antidemocratic than any other outgrowth of the American Independent Party.[72] The young former Wallacites, in effect, went to the extreme of their tendency. In so doing, as various New Leftists noted, they resembled the New Left. *The Guardian* reported:

> [NYA] leaders hit hard at the establishment, the liberals and their elders for botching up the country. "We are more antiestablishment than anyone. . . ."
> The alliance attacked the "criminal politico-economic system of maintaining full employment and buying votes by intervention in alien wars. . . ." The alliance warns rightists of the consolidation of corporate concerns. . . .
> The NYA resembles the New Left also in seeing its primary constituency as young workers and college students. It "vowed" to forge a "revolutionary" alliance of students and young workers to crush the left, stem the "liberal" tide and save a dying republic.[73]

These rightist youth, unlike many of their elders in the Wallace movement, but like the New Left, openly proclaim their opposition to conservative economic principles and "bourgeois values."

We do not concern ourselves with the intricacies of economic conservation. We shall never deny what is needed to those who need it. . . . Those who seek to put bourgeois values over the hopes and aspirations of the people are enemies of the Right Front.

The NYA hopes to unite all American youth in a movement for peace, progress, and the restoration of the rights of the American people.[74]

The Alliance even makes some of the same complaints about American higher education that New Leftist students have uttered. "You are no longer the individual you thought you were; but are now a mere number in a file. . . . Your English professor hardly shows up for class."[75]

The NYA has contempt for George Wallace and many other rightist leaders for adhering to the rules of the political game. They proudly announce their belief in racial inequality by wearing buttons with the mathematical symbol of inequality. They denounce the Jews, Negroes, American Indians, and all other nonwhite races as inferior. They call for teaching the superiority of the white race in "white studies" courses.

The emergence of right-wing extremism among youth is not limited to the American defenders of segregation and white supremacy. In Germany, where the radical right-wing National Democrats secured more electoral backing (4.6 percent) in 1969 than the left-wing movement supported by the New Left students (0.6 percent), "it seems that the young people have infused the [rightist] movement with new strength."[76] A year later, a report on German undercover investigations among right-wing groups reported over half the participants in rightist confrontations "belonged to the younger generation. This response of young people to nationalist agitation is partly an expression of backlash against left-wing supremacy among politically conscious German youth."[77] In France, *Le Monde* reported that "extreme right-wingers are on the move again. . . ."

The fact that students and young people predominate in these new far-Right movements explains the injection of fresh ideas into the shopworn theories of fascism, elitism, and totalitarianism. . . .

Since the May 1968 student-worker revolt in France, certain groups of young right-wingers have been rivaling the Left in condemning the consumer society and the industrial bosses. . . .

Unyielding nationalism is one of the main planks of a rather small group calling itself Action Nationaliste, which draws most of its support from students at the Institute for Studies in Political Science. . . .

Far-Right activists usually do not bother to conceal their taste for violent action and mystery. The Mouvement Jeune Révolution, for instance, revels in secrecy. . . . MJR, like the other extreme right-wing organizations, attracts rightists who "want to do something."[78]

In Italy, second only to France in the extensiveness of student protest in 1968, right-wing extremism in the form of a revived fascist student and youth movement is now again powerful. "Squadrismo," militant violent fascist bands, now operate on some campuses, particularly Rome. "As a fixed fact there seems to be a good deal of truth in the view of those who see the rebirth of youthful neosquadrismo" as springing from the so-called "trauma of the future." Their program has been described as "a bomb underneath the institutions."[79]

The emotive movement of the 1960s is not the first American student expression of sharp discontent with the university and society. Although probably the most powerful one, since, though a minority, it is based on a campus population of close to eight million, it has been preceded by many others which have played a role in changing the university, politics, and cultural practices. Whether one despairs or rejoices about the activities of the current generation-unit of renunciatory youth, any effort to evaluate it must rest not only on comparisons with youth and extremist movements in other countries, but some knowledge of the previous comparable activities of American students is necessary. The next two chapters turn to this effort.

4

Historical Background: From the Revolution to World War I

$\mathbf{M}$any of the explanations for the emergence of student political and cultural protest during the 1960s discussed in Chapter 3 suggest that this event is causally related to structural changes in the university system, or in the ways in which Americans bring up their youth. Thus some writers have pointed to the presumed educational deficiencies derivative from increased university size, or greater concern for research than for teaching. Others have accounted for student patterns of cultural renunciation (drugs, hair, dress, freer sexual practices, etc.) as a consequence of increased parental permissiveness, the unwillingness of adults to discipline children. Some interpretations stress the gravity of the problems facing the nation, especially the Vietnam war, the inability to fulfill the promises of equality made to blacks, and the various ecological pressures stemming from industrialism, metropolitanism, and population pressures, in undermining the legitimacy, the "title-to-rule," of the dominant social institutions.

While all of these factors would seem to have some relationship to the expansion of student unrest, placing the analysis of student activism in comparative and historical perspective challenges the interpretations which seek to account for its current American phase by reference to unique national patterns. Clearly the present wave of student unrest has affected universities and countries in all parts of the world, underdeveloped, Western European, and Communist. Student protest movements have been more widespread and involved a larger proportion of the university population in countries as varied as France, Japan, South Korea, Indonesia, Czechoslovakia, Poland, Senegal, Argentina and Mexico. I have dealt with various aspects of student activism in other countries elsewhere, and do not want to repeat these discussions here, except to note that the similarity in patterns of behavior found in so many different cultural, familial, educational environments suggests that many of the contemporary America-centered interpretations are at best incomplete.[1]

The broad structural explanations, which stress the uniqueness of aspects of the contemporary scene, are also largely stated in absence of any consideration of the history of American campus activism. Much of what has been written is based on the assumption that American students have been quiescent until recently, presumably because their educational experiences were relatively good. In fact, the historical record reveals previous periods in which important segments of the college population have engaged in campus violence, in cultural and sexual experimentation, and in political radicalism. Earlier efforts to explain developments have frequently been stated in almost identical terms with those given for current events. Both in the last decades of the nineteenth century and in the 1920s, many writers urged that the increased emphasis given to research and extramural service activities by faculty resulted in inferior education and consequent student resentments. Similarly, the widespread demand for increased "student power" in the 1890s, and the innovations in cultural and sexual behavior and the disregard for law exhibited by many collegians in the 1920s, were both credited by contemporary analysts to the changes in the American family system, particularly the decline in parental authority. In calling attention to these and other similarities between the interpretations of the past and the present, I am not arguing that any of them are necessarily wrong. But clearly any effort to understand the sources of student behavior in a given time and place must be rooted in a general understanding of the factors in the social situation of university students which encourage particular modes of behavior among them generally, as well as knowledge of the way in which different segments have acted over time and place.

Groups dedicated to change either within society, or more commonly within the university have been relatively frequent among the undergraduate population. There are many explanations, obvious and less obvious, offered particularly in recent years for the special qualities of these students. To summarize generalizations made in the preceding chapters, various elements in their situation — their exposure to familial, religious, and social ideals presented in an absolute fashion, their relative lack of experience with the conflicting pressures derivative from varying value obligations or role demands, the insecurities stemming from being marginal men, in between the security and status derived from their family, and the obligation to find a mate, career, and status of their own — press them to see more clearly and purely the imperfections in university and society. On the other hand, they are freer than other segments of youth as well as older generations to act without concern for consequences to themselves or those close to them. They are footloose, in between engagements so to speak, and with considerable energy to use up. And whatever outlet any particular group of them chooses to use, the ecology of the university — the easy communication among those on a campus — makes it possible for all predisposed in a given direction to find one another, to mobilize that minority of students who are in agreement. Out of their new awareness as members of an intellectual community, out of their detached and advantaged position, students are better able than most of us to recognize the flaws, the inconsistencies around them, and can afford to be offended by them. Sometimes their horizons are limited to the institutions that are close by, the universities themselves, as in much of the nineteenth century; in periods of broad social ferment, however, the world and its problems are their oyster. These statements are as valid for an avant-garde unit of the American student population ever since the beginning of the Republic in 1776 as they are for those of any other nation, as a brief examination of their behavior over time demonstrates.

Protest and Violence on Campus:
From the Revolution to the Civil War

The first record of American students as a protest group may be found in the annals of the American Revolution. As Richard Hofstadter points out: "In nationalist and colonial revolutions college and university students have always played an aggressive part, and to this the American college students were no exception."[2] Samuel Eliot Morison quotes a member of the Harvard Corporation writing in the early 1770s that the students "are already taken up with politics. They have caught the spirit of liberty."[3] The celebrated educational historian W. H. Cowley has described the general reaction of students to the Revolution.

> All of the nine existing colleges either closed down or greatly limited their operations because most of their eligible students had joined the militia or the Continental Army, but more relevant here are instances of students frustrating the British and discomfiting Loyalists. Two such illustrate these numerous harassments: Harvard students drove out of Cambridge the tutor who directed British troops to Lexington and "the shot heard round the world"; the soapbox harangues and the pamphlets written by an eighteen-year-old Kings College undergraduate named Alexander Hamilton helped arouse the mob that, despite his pleas against violence, three weeks later forced President Myles Cooper to seek refuge on a British warship bound for England.[4]

For a half century after the Revolution, students recurrently engaged in protests, some of them quite violent in character, directed *against the universities* for various deficiencies. G. Stanley Hall noted a seven-year-long Harvard outbreak beginning in 1790 against the examination system, and "more serious rebellions" in 1807 and 1830.[5] He also recorded similar events in other universities, and the presence among many faculties of "a fear that the whole student body is capable of being united and arrayed in organization against their authority."[6] Morison concluded: "The typical student of the early seventeen-nineties was an atheist in religion, an experimentalist in morals, a rebel to authority."[7]

At Harvard a series of strikes and other demonstrations occurred in the late eighteenth and early nineteenth centuries against bad food. Many students were expelled, actions which often led to new and more intensive protests. In 1818, four students were dismissed for throwing crockery during a food riot. "Their classmates chose to fight the tyranny of the administration, and, led by young Emerson and many sons whose fathers' names are still remembered as great patriots of the American Revolution, they rallied round the rebellion tree."[8] Emerson was suspended for his role in this affair. In 1823, over half the senior class was expelled shortly before graduation. During that year there had been explosions, the dropping of inked water on tutors, etc. In 1834, the resort to the power of the public authorities by President Quincy to punish riotous students, then as now considered a violation of university norms, brought a drastic reaction from the students comparable to the events of 1969 when police were summoned to Harvard Yard.

> Then, hell broke loose! Quincy had violated one of the oldest academic traditions: that the public authorities have no concern with what goes on inside a university, so long as the rights of outsiders are not infringed. The "black flag of rebellion" was hung from the roof of Holworthy. Furniture and glass in the recitation rooms of University were smashed, and the fragments hurled out of the windows. The juniors, led by Ebenezer Rockwood Hoar, voted to wear crape on their arms, issued a handbill with an acute dissection of the President's character, and hanged

his effigy to the Rebellion Tree. A terrific explosion took place in chapel; and when the smoke had cleared, "A Bone for Old Quin to Pick" was seen written on the walls. A printed seniors' "Circular," signed by a committee who were promptly deprived of their degrees, gave their version of the Rebellion in language so cogent that the Overseers issued a forty-seven-page pamphlet by Quincy to counteract it. . . . Quincy never recovered his popularity.[9]

At Princeton, according to Harry Bowes, student of the history of student rebellions, "following a rebellion in 1806 half the students were expelled. . . . This dealt the college a blow which impaired its usefulness for over a decade. Six rebellions equally violent occurred from 1800 to 1830. During one riot, the students gained possession of the college buildings and defied authorities to try and enter them."[10] On another occasion, after three students were expelled, "for several days Nassau Hall resounded to the report of pistols and the crash of bricks against doors, walls and windows."

Yale also had frequent rebellions culminating in "The Great Rebellion" of 1828, which resulted in the "rustication from the college of some forty students." The University of Virginia, following Thomas Jefferson's enlightened policies, gave its students more freedom than other schools. The university established a plan "under which a board of six student 'censors' would assist the faculty in maintaining order." A series of riots in 1825 undermined the effort. "Three former presidents of the United States who had administered the nation for twenty-four of its thirty-six years [Jefferson, Madison, and Monroe] sat on the Board of Visitors when it met to restore peace, but not even their knowledge and prestige could breathe life into a scheme of self-government that collided with the deeply embedded tradition of student contumacy."[11]

The College of South Carolina is cited in the literature in this field as a more typical example of a Southern school which underwent frequent riots and other disturbances, many protests against poor food and compulsory commons. In 1822, President

Cooper of the college wrote to Thomas Jefferson that "Republicanism is good, but the rights of boys and girls are the offspring of Democracy gone mad."[12] Parents frequently intervened to get a harsh punishment revoked.

Jefferson himself wrote in a letter to George Ticknor of Harvard on July 16, 1823: "The insubordination of our youth is now the greatest obstacle to their education. We may lessen the difficulty, perhaps, by avoiding too much government, by requiring no useless observances. . . . On this head I am anxious for information of the practices of other places, having myself had little experience of the government of youth."[13]

No analysis has been made of the backgrounds of the students who caused trouble in those days. Morison, however, indicates that at the beginning of the nineteenth century, as much later, the sons of the well-to-do were the discontented, while those from less privileged backgrounds took delight in their opportunities to benefit themselves. "If the college atmosphere seemed oppressive to young scions of rich mercantile families, it was Elysium to boys . . . who came up to Cambridge from poor or provincial surroundings after a hard struggle to qualify."[14]

Dormitories were deliberately established at various schools as a means of giving students "a common experience under the protective shelter of the faculty's guiding hand. . . . Group living was supposed to develop self-respect and group responsibility." However, as Bowes points out, the dormitory "also brought students into close proximity usually under poor [living] conditions . . . it was a hatching ground for pranks and plots. In general, dormitories helped to create an atmosphere that invited frustration, peer conformity, and crime."[15]

Although much student "indiscipline" in the first half century after Independence revolved around local college issues, underlying a considerable part of it was resistance to the efforts of the schools to impose a traditional uncritical religious outlook on undergraduates receptive to the intellectual challenges to orthodox Protestantism. Bowes notes that "the 'college fathers' . . . strongly associated the spirit of liberty and self-reliance with infidelity and godlessness. . . . [On one occasion] a number of Princeton students celebrated a triumph over the faculty by breaking into the Presbyterian church, removing the pulpit Bible, and burning it. The leader of the senior class claimed to be an atheist and stated that Godwin's *Political Justice* was his bible. His attitude was quite popular during this period of American history."[16]

The conflicts over the right of the college to impose its religious views and practices on the students were to some degree linked to the domination of most schools by conservative, often clerical, groups of trustees, presidents, and faculty. According to Earnest, in "the early days of the Republic the teaching, except in a few Southern colleges under the influence of Jefferson, was mainly Federalist," in politics, and theologically orthodox.[17] Conversely, Sister M. Kennedy indicates "Deism made rapid inroads among the college students of the day. Disrespect for authority, a sense of impermanence, and liberal theological ideas were heightened and spread by the Revolution. When the intellectual repercussions of the French Revolution reached the United States, skepticism and infidelity became rife and were accompanied by greater rowdyism in the colleges."[18] Many clergymen attributed student unrest to the "vogue of infidelity, Jeffersonianism, and rationalistic philosophy."[19]

The student opposition to rigid discipline within the colleges, as well as to the religious control over them and to the dogmatic beliefs enunciated by many of the colleges, did not constitute generational conflict per se. Rather they reflected and were allied to the liberal forces in the outside world led by Jefferson. These stressed the need for greater freedom from institutional control within the clerically dominated institutions of higher education, as well as the need for a totally voluntaristic religious system in the society as a whole. Morison reports that many of the conflicts within the Harvard Board of Overseers were along party lines, with the Federalists supporting strict authority and the Jeffersonian Republicans arguing for student rights.[20] In the larger polity, many of the Jeffersonians argued that the state was obli-

gated to provide services for its citizens seven days a week — that
it could not deprive non-Christians of their right to receive mail
on Sundays. In 1810, Congress passed a law providing for the
Sunday delivery of the mails. The issue of Sunday activities was
to remain a major one for some decades.[21] In 1830, a Senate
committee report, authored by a future Vice-President, Richard
Johnson, stated explicitly that in the United States religion and
irreligion had equal rights, and that laws proclaiming that the
government should not provide services on Sunday would work
an injustice on irreligious people or non-Christians, and would
constitute a special favor for Christians as a group. The report
enunciated in unequivocal terms: "The constitution regards the
conscience of the Jew as sacred as that of the Christian, and gives
no more authority to adopt a measure concerning the conscience
of a solitary individual than that of a whole community. . . . If
Congress shall declare the first day of the week holy, it will not
satisfy the Jew nor the Sabbatarian. . . . It is the duty of this
government to affirm to *all* — to the Jew or Gentile, Pagan, or
Christian — the protection and advantages of our benign institutions on Sunday, as well as every day of the week."[22]

Such sentiments, of course, outraged the Evangelical Protestant
segment of the community. The Anti-Masonic party, which swept
through the more isolated rural areas of the North in the late
1820s and early 1830s, in many ways represented the first major
backlash movement directed against the cosmopolitan educated
elite who were corrupting traditional values through their power
over politics, the media, and the cultural and intellectual centers. It identified the Masons, the Jacksonians, and the deistic
intellectuals as anti-Christian. Campus religious liberalism,
therefore, was involved in one of the major conflicts of the day.[23]

Bowes concludes his discussion of the period from 1790 to 1830
by saying that student behavior reflected "the growing liberalism
of the age, a liberalism which was impatient with puritanical
restraint and in some cases with religion itself." The universities
tried "to crush what they termed as irreligious, immoral, and
disorderly behavior," but failed. He suggests the internal con-

flicts resulted in "a deterioration of creativity, good scholarship, and inspirational teaching."

Although the succeeding epoch, from 1830 to 1880, witnessed fewer conflicts over discipline, much occurred which also had a contemporary air about it. President Quincy of Harvard "was plagued with the problem of nonconformity of dress by the students."[24] Quincy himself, as an undergraduate, had insisted in 1818: "Resistance to tyrants is obedience to God." He led a forbidden rally around the "Rebellion Tree," and was suspended by President Kirkland for this action.[25] In mid-nineteenth century conflicts with students, the police are described by Bowes as "often guilty of needless brutality and lack of tact."[26] In defense of the police it should be added that the "students make it a point to wantonly insult and exasperate the peelers [police] on every occasion when it can be done with safety."[27]

At the University of Virginia, which had started with more trust in student self-government than any other school in the country, "fear of student violence kept the faculty on edge." But when the boys organized an independent military company and announced that they would resist the "tyrannical movements of the faculty" which ordered them to remove all arms from the campus, the teachers in 1836 out of desperation or boldness ordered a substantial number of expulsions. Two days of rioting ended in compromise: the appearance of the militia upheld the majesty of the law and the retreat of the faculty readmitted the offending students. Ironically, the professor who engineered the compromise was shot to death by a student four years later.[28]

It is difficult to generalize concerning the political and social sentiments of American students in the Jacksonian and pre–Civil War periods. One American, C. A. Bristed, who graduated from Yale in the late 1830s and then went on to study for five years at Cambridge University, during which time he also visited continental universities, concluded "that the majority of highly educated young men under any government are opposed to the spirit in which that government is administered. Hasty and

imperfect as the conclusion is, it certainly does hold good of
many countries. . . ." Bristed went on to argue that the typical
student "sees the defects in the government of his country; he
exaggerates them with the ardor of youth, and takes that side
which promises to remedy them, without reflecting at what cost
the remedy may have to be purchased."[29]

If American students in the 1830s and 1840s were critical of a
mass electoral democracy from a conservative-elitist stance as
Bristed suggests, they did little actively to foster this viewpoint.
During this period, however, a number of abolitionist clubs appeared on various campuses. The University of Michigan had a
secret organization devoted to smuggling runaway slaves into
Canada.[30] The Amherst abolition society included one third of
the student body before it was banned in 1835. Other schools
with such societies included Dartmouth, Franklin, Hamilton,
New York, Williams, Union, Western Reserve, Illinois, Oberlin,
Marietta, Miami University (Ohio), Kenyon, and many others.
Many of these campus groups secured public, and thereby historical, attention because efforts were made during the 1830s to
deny their right to exist. "[I]t appears from a study of the cases
that the infringements upon freedom of opinion in Northern
colleges arose less from fear of the ideas of the [student] abolitionists than from distrust of the *agitative and apparently radical
methods* they employed." The administrative opposition disappeared, since with "the penetration of abolitionism into the
upper levels of Northern society and with its entrance into
politics and the church, antagonism to its discussion in Northern
colleges quickly lessened."[31] Some elite northeastern schools such
as Princeton, Harvard, Yale and Pennsylvania had large Southern enrollments and their administrators sought to avoid internecine warfare on campus. The occasional college straw vote I
have run across indicates overwhelming backing for the Republicans in 1856 and 1860.

There is some indication that Southern students were more
aggressive in fostering their regional point of view than their
Northern compeers. Cowley reports that students often joined
"in molesting anti-slavery visitors from the North and the rare

Southerners who expressed even mild doubts about the sanctity of slavery. In 1856, for example, University of North Carolina students burned in effigy and threatened to tar and feather a professor who supported the newly organized Republican party. In the same year University of Virginia students cheered when their alma mater presented Preston Brooks with a cane like the one he used on the floor of Congress to beat Charles Sumner into invalidism."[32]

After the Civil War, many "disorders in Southern universities . . . resulted from student membership in such organizations as the Ku Klux Klan." The Klan and other white supremacy groups were strong in a number of universities and used terror tactics against campus opponents and Negroes.[33]

Much of the intramural tension in this period, however, did not relate to any political issue. Essentially, students exhibited often in fairly violent fashion resentments against the faculty which were comparable to those expressed a century later. A recent sophisticated history of the American university reports:

> [A] personal relationship [between faculty and students] had seldom existed in the past, and least of all in the mid-nineteenth century. The barrier between teacher and student loomed, if anything, far higher. . . . it had . . . been revealed by riots, the throwing of stones at professors' houses, and in at least two cases by actual murder of a professor. At Dickinson College in 1866, "students regarded the faculty as a species of necessary evil. . . ."
>
> [C]ollege students betrayed many of the symptoms of a deeply disloyal subject population. Why else would oaths of allegiance have seemed appropriate for the students at Yale during the sixties and seventies? Or why would the freedom of students to congregate in large groups sometimes be inhibited by regulation? (e.g., at Harvard in 1871).[34]

Student Power and Radical Politics: The Interbellum Years

The period from the end of the Civil War until the turn of the century witnessed few politically related campus activities, other than efforts to support one of the two major party presidential candidates. There is some suggestion in the historical literature that if political protest was absent among the students of this era, romantic renunciatory, anticommercial and anti-industrial-civilization sentiments were present. "[C]ontemporary observers of the college scene, including those who studied freshman themes for the content of their ideas, agreed that the college student of this period placed high regard upon veracity, frankness, honesty, and such virtues, while opposing hypocrisy and sham." One student editorial in 1872 in a national paper for undergraduates, proclaimed Hamlet as the one character who suggests the ideal of students, for he was "the noble-hearted friend, pure, chivalrous."[35]

This choice of Hamlet as the ideal of American undergraduates a century ago is particularly appropriate for, as Erik Erikson points out, he is "an abortive ideological leader," who exhibits in Shakespeare's portrayal the special identity problems and need for commitment of introspective youth. He "is the morbid young intellectual of his time, for did he not recently return from studies at Wittenburg, the hotbed of humanist corruption, his time's counterpart to Sophist Athens and to today's centers of learning infested by existentialism, psychoanalysis — or worse? . . . He is estranged from the ways of his country . . . and, much like our 'alienated' youth, he is estranged from and describes as 'alienated' the overstandardized man of his day, who 'only got the tune of time and outward habit of encounter.' . . . He abhors conventional sham and advocates genuineness of feeling." And Hamlet's appeal lies precisely in the fact that he is a figure who epitomizes the inherent tragedy of idealistic youth, "that his fidelity must bring doom to those he loves, for what he accomplishes at the end is what he tried to avoid at first. He succeeds in actualizing only what we would call his negative identity and in becoming exactly what his own ethical sense could not tolerate: a mad revenger."[36]

The students of that long-past American age not only sought to identify with heroic and tragic figures, they also expressed their renunciation of the corrupt modern world in the practice common among Yale students in the late 1860s, who "often indulged in primitivistic idylls, camping out for a week or two on lonely islands in the Long Island Sound . . . living after the manner of the primitive savage, the independent barbarian. . . ."[37] In their romantic enthusiasms, these American students resembled the much more full-blown renunciatory groups of German youth who formed the extensive Youth Movement before World War I.[38]

Student demonstrations revived on an extensive scale in the last two decades of the century. They were largely directed "against the doctrine of *in loco parentis.*" Student newspapers demanded that the college "should adjust itself to the liberal changes in the structure of the American family." The *Williams Argo* argued that "Few parents would attempt any such government of twenty-year-olds as do colleges of their students."[39] At a number of schools in this period students forced through public "trials" of their president and secured the removal of many of them. Lincoln Steffens described a successful uprising at Berkeley during his freshman year (1885) there.

> One evening, before I had matriculated, I was taken out by some upper classmen to teach the president a lesson. He had been the head of a private preparatory school and was trying to govern the private lives and the public moral of university "men" as he had those of his schoolboys. Fetching a long ladder, the upper classmen thrust it through a front window of Prexy's house and, to the chant of obscene songs, swung it back and forth, up and down, round and round, till everything breakable within sounded broken and the drunken indignation outside was satisfied or tired. . . . [The president] was allowed to resign soon thereafter. . . .[40]

Students were sometimes instrumental in naming new presidents. Lewis Feuer points to various examples of faculty support for student protest against college administrations and suggests: "Ambitious faculty men who allied themselves with student uprisings found a new avenue for upward mobility."[41] The rebellious students, though expressing a high degree of alienation from their institutions and faculty, showed little interest in national politics, especially of a radical or reform kind. Analysis of campus straw votes indicated that all "over the United States (except, of course, in the South) college students recorded an overwhelming preference for the Republicans. This was true both in the Midwestern land-grant institutions and on the East Coast."[42]

The one source of a politically related controversy during this period was the requirement of the Morrill Land Grant Act that universities benefiting from it must provide compulsory military training. Many students in state universities, those primarily affected, strongly objected to military drill. The University of Wisconsin paper, the *University Press,* argued in 1870 that the American tradition opposed militarism. The most violent protest among the many hurled against such activities occurred in 1886, when students attempted to sabotage the program by breaking in and stealing the stocks and barrels of one hundred muskets.[43] Tensions derivative from the existence of military drill precipitated major student protests at the University of Illinois in 1879–1880, and again in 1889–1891. In both instances, the struggle ended with the resignation of the president.[44] These conflicts, like later ones, resulted in student activists generalizing their antagonism to the power of the faculty and regents. Thus, in 1880, a student paper, the *Vindicator,* "lashed the entire Faculty for twisting truth and using power unjustly, and boldly ridiculed individual professors." It described a typical regent as "a man who builds his house of cheap bricks, bought at reduced rates, on pretense they are for state purposes, and then denies it before a committee of the legislature."[45] During the second conflict, a student paper argued: "It seems inconsistent in this age and country to educate young men and women in republican sentiments and at the same time attempt to govern them by a set of laws in the making of which they have no voice at all. . . ."[46]

Demonstrations against compulsory military drill in state universities apart, almost all of the student protests of the late nineteenth century were manifestly directed against the shortcomings of the institutions as schools, around the issues of discipline, curriculum content, administration power, due process, student self-government and the like. "Disaffected young men rebelled through boycotts, strikes and demonstrations. . . . Frequently the most promising students led the agitation."[47] Then, as now, according to Feuer, they occurred "not in the universities where students were from the lower classes but in the schools of the more well-to-do, not in the universities where the sciences and the practical arts were pursued but in the colleges of the liberal arts." He went on to suggest that class origins made the difference.

> The class origin of the students, indeed, was a decisive factor in their unrest, but in a way precisely opposite to what a Marxist would expect. The Michigan or Illinois [non-protester] . . . came from a home where life's struggle was real and keen; he came to a state university because it was virtually free; often he worked his way through college; he chose his courses with an eye to his liveli-hood. . . . When the obstacles of life are genuine and concrete . . . then there are no surplus energies available for generational revolt.[48]

If the period of student protest in the first quarter of the nineteenth century witnessed the rebellious students pressing for values which they shared with adult Jeffersonians, the wide-spread demonstrations of the last quarter often involved a shared concern with the faculty for a change in university governance. This was also a period of faculty revolt against the absolute power of college presidents.

> Throughout the 1880s and 1890s . . . professors began increas-ingly to identify themselves by academic discipline or as members of a separate, professional class. One sign of this new faculty solidarity was the unprecedented frequency with which faculties as a whole openly opposed their presidents. Another sign was the professors' success in having faculty positions rearranged by intel-lectual disciplines, or departments, rather than individual chairs whose incumbents . . . were responsible only to the president. Yet a third sign was the unprecedented growth that occurred in the formation of professional societies during these years.[49]

Articles published in a variety of magazines read by the elite, the *Nation,* the *Critic,* the *Atlantic Monthly,* the *Forum* and others, contained frequent articles by professors and others concerning the problems of higher education. They dealt with sources of student unrest, the relationship between research and teaching, academic governance, faculty salaries and the like. It was generally recognized that higher education was in a stage of change and crisis. The emphasis on teaching and close faculty contact with undergraduates was attacked as a source of student discontent. It is interesting to note that even before the Civil War, student unrest was explained by "a growing [faculty] minority [as resulting from] . . . the faulty methods of teaching and the uninspiring content of instruction. A small contingent of Americans who had studied at German universities came home to insist that power was better exercised over subjects than over subject schoolboys, that a contribution to philology was far more significant than a contribution to student manners, that the whole emphasis of the college should be shifted from discipline to scholarship."[50] Shortly after the war, the Ann Arbor undergraduate paper, the *University Chronicle,* complained that "the University was not on a par academically with most Eastern universities and ought to admit it." It criticized the university for appointing too many faculty "without tested reputations."[51] These demands for scholars were advanced in much stronger and more general terms as a response to the turmoil of the latter part of the century.

An editorial on "College Discipline" in *The Critic* of July 30, 1881, raised the question why "American youths in college behave worse than . . . German youths." Its explanation for lesser student indiscipline was "the German policy of non-interference by faculty with students" supposedly derived from the fact that German professors were primarily dedicated to research. And both to improve "real learning in American colleges," and reduce student unrest, the editorial writer of *The Critic* argued:

> It must be borne in mind that the modern specialist gains no reputation by merely appropriating the knowledge of the past in

his branch of study; one must continually question Nature and push back the boundary of darkness which on all sides surrounds him. He must mark out a new path of investigation and arrive at new results. The ideal professor is not the mere pedagogue who sits at his desk hearing recitations. . . . The time has evidently come for the return of the latter type to his proper sphere and the establishment in professorial chairs of zealous [research] specialists.[52]

A German psychologist turned Harvard professor, Hugo Münsterberg, argued in the same vein some years later: "A young scholar ought to devote himself to special problems, where he can really go to the sources; instead of that our young instructor has to devote himself to the widest fields, where it is impossible to aim at anything but the most superficial acquaintance."[53]

Faculty defenders argued that excessive emphasis on teaching made for dull lecturers who bored their students and impelled them to dislike their college. In an article published in 1894, "Research The Vital Spirit of Teaching," G. Stanley Hall argued that "excessive teaching palls and kills." Exciting teachers are men whose knowledge "is fresh from the sources, and not second- or third-hand."[54] Münsterberg was to make a similar point:

> The young man who has to conduct twenty "recitations" a week, and to read hundreds of examination books, and to help on the administrative life of the place, begins by postponing his scientific work to the next year, and the year after next, when he shall be more accustomed to his duties. But after postponing it for a few years more his will becomes lame, his power rusty, his interest faded.[55]

Since college presidents and trustees supposedly were primarily interested in assuring that the faculty spent most of their time with students, an objective which some protesting students resented as much as those faculty who sought more time for research, Hall, though a new university president himself, called for faculty self-government. "[The] ideal university . . . is sure to need a larger academic policy shaped more by the faculty, who can be best trusted with the interests of science if their quality is once well established."[56]

Important segments of the students and the faculty were demanding greater freedom, more right to participate in government. A variety of student senates or councils were established for the first time. Undergraduates were allowed to take part in disciplinary committees or boards at a number of schools. These seeming triumphs had some real consequences in the elimination of areas in which colleges claimed the right to act *in loco parentis*. The experiences with shared power through student self-government was much less successful, however, than the increase in faculty influence at major schools.

> But though the students begged loudly for a "New System" when they were without it and complimented themselves on the prospect of running the college, once student government was a reality, the undergraduates lost much of their enthusiasm. There had always been something fraudulent in the idea of student *government*. Students did not, and could not, literally govern the college. The idea of student government was most often a proposition administrations tried to use to harness the rebellious energies of undergraduates. *The Bowdoin Orient* expressed typical disillusionment when it editorialized of Bowdoin's Student Jury, a system colleges throughout the East were clamoring to imitate: "The students do not desire to govern themselves nor is there any logical reason why they should be expected to do so. The faculty is given the authority and the faculty cannot delegate their responsibility." To the *fin de siècle* undergraduate, independence meant freedom from faculty interference in his extracurricular organizations. . . . Students discovered that they did not want to take over the colleges, but rather to insulate themselves from its demands. The grandest independence American students could conceive was their outright rejection of faculty, trustee, and alumni pleas to make a face-saving gesture before the public and reestablish the famous Senate.[57]

The awareness that student participation in the governance of universities involves co-optation rather than shared power, links critics of the campus scene of the 1890s with those of the 1960s. This was not the only similarity that may be found in the writings of the two periods. Then, as now, men differed as to the significance of student indiscipline. Some argued that it was the work of a small minority who did not really represent the feelings of, or the problems concerning, the great majority.

Thus a Harvard professor, N. S. Shaler, in a discussion of "The Problem of Discipline in Higher Education," contended in 1889, in terms prescient of many articles concerning the contemporary student population, that the considerable "public remark as to the evil behavior of Harvard students" was occasioned by the extreme actions of two to three percent which are well publicized, and "carry alarm into the households whence come some twelve hundred normally well-behaved young men."[58]

The controversies among faculty, administrators, and others, as to how to handle the disruptions on campus also resembled current debates. Men differed all during the nineteenth century as to whether to follow Jefferson's advice to reduce external controls and punishments as a means of reducing student hostility, or that of President Josiah Quincy of Harvard who resorted to calling the police and to trying to enforce civil law within the university.

The norm, accepted in many foreign countries, that universities are autonomous and that the police should not be called to intervene in intramural disturbances has always had strong support in the United States, particularly among students. Francis Wayland, pre–Civil War president of Brown, argued that campus unrest would be ended by subjecting students to the same civil penalties and external police power as the rest of society. He pointed out that he had "known college officers to take very great pains to shield students from the consequences of their violation of municipal regulations."[59] Discussions in the public press made the same point during the upheavals of the end of the century. An article by a professor in *The Forum* in 1887 concerning "College Disturbances" stated that they were in some part a result of the notion "that a different code of honor, morals, duty, and conduct belongs to college life from that which attends common life . . . that a college community is to some degree exempt from common obligations and responsibilities. . . . Students — many, not all — act upon the assumption, and the public in too many cases practically concedes it. Practices condemned and punished by the common and statute law are looked upon as allowable . . . in college."[60]

The German emphasis on research and graduate training gradually began to spread among the leading schools. By 1902, Johns Hopkins University, founded as a research oriented graduate school, was celebrating its twenty-fifth anniversary, and was regarded as a great university. Woodrow Wilson, then a professor of politics at Princeton, read an address to President Gilman in which he emphasized the new ideal.

> [Y]ou were the first to create and organize in America a university in which the discovery and dissemination of new truths were conceded a rank superior to mere instruction, and in which the efficiency and value of research as an educational instrument were exemplified in the training of many investigators. . . .
>
> You also first recognized the importance of publication as a function and a duty of a modern university, and by your demonstration of its feasibility and value you set a quickening example which has been widely followed.[61]

Although many academics agreed with Woodrow Wilson that reducing the teaching load and increasing support for research were good for education, these changes were followed by articles in the press which voiced the sentiment of administrators, trustees, and some protesting students in contending that research was interfering with adequate instruction and consequently made for student unrest. An article in *The Educational Review* in 1895 complained that "most young college professors are more concerned with their subjects than with their pupils." Charles Ramsey argued:

> In the zeal for special research which . . . has become the ideal aim of much college instruction, it has come about that only the

most brilliant scholars are chosen to be instructors, regardless of their lack of more strictly professorial preparation and experience. As such instructors are usually promoted, this in turn has also become the ideal method of recruiting professional ranks.[62]

The Nation editorialized in 1900 on "The Decline of Teaching," arguing that it resulted from the fact that it "is the making of books, and not the training of the young in habits of thought and work, that holds out to the teacher of to-day the main promise of reward." *World's Work* suggested in 1901 that research and teaching ought to be separated, that the two interfere with each other. "And in most of our universities the teaching of youth has become less efficient than it once was, and surely less than it ought to be, because of the too common effort to unite it with original research."[63]

An article in *The Atlantic Monthly* in 1902, while recognizing that talented professors ought to be encouraged to engage in creative scholarship, "to explore the farthest boundaries of human knowledge," strongly argued that the passion for research resulted in the neglect of other professorial duties by the large majority who were not genuinely creative.

> Yet the college teachers who really make original contributions to human knowledge are few in proportion to the total numbers engaged in the profession. The passion for scholarship, like that for poetry, does not always imply a corresponding power for production; and because we are glad to release some picked man from the common social obligations and services, and bid him Godspeed upon his adventures, it does not follow that a similar freedom may be claimed by those who stay at home.[64]

Seven years later in the same magazine, Abraham Flexner presented what was to become the classic story illustrating lack of concern for undergraduate teaching.

> I took occasion, not long ago, to ask a college dean who was the best teacher in his institution. He named a certain instructor.

"What is his rank?"
"Assistant Professor."
"When will his appointment expire?"
"Shortly."
"Will he be promoted?"
"No."
"Why not?"
"He hasn't *done* anything!"[65]

A comprehensive and highly praised survey of the operation of *Great American Universities,* published in 1910, generalized following a discussion of the situation of students at Harvard concerning the absence of concern among faculty for undergraduates.

> Here is the weak point of all the great colleges, and even of the smaller ones — the lack of personal contact between teacher and student. It is not due to the influx of an overwhelming number of students because the faculty has generally grown in proportion or more. It is partly due to defective organization and partly to the development of a new school of teachers, who detest teaching, who look upon students as a nuisance, and class work as a waste of time.[66]

The current debates concerning the multiversity, dealing with the involvement of professors in extramural organizations, reiterate points made at the turn of the century. Some welcomed the participation of faculty in such activities; others saw them as interfering with scholarly and teaching duties. The description in any case is familiar.

> [A] newer type of college professor is . . . everywhere in evidence; the expert who knows all about railroads and bridges and subways; about gas commissions and electrical supplies; about currency and banking, Philippine tariffs, Venezuelan boundary lines, the industries of Puerto Rico, the classification of the civil service, the control of trusts. . . . [The] college professor who represents the "humanities," rather than the distinctly

scientific side of modern education, is likewise brought closer to the public than ever before. The newspapers report — and misreport — him. Editors offer him space to reply. Publishers weary him with appeals to write textbooks. . . . The professor's photograph . . . assaults your eye in the marketplace. The college press club and the university's bureau of publicity gives his lecture dates in advance. The prospectus of your favorite magazine bids you inspect his literary qualifications as well as his thoughtful countenance. *Who's Who in America* informs you of the name of his second wife.[67]

Then, as now, participation by professors in political affairs led to their being denounced. Turn-of-the-century comment sounds extremely contemporary.

Within a twelvemonth college teachers have been openly denounced as "traitors" for advocating self-government for the Filipinos. In many a pulpit and newspaper office, last September, it was declared that the utterances of college professors were largely responsible for the assassination of President McKinley. . . . One must admit that a good many college professors have taken the Irish members of Parliament as their exemplars, and are boyishly pleased if they can merely obstruct the business of the House. Miss Evelina Burney once wrote of Sir Philip Jennings Clerk, "He is a professed minority man." This type of man is familiar in academic circles.[68]

This period also witnessed the first large group of academic freedom cases. A number of schools sought to fire controversial professors. The emergence of the "controversial" academic was, of course, not a coincidence. It stemmed from the shift in the conception of the professor from teacher to researcher, "from conserving to searching." Insofar as research, innovation, frontier knowledge began to gain status within academe, faculty members were occupationally motivated to reject the values and lore of the past, to assume that the knowledge and agreed wisdom of the present was tentative, that "tradition was mere opinion and experience, but that opinion improves as society ages and that experience grows stale with senescence."[69]

The growth in explicit reformist political concerns among the faculty and in the intellectual community generally after 1900 was to be paralleled among a small minority of students who became involved in socialist politics in the form of the Intercollegiate Socialist Society (ISS) formed in 1905. By 1908, a conservative English visitor, Alexander Francis, was impressed that the spread of socialism in America had deeply penetrated the intellectual and student worlds.

> If . . . the term "intellectuals" covers all who have had a college career, a considerable number of them may be said to have professed socialism. Socialist societies have established themselves at the universities; and Secretary Taft, speaking at Yale, referred somewhat scornfully to these "dreamers and impracticable thinkers at the universities of this country who would abandon the system lying at the base of modern society." Well, youth everywhere is prone to be full of impetuosity and self-confidence, at once purblind and bold; and in its state of half-culture, undergraduate youth is peculiarly apt to seize with enthusiasm upon a general principle, regardless of its limitations or relations to other principles. But I met not a few professors who hold and teach socialistic doctrines; and it is significant that most, certainly the most extreme, of these have positions in colleges and universities which have received large pecuniary gifts from millionaires.[70]

The young socialist Randolph Bourne, while still an undergraduate at Columbia in 1912, generalized in the same fashion concerning the spread of socialism among undergraduates and the role of the faculty at the leading American universities. "Settlement work and socialist propaganda . . . are now the commonplaces of the undergraduate." And he went on to argue that these tendencies were clearly a function of the university, for "his education, if it has been in one of the advanced universities, will have only tended to confirm his radicalism. . . ." The younger teachers, particularly, rejected traditional values, and Bourne called on the dedicated undergraduate to "ally himself with his radical teachers in spirit and activity. . . . The college thus becomes for the first time in American history a reorganizing force. It . . . now finds arrayed against it, in spirit at least if not in open antagonism, the churches and the conservative molders of opinion."[71]

David Shannon reports that "in the great upsurge of progressivism and radicalism just before World War I, the ISS had chapters in sixty colleges and universities. There were chapters in the major New England colleges, most of the state universities outside the South, and the most prominent Protestant denominational colleges."[72] The ISS had about two thousand dues-paying members, among a national college population of under four hundred thousand in 1912–13. For comparative purposes this may be placed alongside the claim of SDS of six thousand dues-paying members out of a national higher education population of close to seven million in 1968–69.

Once socialism entered the university, student protest enunciated a set of ideological themes and action concerns which have continued down to the present. Upton Sinclair, one of the organizers of the ISS, used the "factory" analogy in his analysis of the operation and function of the university.[73]

John Reed, a founding member of the Harvard Socialist Club, left behind two autobiographical essays which were published long after his death. The first was written in 1912, shortly after his graduation, while the second was drafted five years later. His description of events and ideology has a strong modern ring:

> What's wrong with Harvard? Something is the matter. Numbers of letters from alarmed alumni pour into President Lowell's office every day, asking if Socialism and Anarchy are on the rampage among undergraduates. . . . Old graduates shake their heads mournfully and agree the place is going to the dogs. . . .
>
> [The] group that founded the [Socialist] Club were Fabians, that is, they believed in "permeating" the University with the doctrine which they stood for. . . . The idea was to stir up

criticism, revolt, discussion, opposition, not only of the present
state of things in the outside world, but of the state of things at
Harvard. They wanted to make undergraduates take sides on
every issue that concerned them; to learn what they wanted to
learn, and demand of the Faculty that the "dead wood" among
the teachers be cleared away. . . .

So Lippman and MacGowen, the inner circle of the Socialist
Club, deliberately planned to get control of every organization
that would help them, or at least to be represented therein. . . .
They set themselves enthusiastically to become accomplished
dialecticians, indomitable arguers, to be able to talk, and talk
well, on any subject that might be brought up. . . . [T]he Harvard Socialists turned their theories upon themselves, determined
to work them out at Harvard University. . . .

[W]ithin half a year, the active enrolled members of the Club
amounted to fifty, with about twice as many more interested. . . .

Many of the professors and instructors had become interested
in the various undergraduate movements . . . the Socialist Club
received the warm sympathy and support of the great William
James, of Professor Adams, of Professor S. B. Johnson.[74]

The Harvard Socialist Club, like its campus successors in the
Student League for Industrial Democracy in the 1920s, the
American Student Union in the 1930s, and the SDS in the 1960s,
took as one of its tasks, improving the conditions of Harvard
cafeteria and cleaning workers. The radical group organized in
1908 also set a precedent followed by the others in later decades
for campaigning on local off-campus issues, particularly with
reference to housing conditions in Cambridge and Boston.

Writing in *The New Republic* in 1916, Randolph Bourne
argued that intellectual and student radicalism had become too
popular for their own good. "The real trouble with middle-class
radicalism today is that it is too easy. It is becoming too popular. . . . Let the college man or girl . . . join the Intercollegiate Socialist Society or some similar institution, and discover
how discouragingly respectable they are." He sounded like some
contemporary older left critic of the New Left when he criticized
these groups for being "full of the unfocussed and unthinking,"

and argued that they could most effectively serve the radical movement "by being fiercely and concentratedly intellectual. This is something these organizations have so far failed to do." Bourne went on to urge that "intellectual radicalism should not mean repeating stale dogmas of Marxism. . . . The young radical today is not asked to be a martyr, but he is asked to be a thinker, an intellectual leader." However, Bourne noted that many of the young socialists of his day dropped away when they failed to make contact with the working class. "The young radical soon learns to be ashamed of his intellectual bias, and after an ineffectual effort to squeeze himself into the mind of the workingman drifts away disillusioned from his timid collegiate radicals."[75]

Bourne indicated support for social reform and socialist causes that went considerably beyond the narrow circles of the dues-paying members of the ISS, much as support for the New Left during the late 1960s was more extensive than the two thousand five hundred to seven thousand members claimed by SDS in different years. Another indication of this pattern was suggested at the most conservative of Ivy League institutions, Princeton, by F. Scott Fitzgerald, in his description of life there before the United States entered World War I.

> In his last years at Princeton, Fitzgerald noted that the students around the small tables in the Nassau Inn "began questioning aloud the institutions that Amory and countless others before him had questioned so long in secret." They discussed sex and socialism, and the "social barriers as artificial distinctions made by the strong to bolster up their weak retainers and keep out the almost strong." In "a fury of righteousness" one hundred men resigned from their clubs.[76]

Between 1914 and American entry into the war, there was considerable antiwar activity involving both socialist and campus peace groups. A poll of eighty thousand students in May 1915 on "the question of introducing military drill" in colleges, found that sixty-three thousand voted against it.[77] Opposition to military training in the form of ROTC was, of course, to continue to be a major feature of student activism in later periods, viz., the mid-twenties, the 1930s, and most recently in the late 1960s.

The early twentieth century demand by many college students for relevance, for the opportunity to apply their values in social betterment, met its greatest fulfillment, however, not in radical or antiwar politics but in the participation in settlement work, in direct contact with the poor in the urban slums. Thousands of students and young graduates threw themselves into staffing the rapidly growing number of settlement houses. By 1911 there were 413 of them, three-quarters of which had been formed since the turn of the century. They involved twenty-five hundred residents and another ten thousand to fifteen thousand student volunteers.

> In America, settlements came as an exciting release to the feelings of purposelessness that had frustrated so many college graduates. . . . Settlements in this country were . . . protests by students against learning that was never put to use. . . .
>
> The settlement movement . . . offered students the chance to put the collegiate ideals to work in these cities, just then beginning to dominate national life, and spread their problems across the country. . . . To the early settlement leaders it seemed inevitable that students should predominate in the movement. . . . To Jane Addams it was plain that young people led the reform because they were the ones to feel most fully the lack in their own lives that came from being estranged from the active part of the nation. . . . Students would go into cities ultimately because only there could they save themselves from atrophy. It was their defense against the kind of deterioration into irrelevance that had so frightened their elders in the elite.[78]

Although the settlement house movement clearly involved many Progressives and liberals, it should be noted that some of the most prominent leaders of it, people like Jane Addams, Lilian Wald, and Mary Simkhovitch, were socialist supporters. The outlook of the movement struck an English student visitor in 1908–09 as involving the assumption that "there is no such word as 'cannot' in the lexicon of youth," and that his "favorite motto is 'Do it right now.' Acting on these principles, he is dealing with the vast social problems that beset him through the agency of the various Settlements. . . ."[79]

An analysis of the backgrounds of those active in settlement work points up the similarities among young people who choose the path of reform and transformation of the situation of the poor in different epochs.

> Most settlement workers came from families that were moderately well-to-do. The fact that they were able to enter settlement work at all, especially during the early years, was often an indication that they did not have to earn a living.
> . . . Whatever their occupation, many of the parents were actively involved in reform or concerned with aiding the poor.
> . . . There were some who entered a settlement against their parents' judgment, but the majority inherited a tradition of service. . . . In some cases they felt they were rebelling against their parents, but more often they were translating an inherited impulse to fit a new situation and a new generation.[80]

Campus criticism threw up another wave of protest against pre–World War I American society, the Young Intellectuals. The very term was used to mean a critic of society. As Henry May points out its "origins were partly socialist; the intellectual to the Marxists was the bourgeois who repudiated his class."[81] The groups who so identified themselves came from two streams, midwesterners, and graduates of Ivy League colleges, particularly Harvard, Yale and Princeton. Like those involved in the ISS and settlement houses, "most of these young radicals came from secure upper-middle class families, and for this reason were eager to like and admire the poor, especially, the urban poor, especially the recent immigrants."[82] They flocked to New York, and took up their cause, particularly that of the Jews, who lived in abysmal crowded slums in the midst of extreme wealth.

> The Young Intellectuals . . . turned the conventional hierarchy upside down. Anglo-Saxons, repressed and bigoted, were at the

bottom of the scale; at the top were the Italians, the Slavs, and
above all, the Eastern European Jews of the East Side. Writers of
Puritan ancestry like Hutchins Hapgood, earnest radicals like
Ernest Poole, who was studying Yiddish, found an endless satisfaction in the quarter's crowded streets. . . .[83]

The Young Intellectuals, like many of the student socialists
from whose ranks they frequently came, found the electoral
activities of the growing American Socialist Party prosaic and
boring. Like their compeers in the future, they were attracted to
militant tactics, including violence.

Where the left wing of American socialism merged with the
I.W.W., the Young Intellectuals found a . . . focus for their
loyalty. Syndicalism attracted them because of its appeal for
direct action and also its European intellectual prestige. . . .
Anarchism, the noblest of radical dreams, attracted many of the
Young Intellectuals. . . . The anarchist movement, with its
drama of bombs and spies, outrage and espionage and persecution, had furnished subjects for Dostoevsky, Henry James and
Joseph Conrad.
   . . . The anarchism of Emma Goldman and Alexander Berk-
man appealed deeply to the Young Intellectuals. For one thing,
Russia, and particularly Russian radicalism, had great prestige.
Furthermore, the anarchist leaders hated the halfway measures
and compromise goals of current progressivism or majority socialism. Their morality, like their courage, was absolute. They attacked bourgeois culture, marriage and religion as well as government. In the face of public hatred, they refused to give up their
belief in the propaganda of the deed. Destruction must be justified by the establishment of a new reign of individualism and
brotherhood, mystically combined.
   . . . [Another] revolutionary cause which greatly interested
the Young Intellectuals . . . [was] the revolt in sexual morality.
. . . Neither socialism nor feminism necessarily implied sexual
radicalism. . . . Yet the left wing of feminism and revolutionary
socialism could come together. . . .[84]

The élan of the various student-based movements, both political and settlement house, was destroyed by the war. Their

adherents divided sharply as to whether to support or oppose America's entry, a conflict which continued even after the declaration of war. With minor, though distinguished exceptions, the campus threw itself wholeheartedly into "making the world safe for democracy," and had little time left for other causes.

Any evaluation of the campus-based movements which emerged after 1900 must first recognize that they did not constitute an independent youth or student revolt against the older generation, whether on campus or off. These were also the years of a growing Progressive and Socialist movement which culminated in the large third party votes received in 1912 by Theodore Roosevelt (27 percent) on the Progressive party ticket, and by Eugene V. Debs (6 percent) running as a Socialist. The Socialist Party received over 900,000 votes and had close to 125,000 members in that year. Both the Intercollegiate Socialist Society and the settlement house movement were campus expressions of the same tendencies which inspired mass support for reform and radicalism in the population as a whole. The rapid growth of the industrial cities with their teeming immigrant slums, their corruption and their high crime rate, shocked the sentiments of many middle-class Americans, including a large proportion of their children away in college.

The college faculties, as Francis and Bourne reported, undoubtedly contained many sympathetic to these efforts for social change. The settlement houses "were enthusiastically supported by most of . . . [the] idealist professors."[85] There are no reliable data concerning the politics of college faculty as a group before World War I. One study which dealt with faculty attitudes toward religion did, however, suggest that they were more liberally or radically disposed than has generally been assumed. James Leuba, a psychologist, studied the religious beliefs of randomly selected samples of the membership of the sociological, psychological, and historical societies, and of scientists listed in *American Men of Science* in 1913–14. He reported that the majority in each group did not believe in God or immortality. Although religious and political beliefs are clearly separate, a variety of studies, including some of faculty opinions in the last two decades, indicate a high correlation between religious and political outlooks. Irreligious people are much more likely to have liberal and left-wing views than believers.

There are no comparable data for the nonacademic portion of the population before World War I. The religious census data, however, report that 55 percent of all persons fourteen years of age or older were actual *members* of religious denominations during this period. Leuba was able to compare academic and nonacademic members of the American Sociological Society, and found that the academics were more likely to disdain religion. Perhaps more significant was his finding that the more distinguished professors were much more irreligious than their less eminent colleagues.[86] This result coincides with much more recent survey studies of academic politics which also suggest that academic prestige is associated with more liberal-left views.[87] Seemingly, before 1914, sizable groups of American academics, particularly the more scholarly and creative among them, located disproportionately at the more distinguished schools, were out of step with conventional social opinion. Then as now, therefore, the children of the elite attending such institutions were involved in an intellectual milieu in which a liberal outlook held sway. Those students who sought to act out the implications of such orientations in political clubs like the ISS, or through participation in settlement houses, were not in revolt. Rather, as Randolph Bourne argued, they were probably conforming to the dominant values in the liberal arts in the leading schools.

Leuba collected comparable data on the religious beliefs of students which unfortunately are not as representative of larger populations as his surveys of different groups of scientists and social scientists. He secured 927 questionnaires from "all the students of a number of classes belonging to nontechnical [liberal arts] departments of nine colleges of high rank, and [from] two classes [78 answers] of a normal school." He found that 56 percent of the men and 82 percent of the women in this nonrepresentative sample believed in "a personal God." Less than 10 percent rejected belief in any concept of God. Leuba concluded from these and other data that "considered all together, my data would indicate that from 40 to 50 percent of the young men leaving college entertain an idea of God incompatible with the acceptance of the Christian religion, even as interpreted by the liberal clergy." The rate of unbelief "increases considerably from the freshman to the senior year in college." These findings are clearly less significant than those concerning the faculty, but they do lend weight to the assumption that a substantial minority of American students may have been receptive to radical or progressive ideas before World War I.[88]

The wave of activism and protest among the pre–World War I young was not blamed solely or primarily on the failings of the university, or the teaching of the faculty. Then, as during the 1920s and 1960s, spokesmen for the conventions located the decline in the morality of youth on societal changes which had undermined parental authority. Cornelia Comer bemoaned the effect of the media and the decline of religion and family discipline, which resulted in a *culte de moi* among the affluent young.

> How can anything avail to refine children whose taste in humor is formed by the colored supplements of the Sunday paper, as their taste in entertainment is shaped by the continuous vaudeville and the motion-picture shows? . . . While most vaudeville performances have one or two numbers that justify the proprietors' claim of harmless, wholesome amusement, the bulk of the programme is almost inevitably drivel, common, stupid, or inane. . . . "I don't approve," your fathers and mothers say anxiously, "but I hate to keep Tom and Mary at home when all the other children are allowed to go." . . . In the wrack of beliefs, your parents managed to retain their ingrained principles of conduct. Not knowing what to teach you, they taught you nothing wholeheartedly. . . . If you are agnostic-and-water, if you find nothing in the universe more stable than your own wills—what wonder?
> . . . [As a result] when these young people adopted a philosophy, it was naive and inadequate. They talked of themselves as "socialists."[89]

Two months later, the Columbia junior Randolph Bourne wrote a reply to this attack on the soft character of the badly brought up young radicals. In it, he agreed that home discipline had broken down, but he drew a different conclusion. The youth of his generation could see more clearly precisely because they were freer than previous ones from allegiance to outmoded beliefs. "Having brought themselves up they judge utility by their own standards." He also credited their exposure to the output of the mass media for broadening their horizons. "In an age of newspapers, free libraries, and cheap magazines, we necessarily get a broader horizon than the passing generation had. We see what is going on in the world, and we get the clash of different points of view, to an extent which was impossible to our fathers." And as a result of not having been indoctrinated by an older generation which was certain of its values, Bourne argued that his generation has "retained from childhood the propensity to see through things, and to tell the truth with startling frankness."[90]

5

Historical Background: The Twenties Through the Fifties

If the campus had been a recurrent source of indiscipline, illegal pranks, and unrest, there is no real evidence that any major segment of the student population was alienated from society and polity in the first century and a half of American national existence. But a major generation-unit had its watershed in the 1920s, which Henry May has described as the "decade when the fragmentation first became deep and obvious . . . a period in which common values and common beliefs were replaced by separate and conflicting values."[1] Walter Lippmann referred to the "vast dissolution of ancient habits" in the 1920s.[2] It is not surprising that old habits were dissolving. All of the changes which had been gathering in America, and which are usually described under chapter headings such as "technology," "urbanization," and "mobility," seemed to be coming to a visible head in the 1920s. The 1920 census was the first in which the urban population exceeded the rural population. In the thirty-year generation span since 1890, the number of Americans living in cities of half a million or more had tripled from four to twelve million, while the total population had not doubled. The number of people engaged in manufacturing had doubled. There were millions of people in new jobs, places and proximities.

Education was also spreading out among the American population. The limitation of college training to a small elite was coming to an end. The number of college-age youths attending college shot up from 4 percent at the turn of the century to 12 percent by the end of the 1920s. At the same time, America was beginning to turn the corner of its nineteenth century innocence and euphoria. Basic premises were being laid open to question by the general jarring loose of old associations, marked by the dramatic trauma of World War I.

This state of dissolution lent itself to a revival of the kinds of political protest which had characterized the prewar radical movement of students and young intellectuals. A Marxist analyst, Martin J. Sklar, has recently pointed to the ways in which the strains of the 1920s produced a visible and significant group of radicals among the latter.

> [T]he young intellectuals were conscious of themselves as a distinct group arrayed against the bourgeoisie, its ideology, its values, and its society, . . . Abstractly at first, and increasingly in more specific political terminology, the young intellectuals identified with the industrial proletariat and with the dispossessed generally. They presented themselves as partisan, in varying degrees to socialism. . . . The young intellectuals' outlook assumed that working men and women, and especially the young among them, given the opportunity, would recognize and assert the same objectives as their own, a fuller, richer, deeper personal and social life where work might increasingly become a self-expressive activity. . . .[3]

The moral breakdown also lent itself to another kind of disaffection, which often expressed itself in political terms but was really of a quite different quality. It involved not so much an optimistic passion for social betterment as a disillusioned rejection of the total set of classical rational assumptions on which American and Western society had rested. An identifiable generation-unit of youth began to share this disaffection with a growing class of writers and intellectuals, much the same phenomenon as was to recur in the 1960s.

Similarly to the 1960s, the dominant intellectual spokesmen of anticapitalist criticism came from the children of the affluent whose main concerns were not economic, but cultural and moral. They condemned the class from which they sprang for "dullness, stupidity, aggressiveness in commerce, conformity to the remnants of traditional morality, and a moral opportunism, linked with certain blind convictions about the economic status quo." Many of the students and young intellectuals seized on the Freudian analysis of the sources of moral conformity. Their favorite term to characterize the society was *repression,* predating the influence of Marcuse by four decades.

> For the young men and women of the period the word served as a convenient label for all their grievances against society. It was their feeling that the absurd, exorbitant moral demands which society had made upon its victims had culminated in a national neurosis. Repression became the American illness. With little or no thought of personal responsibility . . . they decided that any force was evil which stood in the way of a full, wholesome, primitive expression of natural impulses. . . .
>
> The idea of repression was soon enough applied . . . to American history and sociology. If repression was a national illness, then all social and moral forces which had led to the neurosis of an entire people must have had this object, to repress the natural life of a people, to shut off the natural satisfaction of healthy desires as the price paid for achieving economic and industrial success. . . .
>
> The proper reaction . . . was to defy [the Puritanical social] . . . code, to act in deliberate scorn of it, and to experiment as much as possible with sexual matters prohibited by it. In some cases this defiance of Puritan morality acquired the characteristics of a primitivism, an attempt to point out the great happiness of people [particularly lower-class Negroes] who were not brought up in terror of sex and who therefore lived a normal, happy, casual life.[4]

The campus-based radical movement was initially in bad shape to take advantage of the disillusionment which characterized some students and many intellectuals. Wartime repression and postwar anti-Bolshevik hysteria had undercut the civil liberties of radicals on and off campus. Socialists and Wobblies were jailed, and professorial opponents of the war were fired. The radical movement first split over the issue of support or opposition to the war. It divided again concerning its reaction to the Russian Revolution and over the efforts to create a Communist party within the United States. Conservatives, on the other hand, moved increasingly towards justifying a repressive stand to prevent the revolutionary wave from reaching American shores. Many in the business and conservative communities argued publicly that college faculties were honeycombed with Communists and Socialists. In February 1919, Edward L. Doheny, an oil millionaire, announced that a "majority of college professors in the United States are teaching socialism and Bolshevism. . . ."[5] In 1921, Vice-President Calvin Coolidge wrote a series of articles on "Enemies of the Republic" in *The Delineator*. His first one dealt with the activities of "Reds" in colleges. The breakdown in the political order which disturbed him was a consequence in part of the fact that "college faculties rebel at the authority of presidents and trustees."[6] And in an introduction to Coolidge's articles, the editor of *The Delineator* proclaimed: "Better a sane hewer of wood or drawer of water in one's family than a University graduate who has nothing more than antagonism to contribute to the service of society."[7] Harry Haldeman, the founder of the Better America Federation of California, commented that his organization was "having students of radical tendencies watched."[8] A study conducted by the ISS of "Freedom of Discussion in American Colleges," reported in 1920 that "an increasing number of schools were (1) prohibiting outside affiliations for political groups, (2) placing increasing restrictions on speakers, and (3) censoring the faculty's right to express liberal opinions."[9] Partly as a reaction to such pressures, the ISS changed its name to the League for Industrial Democracy (LID).

Various campus clubs dropped the name "Socialist Club" in favor of varying titles such as "Social Science Club," "Social Problems Club," "Politics Club" and assorted others.

Such pressures seemingly did not reduce the scope of campus radicalism, since the LID found large audiences for the speakers it toured across the nation. Right-wing attacks seemingly stimulated the more liberal minority to react sharply to the severe postwar repression, to industrial ills, and to militarism.

Antiwar, progressive, and socialist clubs, which invited controversial speakers to the campus, sprang up around the country. As Earnest notes, the issues of free speech occasioned serious controversies in many colleges. "Students demanded the right to hear all sides of every question; conservative alumni, trustees, and citizens objected to colleges becoming a forum for radical views." The Handlins report the spread of "underground student newspapers — *Gadfly* at Harvard, *Critic* at Oberlin, *Proletarian* at Wisconsin, *Saturday Evening Pest* at Yale, and *Tempest* at Michigan — [which] demanded not only the right to ask critical questions but also the right to give the answers."[10]

The renewed wave of meetings, demonstrations, and discussions of campus radicalism led some older intellectuals to once again perceive socialism as the prevailing undergraduate mood. Writing in May 1922, George Santayana reacted strongly to its presence:

> [The] sophomores . . . have discovered the necessity of socialism . . . [They] all proclaim their disgust with the present state of things in America, they denounce the Constitution of the United States, the churches, the Government, the colleges, the press, the theaters, and above all they denounce the spirit that vivifies and unifies all these things, the spirit of Business. Here is a disaffection breaking out in which seemed the most unanimous, the most satisfied of nations; here are Americans impatient with America. . . .
>
> I have made a severe effort to discover, as well as I may from a distance, what these rebels want. I see what they are *against* — they are against everything—but what are they *for?* I have not

been able to discover it. This may be due to my lack of understanding, or to their incapacity to express themselves clearly, for
their style is something appalling. But perhaps their scandalous
failure in expression, when expression is what they yearn for and
demand at all costs, may be a symptom of something deeper: of a
radical mistake they have made in the direction of their efforts
and aspirations. They think they need more freedom, more room,
a chance to be more spontaneous: I suspect that they have had
too much freedom, too much empty space, too much practice in
being spontaneous when there was nothing in them to bubble
out.[11]

Santayana was not alone in voicing complaints about the orientations of the students of the twenties in terms which resemble
the agitated outcries of faculty in the sixties. Thus an Oberlin sociology professor argued in 1922: "Youth is dogmatic. . . . The
enthusiasm of youth may appropriate socialism or free thinking
instead of the traditional faith, but it is likely to have the zeal of
religion, and call bigotry, liberalism."[12] C. Hartley Grattan, a
well-known professor of English, complained bitterly in 1925 that
students judged literature on political rather than aesthetic
grounds.

> The students . . . tend to applaud contemporary writers be-
> cause they are rebels, not because they are artists. . . . And con-
> sequently students tend to neglect really fine writers whose rebel-
> liousness is not so apparent, or but a minor part of their work.
> . . . Then, too, sympathy for a particular social attitude leads to
> the acceptance of bad but congenial writers, and the rejection of
> good but incongenial ones. . . .
> What the college student needs to guard against more than
> anything else is the tendency, in reaction to an even greater
> stupidity, to accept all that is new as good, and all that chimes in
> with his social attitude as best.[13]

Some indication of the renunciatory concepts advanced by the
more radical students may be found in the effort of the editor of
The New Student, Douglas Haskell, to present the policy of his

paper. *The New Student* was the predominant expression of student activism in the 1920s. It was published regularly as a national paper and magazine, once every fortnight through the decade, supported by subscriptions around the country. In many ways, Haskell presented an approach to society and knowledge which was close to that which was to disturb Paul Goodman about his students at the end of the 1960s.

> We do not believe it is any longer possible for the American college to give an education to its students but we still believe it is possible for students to get an education for themselves in American colleges. . . .
>
> With all respect to the older generation, some of us become more and more certain that they cannot feel the chaos as we do. . . . Spiritually, this is an age of ruin — of nausea. We suspect that many of our elders retain the nineteenth century belief in science and knowledge. We cannot share it. We need a faith. . . . At least we know what must go.
>
> Mechanization must go.
>
> A certain scholarly, scientific attitude must go. The values for which we are searching do not seem susceptible of proof, of capture by the "scientific spirit." The faith, the assumptions on which science rests are lacking, hence there are no "social sciences." Moreover we need to look ahead; and creative thought is different in kind from mere knowlege. . . .
>
> We cannot even accept the leadership of the younger [faculty] men. The forces of decay are so strong that we cannot trust a cocksure psychology or a "radical" sociology any more than we could the old hand-dried economics. . . . [although] we still find inspiring friends among our teachers, little as most of these have to give us. . . .
>
> We suspect that there are many individual students who do not care to join organized groups, who nevertheless have ideas better than do many leaders of organizations. Often the sanest imagination belongs to the pure in heart who are not even conscious of any revolutionary tendency. These people should be kept in touch with one another.
>
> Through *The New Student* we are trying to arrange an interchange of ideas between them. . . .[14]

The largest single protest group was probably the Student Christian Movement (SCM) which urged "the correction of such social matters as child labor, industrial strife, poverty, and above all war." W. H. Cowley estimates that the SCM enlisted about 5 percent of the undergraduate population, and that in sum, "during the twenties approximately one student in ten joined a group or groups devoted to examining broad societal problems. . . ."[15] A statistical datum pertaining to the strength of moderate radicalism or progressivism may be found in the results of a presidential straw vote conducted in 120 colleges and universities in 1924 which reported that 14.5 percent of the 51,457 students who completed ballots supported Robert LaFollette, the third party candidate of the Progressive and Socialist parties. This may seem like a large left-wing bloc, but LaFollette secured 16.6 percent of the national vote. The percentages received by the three presidential candidates in this campus poll corresponded closely to that which they secured among the general electorate. Thus Coolidge captured 58.6 percent in the straw vote and 54 percent among electors, while Davis, the Democratic candidate, had 26.9 percent on campus, and 28.8 percent in the nation as a whole.[16] These results would suggest that the campus population strongly resembled the adult world in its politics, that in the conservative Republican twenties, students were also predominantly conservative Republicans. Although this empirical generalization is undoubtedly true, it is important to note that the undergraduate population of this period comprised about 10 percent of the age cohort, as contrasted with close to 45 percent today. This meant that the students were largely from families whose conservative Republican propensities were far higher than that of the general electorate. Hence it is likely that the campus support for LaFollette represented a shift to the left among students as compared with their family politics. Some slight evidence for this thesis may be found in the report of the campus poll which indicates that in a number of colleges, Coolidge's support was lower among seniors than among freshmen, while LaFollette's increased.

A year later, a leading newspaper, the New York *World,* editorialized concerning the "revolt which is going on in colleges and universities all over the country" in terms which indicate that a significant minority of students were involved in various activities. The *World* credited *The New Student* with a major role.

> Revolt against what? That is a little hard to say. In one college there is a revolt against stupid courses, in another against abridgement of free speech, in another against the cheap commercialization of the endowment drives, in another against official interpretations of American history. Always there are the same symptoms: the outlaw student paper, with its devastating satire and cartoons; the speeches, the meetings, the reprisals by the faculty, the mutterings of discontent in the student body. The revolt has been growing for two or three years now; in a loose sort of way it is organized, for it has a magazine, *The New Student,* which circulates widely, and is given over to recording its spicy doings. It has reached such proportions that it cannot be disregarded. . . .[17]

Organized campus protest in the mid-twenties revolved around the issues of peace and the Sacco-Vanzetti case. The disillusionment with the last war brought considerable support for the movement to reduce the scope of the Reserve Officers Training Corps (ROTC) on various campuses. "In 1925, a tremendous agitation began against compulsory military training. . . ."[18] The pages of *The New Student* reported incident after incident on campuses throughout the nation of demonstrations against compulsory military training.

The most important single issue arousing leftist sentiment among intellectuals and students in the mid-1920s, however, was the Sacco-Vanzetti case. The conviction of these two immigrant anarchists for murder in 1921 resulted in a crescendo of protest among liberals and leftists around the world. Gradually, a large proportion among those so inclined became convinced that the majesty of the American juridical and police system had been deliberately mobilized to execute two innocent men. The conflict between the protesters in the American intellectual world and the powers enlarged the cleavage between the two to the point where each was ready to believe the worst about the other.

> Thus when writers and professors begin to voice . . . doubts, it seemed to many conservatives only another proof of dangerous radicalism among the intellectuals. And the writers and the professors, bringing out fact after fact which showed the prejudice and perjury involved in the conviction, came increasingly to feel that the leaders of business and government were not interested in evidence but only in teaching the radicals the brutal lesson that there was no room for dissent in America.[19]

Since the trial took place in Boston, Harvard was much involved in the protest on both faculty and student level. President A. Lawrence Lowell chaired a three man committee appointed by Governor Fuller, which concluded that the two anarchists were guilty. "The case . . . emphasized the dichotomy between the professors and the powers that ruled the academic community. . . . The socially and politically aware members of the academic community were imbued with a deep distrust and hostility to the conservative elements . . . in the church, business, and government. . . . Many a student who knew nothing about the trial of Socrates became deeply stirred over that of Sacco and Vanzetti. . . . [T]housands of them came to believe it important to know more about shoemakers and fishpeddlers."[20]

Much of the activity against ROTC, the execution of Sacco and Vanzetti, American military intervention in the Caribbean, and a myriad of other issues reported during the 1920s in *The New Student,* seemingly involved white students in the more prominent universities and colleges. Schools like Harvard, Dartmouth, Yale, Wisconsin, California, appear frequently. In this respect also there has been seeming consistency in the sources of collegiate activism. Another group which was to figure prominently in the activism of the late 1960s also entered the campus unrest scene during this decade, the Negro students.

As during the 1960s, campus protest by black students cannot be viewed primarily as an outgrowth of their situation in the university. The decade of the twenties was also marked by racial violence, most of it initiated by whites; but Negroes fought back, killing whites in Chicago and other cities, using guns in the black belt in the South. The concept of the "New Negro" who would stand up and demand his rights emerged. Black nationalism which called on the Negro to "reject whiteness, to see the beauty of his own skin" became a major tendency.[21] Marcus Garvey, who totally rejected white culture, became the head of the largest Negro political organization that had yet appeared, the Universal Negro Improvement Association, one which was much bigger than any of the current black power groups. He proposed that Negroes leave the corrupt white civilization and go to their homeland in Africa.[22] Negro writers gave voice to the new militancy in novels, plays, poetry, and belligerent anti-white articles. It is not surprising, therefore, that Negro students also exhibited some of the aggressiveness. Contemporary description of Negro unrest in the twenties points up the relationship between economic security and the potential for campus disturbances.

> The recurrence of disorders ranging from summary expulsions of individual students to wholesale student strikes in Negro colleges will tell even the most casual observer that something is radically wrong. . . . One thing is certain: The Negro student is not what he used to be.
>
> . . . [S]tudent strikes have come to be regarded as an unavoidable and periodic liability of the white college. Not so the Negro college. . . . Economically bound by almost impregnable fetters, the Negro student had no time for anything but the acquisition of a meager education. . . . [H]e was generally so poor that what leisure time was his had to be spent working at odd hours. . . . Then came the War. With it came a tremendous betterment of the economic conditions in the southern Negro home. More students came to college. Fewer found it necessary to work their way through school. The radio, the newspaper, the moving picture, the spread of liberal ideas, and the *élan vital* of the Negro Renaissance developing into the concept of the "New

Negro," all conspired to send to the threshold of the Negro
college a new type of student, wholly unprecedented.

There were strikes at Fisk, at Hampton Institute, [three] at
Howard . . . at Kittrell, at St. Augustine, and at Knoxville
College. There have been revolts almost equivalent to strikes in
nearly every Negro college in the South. These were obviated in
many instances only by wholesale expulsion of large parts of the
student body.[23]

A recent study of the 1927 Hampton Institute strike basically
agrees with the earlier account. Edward Graham notes that by the
winter of 1927, "Student strikes had already reached epidemic
proportions at Fisk, Shaw, Howard, Lincoln (in Missouri),
Florida Agricultural and Industrial Institute and elsewhere."
The Hampton strike, which demanded a better faculty and a
relaxation of parietal rules, was broken and many students were
expelled. Those most deeply involved serving on the Protest
Committee were drawn heavily from among the superior students in intellectual and leadership-ability terms. Success at
other schools and in subsequent careers indicated that those who
had led the strike were "probably one of the most talented
groups ever to leave a college or university campus."[24]

On the campus the rejection of the prewar past was most
widely expressed through new forms of personal behavior: short
skirts, freer relations with those of the opposite sex, violations of
the law banning alcoholic beverages. Kinsey has documented one
aspect of the break in statistical terms in his report that a big
jump in the proportion of females with premarital sexual experiences occurred in the 1920s.[25] Seemingly, the proportion did not
increase again, at least among college students, until the 1960s.
Earnest, in his history of college life, concludes that this period
witnessed a general break with the conventional verities, even
among the large apolitical and unintellectual majority.

Thus without intellectualizing it, a host of boys and girls in the
early 1920s instinctively knew that the platitudes about honesty,
democracy, chastity and religion did not represent the truth

about American life. They knew that kikes and wops and niggers were outside the pale — in fact, many of the college students agreed that they should be. . . . With the coming of prohibition they knew of the liquor in country-club locker rooms or in the family cellar. . . . What the defenders of the established order overlooked was that the youth has an instinctive hatred of bunk.[26]

The result was a revolution in manners and morals. This was evidenced by new dress styles, the open flaunting of sex and liquor, and the strong objections voiced to conventional religion. But the avant-garde elements among intellectuals and students not only rejected the traditional mores; they also expressed their renunciatory tendency through general opposition to rational political society — not just the pathology but its very concept. This is sometimes difficult to perceive, because the range of expression was so broad. There was nihilism, sheer bohemianism, Dadaism, whose motto was: "I do not wish to know whether there have been men before me."

> A . . . revulsion against civilization broke out . . . in the black humor of the Dadaist movement. . . . Dadaists gave lectures from within diving helmets to the sound of clanging bells and held exhibits in public urinals. Their assaults on a victim-public were exactly like the "happenings" reinvented here in the mid-sixties. . . . Dadaism took its slogan "destruction is also creation" from Bakunin, and its poetics from Rimbaud.[27]

In reviewing campus culture during this period, Oscar and Mary Handlin conclude that rebellion "became a conventional student posture." They also describe a dominant mood reflecting a radical rejection of the past in terms both of ideology and personal behavior.

> Intellectually, it took the form of a call for liberation "from the entanglement of mere traditional authority and provincial prejudice" and for the discard of the millstones of "dead formalism in religion, and narrow thinking in social relations." The de-

mands were peremptory: "Saccharine Sunday-school religion, blatant Fourth-of-July patriotism, inherited class bias — all must fall." A pronounced shift in patterns of personal behavior expressed the same impatience with institutional restraints. The lost generation — self-proclaimed — flaunted its interest in sex and whiskey in defiance of the Puritans and of the prohibition laws and provided a compelling model for college youth.[28]

But though their elders who had gone through the war often referred to themselves as the "lost generation," the students of the twenties went far beyond them in rejecting tradition. For the first time in America, the concept of the generation gap, of the sharp difference in values between the young, particularly the college students and their elders, appeared as a general notion. And interestingly, then as during the late 1960s, age thirty was taken as the dividing point.

> The greatest gulf, however, was that between generations. Parents, and faculty members over thirty, found the younger generation incomprehensible, while youth regarded their elders as either hopelessly incompetent or as pious hypocrites. Probably never in American history had two generations found it harder to communicate. One of the characteristic lacunae in the work of F. Scott Fitzgerald is the absence of characters over thirty. . . . In an introduction to a collection of Fitzgerald's short stories, Malcolm Cowley explains this gulf on the ground that "the elders were discredited in their [the younger generation's] eyes by the war, prohibition, by the Red scare of 1919–1920, and by the scandals like that of Teapot Dome."[29]

Recognition that an important part of the college population had rejected the traditional values of the society resulted, in each affected period, in an analytical literature which tried to specify what went wrong. "Why is the Younger Generation so different?" One such effort by a journalist resembles both earlier and later writings in stressing social changes which reduced the "sense of parental responsibility." Urbanization, John Gavit argued, brought about a sharp reduction in time spent by parents with children, a reduction in "the sense of responsibility to neighborhood public opinion and standards," and a greater involvement in formal pleasure-seeking activities by the parents. In addition, many of the older generation who advocated "law and order" and condemned sexual immorality and radicalism were engaged during the decade in "openly flouting the Constitution and the law in the matter of Prohibition." And Gavit concluded:

> People, young and old, whose home experience has given them no standards, or no self-control with which to enforce such as they have, always go to pieces when superimposed restraints are lifted. . . . There is no absurdity more futile than that of saying to a young person: "Do not follow my example; do what I *say*." . . .
> Whose fault is it if the young people are coming to college with the most casual ideas of purpose and responsibility? The lamentable characteristic of the typical college student is not that he has "radical" convictions, but rather that he has so poor an outfit of convictions on any subject.[30]

Writing at the end of the twenties, Christian Gauss, dean of the college at Princeton, pointed to the general pattern of protest "against restraints — against all rules and regulations," and the widespread demand that "the colleges be turned over to the students and be run by undergraduate committees." He argued that since such behavior could be found around the country on highly different campuses, the explanation could not be "merely collegiate," that the student reactions must be "the reflections of some underlying condition in the country at large."[31] And he found the answer in the rapid rate of social change which produced what a writer in 1970 would call "future shock."[32] The youth of the twenties were faced with a long list of "inventions and conceptions which began to affect our way of life after 1900."

> We can repeat only a few of them here — such as the long-distance telephone, wireless, jazz, bobbed hair, brain storm, the bootlegger, the hijacker, the airplane, the airship, antitoxins, the

flapper, camouflage, propaganda, the automobile. . . . The most popular amusement to-day is the cinema; it, too, has had its effect. The boy or girl who comes to the college, and who has been attending the movies for the past six or eight years, has seen far more life than the ordinary undergraduate of 1895 ever dreamed of. . . .

We have changed our world from top to bottom, and where things have changed so rapidly, society is usually in for a long and often painful process of adjustment.[33]

Much of the efforts by those concerned with higher education, both academics and students, to explain campus discontent in the twenties, however, like those of the sixties and early seventies, did not focus on extramural social tensions and technological changes, but rather placed the blame on the presumed failings of the educational system, itself, to do a good job of teaching and relating to undergraduates.

A committee of Dartmouth seniors submitted a report to the president of the college in 1924 informing him of needed changes. They objected strongly to "the impersonal relationship between teacher and student, the present classroom, lecture-hall, and final examination system of education." They proposed to replace classroom activities by freeing the students to learn through independent reading in all subjects, such as the social sciences and humanities, in which there are a variety of points of view. The professor's role should be to discuss the books after the students have read them, not to lecture at the students or to impose an overly integrated point of view.[34]

Attacks on teaching methods and the lack of close relations between faculty and students tended, then as in more recent years, to be linked to the growth of universities. Thus *The Daily Nebraskan* complained that "the University has grown immensely" and "classes are now so cumbersome . . . that personal contact is impossible."[35] The editors of *The Vagabond* of Indiana University noted with dismay: "In all our institutions of higher learning there is a tendency toward Gigantism, the worship of Bigness, which regards the success of the school as

proportionate to its enrollment, the acreage of the campus . . .
and number of men on the faculty."[36] A Wisconsin professor
eloquently portrayed the grievous lot of the undergraduate in
the large state university of 1920, in terms which sound like
Mario Savio talking of Berkeley in 1964.

> The student is admitted by thousands, registered by a vast
> clerical machine, assigned to courses, divided into sections, lec-
> tured to, quizzed, tested, examined; he is warned by his instruc-
> tor, warned through his parents; . . . he is limited in the
> number of his semester hours, limited in his elections, limited in
> his "student activities," limited in his social life; he is recorded,
> card-indexed, filed, questionnaired, statisticized, and his docu-
> mentation is kept in a safe.[37]

The concern for better teaching and more personal contact
between faculty and students was not limited to criticism about
the size of the universities or classes. The discussion begun in the
latter decades of the nineteenth century about the effect of
increased emphasis on research on teaching filled many pages in
the 1920s. Essentially the specific arguments and proposed solutions were much the same as those advanced earlier and which
continue to be proposed today. Thus Frank Spaulding argued
that "great teachers" have almost totally disappeared because in
"appointments and promotions the primary question is not how
successful the man is as a teacher, but what has he done in
research in his subject, what has he published?"[38] In his 1925
presidential address to the Modern Languages Association, William Neilson complained that graduate education is planned
"for the production of scholars, hardly at all for the training of
teachers."[39] Writing in 1928, Addison Hibbard of the University
of North Carolina reported that "probably at no time since the
beginning of higher education in America has the criticism of
our colleges and universities been so general and so bitter as it is
today." This was largely because of the lack of interest in teaching, which he blamed not only on the greater rewards for research but on the considerable growth in rewards in terms of

publicity and outside income: "Extracurricular service — popular lectures given by faculty members, field research, help of one
kind or another to outside organizations."

> Professors are great makers of textbooks in or out of their
> field — and students in their classes keep on buying them.
> Teachers of science serve the State and private corporations in
> countless ways: the psychologist and penologist are advisors to
> State departments; sanitary and civil engineers give advice to one
> commission or another; the geologist and forester advise on con-
> servation and mineral deposits; public health measures take the
> time of the university medical staff; the United States government
> now and then calls for a man to serve in one capacity or another;
> this corporation or that asks for chemical analyses of some of its
> by-products; State legislatures ask that surveys be made; . . .
> [P]rofessors gain a reputation in a field and are called upon for
> commercial lecturing; magazines, newspapers, publishing houses
> urge men to write of their specialities.[40]

The president of Hibbard's university, Harry W. Chase, who
had earlier presided over two other universities, argued persua-
sively in 1924 in terms that had been used a generation before
him, and which were to be used half a century later, that the
emergence of a national research-oriented professorate had created a "new" problem of loyalty for the university.

> [I]t seems to me that individual faculty members today are less
> deeply rooted in the soil of the institution they serve, less com-
> plete in the identification of their interests with its development,
> less concerned about it as an institution, than were the men who
> came into university faculties a generation ago. . . . [W]e have
> lost something of the deep sense of personal attachment of an
> earlier day. And this loss seems to me to constitute an important
> problem for those who are concerned about the most effective
> functioning of universities.[41]

The solution to the problem of the "truant professors" was to
enhance the status of teaching as such, in particular by creating

new highly paid "superprofessorships," not for research competence but for men proven "preeminent *as a teacher.*" The young
Robert Hutchins in his inaugural address as president of the
University of Chicago in 1929 addressed himself to the same
dilemma, how to get first-rate teachers who stuck to the classroom. He, too, advocated higher salaries. He also proposed,
however, that the graduate departments of his university undertake "to devise the best methods for preparing men for teaching." He intended to place "a new responsibility upon the
departments, that of developing ideas in college education."[42]

The most popular explanation for inadequate teaching, for
faculty involvement in research and consulting activities, and for
inadequate resources, among radicals of the 1920s, both students
and others, was the control of the university by reactionary
trustees, almost all of whom were big businessmen, who could
determine the internal decisions through the absolute campus
power of their appointee, the president. This thesis was presented in elaborate detail, campus by campus, by Upton Sinclair,
in his book *The Goose-Step,* widely circulated among undergraduates of the decade. Yet some radical intellectuals closely
acquainted with the workings of the university tried to challenge
this simplistic approach, much as was to occur with respect to the
revival of such interpretations in the 1960s. The *Freeman* magazine, then one of the most important liberal-radical organs, ran a
series of articles on problems of higher education during 1922–23,
directed in part to clarifying these issues. In discussing the role of
the president, Somnia Vana argued that "nothing could be
further from the truth," than the image of the all-powerful role
of the president who could prevent heresy and intimidate the
faculty. A new president "finds a mesh of academic rights, titles,
and privileges before him. . . . His chief business is to raise
money by collecting it from those who have it." He is expected to
remain outside of academic issues, particularly if they affect
policies within departments. Any interference by him with "departments is usually hotly resented." In terms which closely
resemble Clark Kerr's analysis of the behavior of the president in

The Uses of the University, published over forty years later,
Vana argued that the president's principal function is "constantly mediating among contending academic interests," that he
must have "a talent for manipulation." The difficulty with
reforming academe, argued this 1920s student of American university life, was not that it was controlled by the reactionary
affluent, but that there were within it so many vested interests
protected by "all kinds of customs, laws, compacts, understand-
ings, agreements, promises, and obligations, created by years of
conscious, unconscious, and subconscious operations. It is a vast,
magnificent, and historic tangle. About all that the mighty
gentleman who presides over it can do, is to stand on a height
above it and squirt perfume on the ensemble."[43]

Cultural Conformity: The Thirties Through the Fifties

The emergence of a pattern of seeming renunciation of the
behavior of their elders by an important segment of the college
generation was curiously inhibited by the Depression of the
1930s. As noted earlier, two radical sociologists recently suggested:
"The collapse of the counter-culture of the 1920s in the face of
economic depression suggests that one must eschew any linear
theory of societal change."[44] That traumatic event did, of course,
stimulate major political changes among both students and intellectuals.

"Straw polls" taken on college campuses each presidential
election year point to a marked shift from the 1920s to the 1930s.
They show that the G.O.P. had a substantial majority among
students in the twenties, but lost this position in 1932 and 1936;
the Socialists received 18 percent nationally in 1932. Of course,
these straw polls are not reliable estimates of the opinions of the
campus populations since they dealt with returns from a small,
self-selected number of colleges and students. (The 1936 returns,
for example, were based on ninety-two colleges and 80,590 ballots
out of a student population of more than one million.) A recent
report on the results of various academic surveys of student

political attitudes on assorted campuses at different times in the 1930s concluded that "students expressed more liberal views toward economic planning and change than their counterparts before the Depression and this liberalism increased during the four years of college attendance. Polls repeatedly showed that President Roosevelt was held in high regard among the younger generation." *A Literary Digest* poll of college students across the nation in 1935 found that those who replied favored Roosevelt's policies by two to one.[45]

The American Student Union, formed in 1935, as a coalition of Socialists, Communists, and liberals, was to report twenty thousand members out of a student population of over one million, clearly proportionately much more than has ever been claimed by all the radical student groups in the hectic 1960s. In April 1934, twenty-five thousand students were reported to have taken the Oxford Pledge against participation in war during the student antiwar week. By April 1935, 185,000 students were counted as participants in such demonstrations. Peace Day or Peace Week demonstrations in the late thirties are reported to have included several hundred thousand students.

A comprehensive academic study of the student movement of the early thirties, that by George Rawick, concludes that it "received its major impetus from the antiwar movement." Polls of students indicated that the strength of pacifist feeling was much greater than the following of the organized groups. Thus in one Ohio college sample in 1932, one third of the students said they would be conscientious objectors in a future war; and one quarter reported they might take that position; while only 41 percent said they would definitely go if drafted in a war. In 1933, a national poll of seventy colleges found that 39 percent of those queried stated they would not take part in any war, while 33 percent said they would fight only in the event the United States was invaded. A larger, more systematic, though still inherently unrepresentative poll of student opinion on foreign policy issues was conducted by *The Literary Digest* in 1934–35. Ballots were returned by 112,607 students out of the 318,414 who received them. The large majority of those who replied took a strongly peace-oriented position. Thus, 82 percent said they would not bear arms if the United States were involved "in the invasion of the borders of another country"; 63 percent disagreed that "a national policy of an American navy and air force second to none is a sound method of insuring us against being drawn into another great war"; 91 percent favored "government control of armaments and the munitions industry"; and 82 percent supported "the principle of universal conscription of all resources of capital and labor in order to control all profits in time of war."[46]

As in the 1920s and the 1960s, a second major set of concerns was "free speech." "It is significant that amongst the chief issues of contention [during the 1930s] was the student's right to political activity at all: bans on speakers, censorship of student newspapers, punishments for demonstrations, were frequent *causi bellicum*."[47]

The Communists, who were particularly influential in the leadership of the American Student Union, the American Youth Congress (with a claimed membership of affiliated groups including over five million youths), and the Southern Negro Youth Congress (claimed membership of five hundred thousand youths), lost most of their influence by 1940 as a result of shifts in the party line related to the Soviet Union's foreign policies.[48] The Young Communist League itself reported a membership in 1939 of twenty-two thousand youth, student and nonstudent.

The Communists and the various student and youth groups which they eventually dominated kept the potentially alienated within the political system. The CP, following the international Popular Front line of the Comintern, insisted on supporting Franklin Roosevelt, the New Deal, the Democratic Party, and an aggressive anti-Fascist foreign policy. These policies, together with involvement in the campaigns to organize workers by the CIO, attracted the largest portion of college dissenting youth, who could thus link a super-rational ideology with support for the underdog in the form of unorganized workers, persecuted Jews, and the Loyalists in the Spanish Civil War. And the rational in-system politics of the Communists and the liberals, who were encouraged to remain so by the CP, discouraged any thrust toward cultural innovation. Ironically, then, the very considerable power of the Communists within intellectualdom and the student movement severely weakened the pressures towards renunciation of American culture and polity. The dominant "radical" group held back the formation of a generation-unit which would have rejected the premises of Western political society, then being undermined by the greatest depression in history.

> The Communists set the tone for the student movement of the thirties . . . because they had the advantage of numbers, because they offered the weak the impression of strength, and because they had a church which no one else could match. They offered in short an available escape from the reality. Most students, of course, managed to bear reality quite well enough to be apathetic about any avenues for escaping it. The Communists were a tiny fragment of the whole, but they were a majority of the committed. To reject them meant to surrender even the illusion of strength and condemn yourself anew to that alienation which had moved you to commitment in the first place.[49]

Although the Communists were always a relatively small group on and off the campuses, many individuals passed through the movement, particularly in the 1930s, and again during the period of the American alliance with Russia in World War II. Estimates of the number range as high as 750,000 different individuals. "Party members stayed for short periods; they might be active for shorter periods, and a good many didn't even pay their dues regularly."[50] What makes the figures concerning large rapid turnover within the CP particularly relevant for an analysis of student politics is that the overwhelming bulk of those who joined were of college age. "The peak age appears to be 18–23. In fact a majority of the rank and file have not only joined but have left the party by the time they are 23. The late teens seem to be an especially susceptible time."[51] It seems clear that "the proportion of party members who have been to college is very high. Even more striking is the great number of graduate degrees among them."[52]

Given the findings that the Communists were heavily composed of people recruited from those who attended college, it is not surprising that the membership, particularly during the period of massive recruitment in the 1930s, was heavily white collar and professional. Party leaders who were committed to building a proletarian party frequently expressed their dismay at this fact, and sought to get students and college graduates to take jobs as manual workers.[53] The family backgrounds of the party members resembled those reported for New Left activists in the 1960s.

> They have been brought up, in general, in comfort and often in luxury. They are the children of professional men or more than usually successful businessmen, bankers and ministers. In fact, the Communist Party in America seems to be such a highly educated, non-manual laboring group that at times there would seem to be more rejoicing in its headquarters over the recruiting of one common laborer than over ten Ph.D's.[54]

The Communists also resembled the current student activists in "that a large proportion of its members were of Jewish origin."[55] Parenthetically it may be noted that attitude surveys among college students during the 1930s which sought to locate the correlates of liberal-left to conservative beliefs generally reported comparable results to those of the 1960s. The more liberal students tended to come from relatively well-educated professional families disproportionately Jewish or irreligious, and tended to major in the social sciences.[56] "A definite linkage with father's and mother's political attitudes was established, not supporting the view that student radicalism is primarily a protest against parental conservatism. . . . The most striking factor . . . was the rather high correlation between college scholarship and radicalism. . . ."[57] The strength of the latter relationship led Gardner Murphy and Rensis Likert to try to answer the question: "Why is the bookish student more radical?" They concluded that modern intellectualdom and radicalism are closely related.

> The answer lies in a study of the modern temper. The whole whirl of the first third of the twentieth century is definitely a radical whirl, and this is particularly true of the postwar period. To be bookish in this era has meant to steep oneself in the disillusioned gropings of postwar thinkers, most of whom, from philosophers to lyricists, are clearly "radical" in the everyday sense of striving to find a new base for the relations between men. . . . The literary groups to which these men belong, the day-by-day conversations in which they train one another to think and to feel, are full of the modern doubt and disquietude, and, even more frequently, of the modern challenge and rebellion. To be bookish today is to be radical. . . .
>
> This is our theory, and it is nothing more; but it is supported by many straws of evidence. We . . . note that "books" are the one thing *besides parents* that are credited by [radical] students with consistent and powerful influence, and that radicals make mention of books and magazines more frequently than conservatives do, as factors to be underscored in the shaping of their attitudes. If our hypothesis is correct, the preferred courses of radicals will be those which emphasize wide reading as against those emphasizing laboratory work, mathematical calculation, or the acquisition of practical skills. A glance at Tables 34 and 35 [in the Murphy-Likert book] will show that the courses meeting this specification, such as philosophy, psychology and English literature, yield the expected results.[58]

Clearly the New Left of the 1960s recruited activists from the same social pool as did the Communists and other radicals of the 1930s and early 1940s. In fact there is some evidence to suggest that the activists of the 1960s, born for the most part in the 1940s, are to an extent the actual children of radicals and fellow travelers of the earlier generations.[59] Given the educational, occupational and cultural background, it is likely that the overwhelming majority of their children went to university. And studies cited in Chapter 3 report a family history of political activism and a left-liberal ideological outlook in the background of the contemporary crop of collegiate radicals.

While there can be little question that the decline of renunciatory tendencies and the failure of campus radicalism can be blamed in large part on the Communists and their effort to gain support for the Soviet Union's foreign policy, the one comprehensive effort at a national representative sample (1220) of college youth, conducted for *Fortune* in the spring of 1936, documented both the decline of the cultural renunciation which had characterized the twenties and the limited appeal of political radicalism. Concern with their economic future brought a yearning for security, for a job with tenure. *Fortune* worried that the students were too willing to do what they were told to get and hold a job, and raised the question, "Are good corporation heads made out of tractable material?" It found that the "family as such is no longer an object of derision, as it was in the early twenties. Fathers and mothers are listened to once more. . . . Deference to the advice of father is part of the general yearning for security among the young." Politically, there had been a sharp shift to the left, as compared with the surveys of campus opinion in the midtwenties which had found Republican majorities. By the mid-thirties, "liberals and democrats. . . . form the thick equatorial bulge of the [campus political] turnip. . . ."[60] An examination of the unpublished detailed report of the survey does indicate that many of the students did favor structural changes. Close to one quarter (24 percent) of those interviewed, when asked about various terms which "suggest ideas toward which you feel sympathetic," picked "socialism" as a positive term and 6 percent said "communism," as contrasted to 15 percent for "conservatism," 45 percent for "liberalism," and 2 percent for "fascism." Over two thirds indicated that they favored changes in the Constitution to enable people "to live comfortably . . . even if this means a revision in our attitude about property rights." Yet close to 90 percent indicated their belief that "there are plenty of employers who will give you satisfactory promotion in due course if you work hard and learn your job well."[61]

Fortune's reporters who visited many campuses were impressed with the relative weakness of the organized radical groups. The politically active and concerned are described as numbering at most between 5 and 10 percent. The exaggerated image of campus radicalism is sustained because the "college newspapers are often far to the left of the undergraduate bodies." In this respect, of course, the sixties resembled the thirties. There are other comparable patterns which are an outgrowth of similar peakings in the cycle of concern for political reform in the two decades. The college athletic and fraternity type social events lost appeal in favor of a more positive concern for relevance in courses. "Students have been flocking to history, economics, and sociology courses. . . ."[62]

Radical political activity in the 1950s was notable by its absence. Liberal and left student organizations either passed away or existed with tiny memberships and small agendas. A number of conservative campus groups acquired considerable publicity in the national media, as supposedly representing the new campus mood.

Why was there such political quiescence on the campuses during the 1950s? Many who have written on the problem have suggested that it reflected the coercive pressures on the adult world, particularly faculty and other intellectuals, imposed by the various aspects of the phenomenon known as McCarthyism. Professors were fired at a number of institutions for refusing to take loyalty oaths, or for failing to answer charges that they had been or still were members of the Communist party. Relatively little was done to defend the civil liberties of those charged with being Communists, in part because few of them ever tried to defend their rights to be Communists or radicals. Rather the tactic that was followed — of "taking the Fifth Amendment," of refusing to answer questions concerning political beliefs or memberships on the grounds of possible criminal self-incrimination —

made a civil liberties defense based on the First Amendment right to hold and espouse unpopular beliefs difficult. The issue in most cases became a detective story one; was the individual under attack actually a Communist, not whether he had a right to be one. In all previous periods of repression of radical opinion, those involved had vigorously defended their right to be political radicals, and by so doing had created *causes célèbres* around which others could rally. In addition, the first four years of the fifties, 1950–1954, were not only the era of repressive McCarthyism which intimidated many; more importantly they were the years of the Korean War, of a war perceived as having been started by an invasion of a non-Communist state by a Communist one. Wartime sentiments and pressures presumably also held critical sentiments in check.

But the interpretations which see the low ebb in student and other forms of radical activism as a response to repression are inadequate, since much the same pattern occurred among the students and intellectuals of Western Europe and Canada. Polls of student opinion in Britain revealed conservative majorities. The London School of Economics, once the principal stronghold of radicalism in the British Isles, was frequently described in this period as having become conservative or at least apolitical. Canadian students and intellectuals, clearly out of McCarthy's reach, showed close political resemblance to their American brethren. *The Canadian Forum,* the Canadian magazine which most resembled American ones like *The Nation, The New Republic,* or *The Progressive* in its outlook, and which had been outspokenly socialist in its sympathies during the 1930s and 1940s, became increasingly critical of socialism as an ideological outlook during the 1950s. In many European countries, socialist parties modified their programs so as to eliminate references to the class struggle or to the traditional goal of a socialist society, with little or no opposition from their intellectual or campus supporters.

The left-disposed segments of the students of the 1950s were caught up in a political era that inhibited deep political commitments and political activism. The experiences of the 1930s, and the behavior of the Communist states both internally (overt anti-Semitism, new purge trials), and in foreign policy (the Czech coup of 1948, the Berlin Blockade, the North Korean attack) made them, as well as their intellectual elders, suspicious of simple answers to complex problems. Fear of the aggressive power of monolithic Communism played the same role in the late 1940s and the 1950s that fear of Nazism had played during the late 1930s and early 1940s. The "lessons" preached by the Communists to other radicals during the 1930s were applied to Stalinism. To resist the totalitarian threat, liberals and non-Communist leftists, in effect, adopted the tactics advocated by the Communists to fight fascism against Stalinism, namely to concentrate on defeating the expansionist enemy, even to the point of sharply reducing criticism of the status quo in one's own country. For a second time, Western intellectuals accepted a defensist rather than a critical posture. Few proposed radical answers to current domestic problems, and still fewer were raising any important questions about inequality, poverty, or power. The students under these circumstances turned inwards. They became concerned with their psyches, their personalities, and their feelings. The fact that *The Catcher in the Rye* was a collegiate best seller in the 1950s should occasion no surprise.

Yet it would be a mistake to reach a conclusion from the presence or absence of an activist campus minority in any given period concerning the viewpoints of the student population. Clearly, the behavior of the very small minority of politically involved or avant-garde oriented students at any point in time must not be taken as typical of the attitudes and values of the generation cohort. During the 1920s, in spite of the concentration of attention on those engaged in cultural revolt, and the increase in premarital sexual relations from approximately 15 percent to close to 30 percent of the female population reported by Kinsey, studies of religious attitudes of college students revealed a commitment to religiosity among the great majority. The national poll of campus voting preferences in 1924 found that the large majority of the students participating in this straw

vote were for Calvin Coolidge. The 1936 *Fortune* poll pointed up
the minority status of the radicals of the thirties.

If it is proper to stress the unrepresentativeness of those who
set the dominant mood on campus during the 1920s and the
1930s, it should also be noted that there was considerable student
support for unpopular views during the 1950s, even though there
was relatively little action. Thus a national survey of a sample of
male college students taken in April to May 1952 revealed considerable opposition to the Korean War. Thirty-three percent
expressed outright opposition, 19 percent were uncertain, and 48
percent favored our policies in Korea. Less than a fifth (19 percent) stated that they never had felt the war "is not worth fighting." Only 10 percent indicated that they would like to serve in
the military.[63] To place these results in perspective, it should be
noted that a majority of American students still supported the
Vietnam war as late as 1967.

Evidence that the dominant mood in academe was not conservative even during the height of McCarthyism and Eisenhower
Republicanism may be adduced for both students and faculty.
The most comprehensive analysis of student opinion in the early
fifties found that liberal opinions were more prevalent the higher
the class in school, suggesting the liberalizing effect of the university.[64] A survey of faculty opinion in October 1956 reported
disproportionate backing for Democratic and leftist third party
presidential candidates in the 1948 and 1952 elections and in
vote intention in 1956. In 1948, Harry Truman received 50 percent of the academic ballots, while Henry Wallace, the Progressive candidate, and Norman Thomas, the Socialist, took about
ten percent. In 1952, when Eisenhower was sweeping the country,
Adlai Stevenson received 54 percent of the professorial vote, and
various left minor candidates had two percent. In 1956, the
Stevenson percentage among faculty rose to 60 percent.[65] Since
propensity to support liberal or left candidates varies with discipline and with school quality – the liberal arts fields, particularly the social sciences, and the more prestigious schools, as
noted earlier, are more liberal – the support for Stevenson or

left-wing candidates was undoubtedly much higher in the major centers of academe. A comprehensive survey of the opinions of social scientists completed in 1955 revealed that the Republican candidates in 1948 and 1952, Thomas E. Dewey and Dwight Eisenhower, took only 28 and 34 percent of the vote. The overwhelming majority of the social scientists supported the academic and political rights of Communists and other radicals in the midst of McCarthyism.[66] Since backing for these views and for political liberalism and radicalism increased with quality of university, it is clear that the more intellectually oriented students of the 1950s were in an environment in which prestige was associated with opposition to conservative views.

Perhaps the most telling report concerning the mood on the American campus during the 1950s are the conclusions reached in a book by a conservative, M. Stanton Evans, concerning the conservative revival during the decade. In general, Evans emphasized all the evidence from pre-election straw votes, formation of conservative clubs, and student reactions to various issues, to point up the magnitude of right-wing strength. The evidence clearly pointed to the greater political conservatism among the campus population during the early and mid-fifties as compared with the previous two decades. Eisenhower had widespread student support. Yet all during the period, sizable minorities expressed attitudes toward the role of government, welfare, and foreign policy, which can be best described as left-liberal and even socialist. And in summing up the results of various opinion studies made during the fifties, Evans concluded that the dominant student mood "is permissive, antireligious, and relativist in the realm of ethics; statist in the realm of politics; anti-anti-Communist in the *sui generis* crisis which grips our age. In a word, it is liberal."[67] These conclusions, it should be noted, were derived more from studies of the late fifties than from the early years, and may help to explain the rapid growth of civil rights, antiwar and leftist activism in the following decade.

A summary of the findings from various surveys of student opinion completed during the 1950s compared the characteristics associated with liberal or left social attitudes in that decade with those found in the studies of the 1960s, reported in Chapter 3, and concluded "that liberal or left students in each decade are recruited from similar sociological reservoirs,"[68] as were those of the 1930s. That is, those on the left side of the ideological division were more likely to be in the social sciences or humanities, to be Jews rather than Christians, to report higher grades, and to come from Democratic rather than Republican family backgrounds.

This brief survey of American campus discontent and politics is not designed to prove any general thesis concerning the cyclical sources of such behavior. The repeated periods of student unrest and political activism have given rise to various efforts to account for a given wave of protest. The similarity in causal analysis among them is striking. Most commonly, commentators assume that the contemporary discontent is a consequence of a structural trend, which has had as its inevitable results the contemporary state of affairs. From Cornelia Comer writing in *The Atlantic Monthly* of February 1911 to the editor of *The New Student* in October 1923 to Margaret Mead and Kenneth Keniston, in 1970, writers have pointed to the ways in which new and rapidly changing modes of communication and technology have upset standards, have reduced the influence of older generations, and have led students to look for new values and to support radical change.[69] The analyses of the changing characteristics of the university which presumably result in student unrest also have repeated themselves, often using identical explanations for close to a century.

Two studies of published material dealing with the role of the professor, one comparing articles from the 1890s to the late 1930s, and the other comparing turn of the century comment with those made in the late 1940s and 1950s, demonstrate this continuity in detail.[70] Veysey's analysis of the *Emergence of the American University* before 1910 argues that student complaints about faculty have been continuous and similar under varying conditions and teacher-student ratios — the small nineteenth century college or the large research and graduate-oriented university, the lecture or the tutorial system. He points up comments suggesting an inherent "class" tension between students and faculty and administration.[71] Given the presence of discontent, commentators have indicated comparable intra- and extramural causes. The campus-located causes take the form of inadequate teaching — overspecialized (or underspecialized), irrelevant to personal or social concerns, impersonal (although there was a time when relations were viewed as too close) — and also, at least since Jefferson's day, too tight institutional control. The solutions have also been similar. A multitude of articles written from 1900 to 1970 have called for greater rewards to teaching as compared to research, for special graduate programs to train college teachers, for a degree other than the Ph.D. for those who prefer to teach, for various programs which would end the lecture system, for more freedom for students to choose their courses and programs of concentration, for more generalized and socially relevant courses, for senior professors to teach elementary classes, and for greater student participation in the governance of the schools.

Off-campus factors are presumed to have resulted in a much higher degree of permissiveness and resultant lack of emphasis on basic morality than was experienced by the previous generation, as a result of larger social adjustments which have undermined basic beliefs. These usually have been the result of changes in the media, leisure activities, and pace of transportation: first, the rise of the penny press, the silent movies and vaudeville; later, radio and the automobile; and currently, television and the jet plane. Each older generation is convinced that the rate of change which has occurred in the last decade or two is the greatest in the history of mankind, that it has upset moral values, and that, consequently, young people have become more likely to follow their impulses or new pure ideals than at any previous time. If any solution has followed from such diagnoses, it has been to urge a speedup in the pace of political responses to the new moralistic demands of young people and to give them more of a share in the decision-making system.

The explanations for student unrest which focus on specific historical events also have in common an insistence that the experiences faced by a given student generation represent the greatest challenge to the American Creed that has been experienced in modern times. Thus, the radical wave before World War I was viewed as a response to the rapid growth of crowded, corruptly run cities, inhabited by hordes of immigrants living in abysmal poverty close to fantastic wealth. And in fact, the immigrant ghettoes of the East Side of New York were much more densely inhabited than the slums of Harlem today. The spread between the income of day laborers and the untaxed wealth of the *nouveaux riches* industrialists was also much greater than at present. Governments did almost nothing to aid the unemployed and poverty-stricken, who also were proportionately more prevalent than currently. The period from 1870 to 1914 did witness immigration at a rate of over a million a year, much of which was settled in the urban slums. There can be little doubt that the Progressive, Socialist, and settlement house movements, all of which were represented among the campus population, were an earnest of the tensions created by the gap between the nineteenth century American ideal of a society of independent yeomen, and the reality of the machine-run immoral dirty city.

The generation which came of age during the 1920s was also convinced that history had dealt a body blow to the American dream. The promises of the war to end wars, "to make the world safe for democracy," proved to be hollow. The immediate postwar era was characterized by a wave of political repression against dissenters, the passage of immigration restriction legislation which was nativist in intent, and specifically designed to limit Catholic and Jewish migration, violent race riots in many cities, the rise of the multi-million-membered Ku Klux Klan, legislative efforts to prevent the teaching of evolution in many states, and the dismal failure of the Prohibition Amendment, as large segments of the middle class and their college-student off-spring openly violated the law by patronizing racketeer boot-leggers to get their liquor.

The collapse of economic institutions, widespread bank-ruptcies, evictions from farms and homes of those who could not pay their mortgages, and from 15 to 20 million unemployed, all gave the students of the 1930s a set of domestic experiences strong enough to undermine faith in American institutions. Abroad they witnessed the seizure of power by the Nazis in Germany, the revival of religious persecution on a scale not seen for centuries, the expansion of totalitarian rule through force and war in Austria, Czechoslovakia, Ethiopia, Spain and China, with little opposition from the United States or other democratic countries. And the promise of Communism turned to ashes with the state-created famines of the early thirties, the purge trials and large-scale imprisonments in concentration camps of the late thirties, and the ultimate conclusion — collaboration between Hitler and Stalin to eliminate the independent states between their borders — an event which precipitated World War II. The youth of the thirties, too, could and did cry out that no other modern genera-tion had their experience of such a series of catastrophic value-challenging events.

Post-World War II generations have obviously seen much to make them query the worth of the larger social system. World War II, like World War I, left in its wake more extensive authoritarian regimes. The nuclear bomb, and the emerging cold war, meant all those who have come of age since 1945 have lived under threat of annihilation. Hot wars in Greece, Korea, the Middle East and Vietnam, made concern for peace a constant interest. Poverty in the underdeveloped world and at home was raised to mass consciousness. The struggle of the blacks in the United States for equal rights reached a level of intensity prob-ably not matched at any time since the Civil War. The failure of the United States to defeat a small impoverished Asian enemy undermined the American self-image that its foreign policy is designed to further the right to self-determination. Once again a major segment of American collegiate youth demonstrated their disgust at the failures of the society by various forms of personal and political protest.

The response of the alienated youth of the late 1960s to the changes and events they have experienced is undoubtedly greater and more intense than occurred in the earlier periods of this century. In part, the difference is produced by greater numbers, nationally, as well as on given campuses and in particular areas. Given almost eight million students in institutions of higher education in 1971–72, the small percentage of the thoroughly alienated constitute a much larger absolute mass base for aggressive student protest than has ever existed in any country at any time. The Boston metropolitan area, for example, has about 250,000 students in fifty-five colleges. Some of the protest groups, both white radicals and black militants, recruit from all over the metropolis for demonstrations on a given campus.

The willingness of discontented Americans to violate the law, to use confrontation tactics, and even on occasion to resort to violence, is not new. The students of the early nineteenth century engaged in serious campus violence. Labor movement organizers and radicals blew up buildings and used dynamite to gain their ends around the turn of the century. Blacks and whites fought each other with guns in the early twenties. During the 1930s, striking workers occupied factories in massive industrial sit-ins, while militant farmers brought their guns to prevent foreclosure sales at neighboring farms.

It is difficult to evaluate the severity of the recent pattern of polarization as compared to past waves. Clearly higher education has been affected more severely than at any previous time. The concentration of disaffection and alienation among students and younger faculty in the best universities and colleges of America has had an impact far beyond the campus. They are regarded by many who do not agree with them as the voice of their generation, a role which gives them considerable influence on those sections of the elite which are oriented towards the intellectual and university communities. Regardless of how small or disorganized the various radical groups are, there still is a "movement" today which includes the hundreds of thousands who read the "underground press," attend demonstrations and rallies, and give close moral support to the more violent militants.

The escalation of protest on the left and the right during the late 1960s does not necessarily mean a renewed period of growth in political polarization, or even its maintenance at a high level in the 1970s. As noted earlier, there is no doubt that both activism and radical sentiments declined considerably during the 1970–71 academic year. As David Riesman pointed out in his commencement address at the University of Pennsylvania at the end of the year, this change may reflect a new phase in the "recurrent cycles of activism and withdrawal" which have characterized student behavior. The brief look presented here into the history of campus-related unrest and protest should force us to be humble both about our ability to understand and to predict waves of discontent. Heightened social, political, or educational tensions seemingly bring a number of academic, societal and political reactions which reduce the sources of particular crises. Marxists in their historical analyses of revolutionary strategies have been well acquainted with the ebbs and flows of their potential strength. Marx, Engels, Lenin, and Trotsky each pointed up the necessity for revolutionaries to moderate their tactics during conservative tides, to avoid giving reaction the excuse for repression by the "adventurist" or "putschist" tactics of the left.

But whatever the future of the current wave, this American record does lend support to those explanations which stress the inherent potential of students as the most available social base for innovative forms of cultural behavior and aggressive political action dedicated to the attainment of "absolute ends." It reinforces the conclusion that the student population is the most volatile and most easily mobilizable of all social strata. Whether, and how, and for what causes it is mobilized will depend on specific events, on changes in the larger climate of opinions and custom within intellectualdom and the polity and society generally. Foremost among the forces in the adult world which affect student reactions is the faculty. Some analysts have even argued that faculty discontents and policies are at the heart of student reactions.[72] But this relationship, even between faculty and student radicals, is not a simple one. The following chapter turns to a discussion of some aspects of this.

6

Faculty and Students: Allied and in Conflict

The descriptions of student activism in the 1960s, as well as over the previous century and a half, have indicated an alliance between student and adult protest. The early nineteenth-century undergraduate opponents of orthodox theology found support from the Jeffersonians on the Harvard Board of Overseers as well as in other institutions. Student abolitionists were allied to older activists in the movement. The waves of student rebellion against parietal rules and the absence of student government in the last two decades of the century were clearly linked to the changes in the role of the faculty which led many professors to demand more intramural power and freedom. The various types of student political protest from the Intercollegiate Socialist Society of the first decade of the present century down to the Students for a Democratic Society of the 1960s were each, in turn, related to trends in the adult world, particularly among faculty. In a real sense, therefore, student rebellion has not been a generational revolt, but rather has represented the undergraduate contribution to social and political tendencies which have been present within each age group. The students, for reasons discussed earlier, have frequently been the most militant, the most extreme, the least disciplined, the most uncompromising segment of the ideological grouping of which they have been a part, but it is rare that any student movement has occurred without counterparts in the larger intellectual world.

Faculty participation in stimulating or supporting current student unrest has been documented in various surveys conducted by the American Council on Education. A comprehensive analysis of demonstrations which occurred at 181 institutions during 1967–68 found that faculty were involved in the planning of over half of the student protests which occurred. In close to two thirds of them, faculty bodies passed resolutions approving of the protests.[1] Faculties have clearly been bitterly divided on the issues involved in campus unrest, but a detailed investigation of the sources of faculty political involvement points to predispositions among professors to sympathize with student activism, as well as to the existence of basic tensions between student radicals and faculty supporters which result in faculty backing being short lived for student protest on any given campus.[2]

Intellectuals, who, as noted in the first chapter, are concerned with creation and innovation and are partisans of the abstract and the ideal, have a predominant sympathy for causes and ideologies which reject the status quo in their particular society and wing. Such orientations need not be political, and they may be right-wing or left-wing. Daniel Patrick Moynihan has advised Richard Nixon that since "about 1840, the cultural elite have pretty generally rejected the values and activities of the larger society. It has been said of America that the culture [the intellectual elite] will not approve that which the polity strives to provide."[3]

This comment of Moynihan's errs on the side of being too parochial. Similar judgments concerning the inherent tendency of the intellectuals to oppose the system have been made at different times by writers as diverse as Joseph Schumpeter, Robert Michels, Karl Mannheim, Reinhold Niebuhr, Sidney Hook, Richard Hofstadter, Lewis Coser, Richard Flacks, and many others. One hundred years ago, Whitelaw Reid, then the new young editor of the New York *Tribune,* presented what has become a frequently expressed thesis concerning the relationship between the academy and the rest of the elite, one which resembles Bristed's 1840 statement concerning the oppositional tendencies of students discussed in Chapter 4.

> Exceptional influences eliminated, the scholar is pretty sure to be opposed to the established. The universities of Germany contain the deadliest foes to the absolute authority of the Kaiser. The scholars of France prepared the way for the first Revolution, and were the most dangerous enemies of the imperial adventurer who betrayed the second. . . . While the prevailing parties in our country were progressive and radical, the temper of our college was to the last degree conservative. As our politics settled into the conservative tack, a fresh wind began to blow about the college seats, and literary men, at last, furnished inspiration for the splendid movement that swept slavery from the statute book. . . . Wise unrest will always be their [the scholars] chief trait. We may set down . . . the very foremost function of the scholar in politics, *To oppose the established.*
>
> . . . As for the scholar, the laws of his intellectual development may be trusted to fix his place. Free thought is necessarily aggressive and critical. The scholar, like the healthy redblooded young man, is an inherent, an organic, an inevitable radical. . . . And so we may set down, as a second function of the American scholar in politics, *An intellectual leadership of the radicals.*[4]

And most recently, the most significant conservative in American academe, Milton Friedman, has approvingly quoted an unpublished manuscript of his equally conservative economist colleague, George Stigler, to the same effect as Whitelaw Reid:

> The university is by design and effect the institution in society which creates discontent with existing moral, social and political institutions and proposes new institutions to replace them. The university is, from this viewpoint, a group of philosophically imaginative men freed of any pressures except to please their fellow faculty, and told to follow their inquiries wherever they might lead. Invited to be learned in the institutions of other

times and places, incited to new understanding of the social and physical world, the university faculty is inherently a disruptive force.[5]

Much of the discontent during the last decades of the nineteenth century was expressed as conservative disdain for the crude materialism of *nouveaux riches* businessmen and the vulgarity of taste in democratic society. Increasingly, however, during the twentieth century, the critical stance of the intellectuals, including first the social scientists and later the humanists within the university, took the form of a predominant sympathy for antiestablishment, liberal-left positions. Opinion studies, the earliest of which date back, as noted in Chapter 4, to before the First World War, indicate that American academics as a stratum, have been much more likely to express liberal opinions in religion and politics than other strata. They have lent disproportionate support to atheistic, antiwar, civil rights, civil liberties for deviants, liberal Democratic, and third party causes.[6] Given this relatively consistent outlook among the pacesetters of the academic and intellectual world, it may be argued that faculties should have shown much more support for student protest than in fact emerged. A look at some of the reasons for faculty opposition may help explain the growing tension between faculty and student activists.

The most obvious and important source of division in faculty response is linked to variations in faculty roles. Professors clearly differ in the extent to which they are involved in creative, intellectual, scholarly, and hence critical functions, as contrasted with teaching, professional, and applied activities. Most faculty employed in the twenty-five hundred institutions of higher learning in America are primarily teachers, not scholars, and hence more dedicated to the passing on of the existing tradition, not the enlargement or critical rejection of it. Second, disciplines vary in the degree to which they are "intellectual." The more intellectual fields, those more dedicated to the value of knowledge, art, basic research, as valued goals in themselves — the liberal arts fields — tend to recruit or produce practitioners on both the student and faculty level who are sympathetic to antiestablishment reform or radical positions. Conversely, the more practical fields, such as engineering, education, business, and agriculture, include on all levels the more conservative.

Given the relationship between intellectual creativity, commitment to innovation, and political criticism, it is not surprising that a variety of surveys indicate that the most successful scholars in all fields, those most dedicated to research and to national intellectual activities rather than teaching and local campus affairs, tend to be the most liberal or left-wing members of academe. This pattern results in a high correlation between the academic quality of institutions and faculty predilection for liberal-left politics.

The particular disciplines and universities which have the highest proportion of students inclined to the left politically and involved most heavily in campus demonstrations are the same ones whose faculty members have the most sympathy for the values and causes espoused by the students. Hence, as we have seen, the "gap" between student and faculty political orientations, like that between parents and their offspring, is relatively small. The liberal-left children of liberal-left parents study subjects and are in colleges where teachers are also among the more left-disposed among American academe.

Analyses of faculty opinion agree that the most important single determinant of attitude toward given campus demonstrations, or student activism generally, has been personal political outlook. The more liberal-to-left a professor is on wider social and political issues, the more likely he is to support radical student activities. The principal factors modifying this generalization are the related ones of age and longevity at a given institution. Within the same political category, e.g., faculty holding radical or liberal opinions, the older ones and those who have been at a given school longest are least likely to back campus demonstrations or locally relevant campus demands.

But, most student activists, even the more moderate among

them, sharply challenge the description of their faculty as a critical, antiestablishment group sympathetic to the same ideals as themselves. For in spite of the initial endorsement through faculty-meeting resolutions of the objectives of given campus protests, the activists find a lack of commitment to the endeavors of student protest movements even by those faculty who *are* intellectually oriented, critical of the status quo, and liberal-left in their political ideology. A study of opinions of a sample of social science faculty who had signed various advertisements against the Vietnam war validated the impressionistic complaints of the activists, for only 21 percent of this group of antiwar professors indicated that they approved of the student demonstrations that had occurred at places like Columbia, Cornell, Harvard, and San Francisco State.[7] These liberal-left faculty seem to justify the charge levied by many student activists that the faculty, like their parents, are hypocrites, that they do not act in ways congruent to their proclaimed beliefs.

It becomes necessary for the liberal faculty to explain themselves to their students. The conservatives will obviously oppose the politicization of the campus from the left, but theirs is not a relevant objection to leftist students. There are important reasons why scholars have opposed politicization, regardless of their political ideology, which derive from the very nature of scholarship. And just as it is possible to argue that a critical antiestablishment stance is inherent in the functions of the intellectual and the university, it is also possible to urge that the university cannot accomplish its task if it becomes a center of political advocacy. This is a view not easily or normally understood by morally concerned, politically dedicated students.

Politics and scholarship are highly different types of human activities, even though many scholars are also political actors and some men shift from a political to an academic career or vice versa. Many radicals fail to recognize the major differences between scholarship (both teaching and research) and politics (relevance). Both activities also involve the same types of actions, namely, writing and lecturing. Many academics, of course, are experts in policy-relevant fields and may be called upon to advise policy makers. Yet, in spite of the considerable overlap in activity and concern, the differences between the roles are greater than the similarities.

The political activist, whether a member of SDS or a leader of the Republican party, is expected to be an advocate. One of his major tasks is to mobilize support behind his group or party. To do this, he presents a point of view which emphasizes all the arguments in its favor, which ignores or consciously represses contradictory materials. In a real sense, the political activist is like a lawyer, whose obligation is to make the best case possible for his client. Inherent in the effort to gain a following and to win power is the need to simplify, to insist that the policies fostered by the group can eliminate evil, can gain the goals of the group, whether these be the ending of a war, the elimination of corruption, the end to depression or inflation, law and order in the cities, the end of poverty, the elimination of ethnic-racial discrimination, social equality, religious morality, mass participation, and so forth. The political leader who points out that life is complicated, that he is uncertain about the way to end practices which his group regards as evil, will not last very long in the role. Political leadership calls for decisiveness, for the ability to make decisions quickly on the basis of limited knowledge, with the awareness that there is a good possibility that the action will be wrong.

Scholarship, clearly, emphasizes the opposite characteristics. Ideally, or normatively (which by definition means major discrepancies from any given practice), those involved will be concerned with careful and extensive studies of the broad range of human knowledge. A scholar should consider all existing points of view and all available evidence before reaching a conclusion. He is expected to take his time in coming to a definitive conclusion before publishing his findings as knowledge. One of the worst things that can be said about an academic is that he publishes too quickly, that he rushes into print before he has exhausted the possible areas of inquiry. A scholar is normatively required to present contradictory evidence, to point to any methodological weaknesses in his materials. In attacking a research problem, he is initially required to complicate the issue, to introduce as many factors as appear at all relevant. Thus scholars writing on issues of race relations, equality, poverty, inflation, foreign policy, war, etc., tend to emphasize the indeterminate character of knowledge in these fields, the fact that the evidence rarely justifies any simple cause and effect relationship.

The dialogue between the scholar and the activist must inevitably be one in which the former undercuts the will of the latter to act, if he remains in the academic world. Or conversely, if the scholar takes to the hustings, he must cease being a scholar. There are, of course, considerable areas of overlapping usefulness. Any good political leader will want to have as much information as possible about a given topic before he makes a decision. He may call upon the scholar for policy-relevant research, which he wants to be cautious, to err, if at all, on the side of complexity and conservatism. The politician will often still have to make a decision, which assumes an ability to predict consequences with great probability, even when the extant knowledge implies a very low order of predictability about outcomes of different policies. Ironically, in his use of the scientific policy-adviser, the politician, therefore, is not looking for originality, but for "safety." He calls upon the scholar in much the same way as he might ask an engineer to plan a new bridge. The latter will always put in a great safety factor to make sure the bridge will not fall down. For this reason, the most brilliant and prestigious scholars may not make the best policy advisers. For the highest rewards in intellectual life are generally given for originality, for new ideas, for theoretical breakthroughs, not for valid replications, for proof that an existing proposition is valid.

The scholar, even when concerned with applied politically relevant problems, is committed to the notion that visible forms of behavior which can be described in common sense layman's terms can be better understood as the product of a complex set of underlying relationships which must be treated analytically in an effort to synthesize such linkages. A variety of seemingly disparate behaviors can only be identified as having common causal elements through use of abstract theoretical models. Hence science will insist that a cure for cancer will never be found if everyone interested in the disease becomes a surgeon; rather that an ultimate solution requires basic research on genes, cellular growth patterns, body chemistry, and so forth. Concern with racial tensions does not mean that every social scientist should concentrate on attacking racism or documenting its punitive character in economic, psychological, or sociological terms; it also requires detailed investigations into the underlying processes which make discrimination a characteristic of every multi-group society, of the functions of intolerance, of its effects on the abilities of those subject to discrimination to interact effectively, and so forth. The scholar involved in basic research will often deliberately separate himself from any substantive (policy-relevant) problem so as to be free to look for more abstract levels of generalization. This point has been made effectively by the radical historian Christopher Lasch, who finds the work of Erving Goffman on stigma and "spoiled identity" particularly useful in analyzing the behavior of leaders of Negroes and other socially oppressed groups:

> Goffman deliberately excludes the race problem from his analysis of "spoiled identity," on the grounds that established minorities do not provide the best objects for an analysis of the delicate mechanisms surrounding the management of stigma. . . . At the same time an understanding of face-to-face relationships drawn from quite a different perspective throws unexpected light on certain aspects of race relations — notably on the role of "professionals." As Goffman notes with his usual acuity, traditional fields of study such as race relations are areas "to which one should apply several perspectives"; and "the development of any one of these coherent analytic perspectives is not likely to come from those who restrict their interest exclusively to one substantive area."[8]

These differences between scholarship and politics are particularly significant for the social sciences, and to a lesser extent for the humanities, since matters of academic concern in these disciplines are often also political policy issues. As has been noted, many students who take social science courses or decide to major or do graduate work in these fields often do so because of the subject matter, because they see ways of enhancing their political objectives. Hence the interest of many students in these disciplines is not that of the scholar but of the politician, of the political activist. Such an interest is clearly a valid one, much as is the interest of the pre-engineering student in physics, or the premedical candidate in biology. But the activist-oriented social science student often wants his research-involved professor to join him in his efforts to gain social change by immediate political activities.

If students do not understand these differences between scholarship and politics, they must be taught them. But since most students will not become scholars, there is no reason why we should expect or try to force them to accept scholarly values for themselves. They should be encouraged to be as political, as relevant, as they wish *outside* the classroom. The demand for relevance is a political, not a scholarly demand. When students demand "relevant" courses, they are asking for courses which involve advocacy, or which see the faculty members acting as policy advisers. Efforts by faculty to be "objective" in courses which bear on politics are often regarded as forms of escaping from an obligation to fight evil, or even of supporting the system. And the committed activists, regardless of ideological stance, regard any claim to objectivity as pretense, as an effort to conceal the ideological commitments, the value preferences, and the biases which all men have.

Many social scientists, on the other hand, will argue that precisely because their fields touch so directly on politics and are involved with subjects about which they, like all aware men, have strong feelings, it is important to try to separate their values from their research *as much as possible*. The effort to engage in objective scholarship is clearly much more difficult in the social sciences and humanities than it is in the natural sciences.

This stress on the problems of scholarship in the social sciences and humanities does not mean that any such thing as objective or value-free scholarship occurs in any pure or absolute sense. Practically every major writer on these methodological problems has recognized that personal values, variations in life experiences, differences in education and in theoretical orientation, strongly affect the kind of work which men do, and their results. Such differences enter first into the choice of problems, then they affect the variables dealt with, the rigor with which they explore alternative explanations for given phenomena, and the like. Max Weber, who is frequently credited with being the major exponent of value-free, politically neutral scholarship in the social sciences, clearly enunciated the impossibility of such work. He argued, in fact, that the concept of ethical neutrality was spurious, and that those who maintained this "spuriously 'ethical neutral'" approach were precisely the ones who manifested "obstinate and deliberate partisanship."[9] He stated unequivocally that all "knowledge of cultural reality, as may be seen, is always knowledge from particular points of view."[10] He pointed out that the "significance of cultural events presupposes a value-orientation toward these events. The concept of culture is a value-concept. Empirical reality becomes 'culture' to us because and insofar as we relate it to value ideas."[11]

Weber was a highly political individual. He was an active partisan, wrote and spoke as a politician, intervened directly and often in political matters. He stressed that every professor had a personal "party-line." Because of this, and even with his general recognition of the role of personal values in affecting what we see as problems and facts, and his deep political involvements, he insisted that teachers and scholars were all the more obligated to try to be as objective as possible in their teaching and scholarship. A teacher, knowing something about his own political biases, should consciously try to negate them in class by presenting more materials contradicting his opinions than supporting them. He should make his values manifest to those who read his works or listen to his lectures. As a teacher, he must set

> . . . as his unconditional duty, in every single case, even to the point where it involves the danger of making his lectures less lively or attractive, to make relentlessly clear to his audience, and especially to himself, which of his statements are statements of logically deduced or empirically observed facts and which are statements of practical evaluation.[12]

As a methodological precept, Weber suggested that scholars should be more disposed to accept as valid findings which challenged their values and preconceptions than those which agreed with them. Clearly, he assumed that scholars, regardless of their efforts at objectivity, will be prone to recognize results and deductions which indicate they are right rather than the opposite. Hence, if science is to progress, particularly the strongly value-laden social sciences, great care must be exerted to reduce the impact of personal preferences on research results. The ultimate test, however, of scientific validity is the exposure of research results to the community at large. Any given scholar may come up with erroneous results stemming, in part, from the way in which his values have affected his work. But the commitment of scientists to objective *methods* of inquiry, the competition of ideas and concepts, will heighten the possibility of finding analytic laws which hold up regardless of who does the investigation. "For scientific truth is precisely what is valid for all who seek the truth."[13]

These are complicated methodological issues which have concerned scholars for many decades. They are not issues which should be of any great interest to the politically involved, students or others. Yet the politically concerned students live in the university. It is their home, their political base, and they, not unnaturally, want others in the institution to join them as allies in their morally justified political efforts to eliminate evil. Faculty who seek to deal with politically relevant matters in any "objective" fashion, who refuse to engage in advocacy, who point up the complexities involved in any causal treatment of the subject, necessarily become enemies; they are seen as partisans of the status quo who, if listened to, reduce the commitment to moral action.

The argument against overt political involvement by the university or the faculty as a body must also be dealt with. Karl Marx himself included as a plank in the program of the revolutionary movement: "Government and church should . . . be equally excluded from any influence on the school."[14] This issue is linked to the historic struggles of universities to free themselves from clerical and state control. In demanding and securing freedom from such controls, the university argued that its members as individuals must be free to come to any conclusion about topics relevant to religion or politics. In turn, it implicitly committed itself *officially* to ignore religious and political commitments in making appointments to its faculty, or in its formal policies. This meant that a university could appoint men who agreed with one political or religious point of view, who were liberals, atheists, radicals, or conservatives, as long as they never spoke out as a corporate body on such issues. In the United States, conservatives like William Buckley, Ronald Reagan, and others have argued the need for political balance, that is, for more conservative professors to reduce the predominant liberal-left dominance within liberal arts faculties in major universities. Others denounce the university faculty for being disproportionately composed of agnostics and atheists. And today, they are joined by student radicals who argue that more radicals should be named to academic appointments.

The university can only fight off such renewed demands by political and religious groups by insisting that the only formal criteria for appointment be scholarly, and that, even if this results in a faculty weighted toward any given side in extramural conflicts, the university and its faculty do not use their corporate prestige as a weapon in such extramural conflicts. Of course, such a formal position does not mean unpoliticized or neutral universities. That is impossible. But as Robert Wolff, the Columbia philosopher who co-authored *A Critique of Pure Tolerance* with Herbert Marcuse and Barrington Moore, points out, the myth of the apolitical university, though a myth, serves to protect unpopular minorities, that is, radicals. To insist that the university make manifest its politics would "have reactionary rather than progressive consequences. . . ." As a radical he argues against pressing the faculty to vote on political issues:

> [T]he politicization of the university invites . . . the ever-present threat of pressure, censorship and witch-hunting by conservative forces in society at large. The universities at present are sanctuaries for social critics who find it very hard to gain a living elsewhere in society. Who but a university these days would hire Herbert Marcuse, Eugene Genovese, or Barrington Moore, Jr.? Where else are anarchists, socialists and followers of other unpopular persuasions accorded titles, honors, and the absolute security of academic tenure? Let the university once declare that it is a political actor, and its faculty will be investigated. . . . It is a bitter pill for the radicals to swallow, but the fact is that they benefit more than any other segment of the university from the fiction of institutional neutrality.[15]

Barrington Moore, perhaps the most radical American sociologist, has defended the idea of a politically open university, not only on the grounds of political utility, but also as a basic principle.

> Nevertheless the general situation does create a dilemma for those of us who find ourselves in passionate opposition to the general drift of American society — a position often reached with uneasy astonishment. As students and teachers we have no objective interest in kicking down the far from sturdy walls that still do protect us. For all their faults and inadequacies the universities, and especially perhaps Harvard, do constitute a moat behind which it is still possible to examine and indict the destructive trends in our society. . . . The faculty's overwhelming commitment to free speech in the university community is part of this

moat, perhaps its most important part. To attack it heedlessly is irresponsible and self-defeating. That is so not merely because we who are vehemently opposed to many basic trends in American society may badly need its protection from time to time. The principle is important in its own right.[16]

The need to separate formally the political concerns of scholars as citizens from their academic role was held up at the convention of the American Historical Association in Washington at the end of December 1969 by three prominent historians who have attested to their personal involvement in dissident politics. The leaders of a fight against a resolution which would have placed the association in formal opposition to the Vietnamese war were Eugene Genovese, H. Stuart Hughes, and C. Vann Woodward. Genovese, who is probably the leading Marxist historian in the United States, lost his position at Rutgers University five years earlier because of his open advocacy of a victory for the Viet Cong. Hughes, who has been president of the peace organization SANE for many years, ran for United States senator from Massachusetts on a third-party peace ticket. Woodward, the leading historian of the South, has spent considerable time in civil rights activities. He was also prominently involved in the early meetings which established the Socialist Scholars Conference some years ago. These three men successfully argued, in opposition to the proposals of the "radical caucus," that the historians were morally obligated not to confuse scholarship and politics. They felt that radicals must defend scholarly institutions from politicization, even when these efforts came from young leftists.

Both Hughes and Genovese have published strong statements emphasizing their belief as political dissenters in the separation of politics and scholarship. Thus Hughes states:

> The social wrongs that may be committed by the university, such as being a bad landlord or aiding the "military-industrial complex," are not to be corrected by turning it into a social service institution. There are other institutions better equipped

to do that. If you lose the "ivory tower," you've lost the university. . . .

Just because a minority of conformist professors corrupted our universities through their tie-in with the "military-industrial complex" . . . just because one minority misbehaved is no reason for us, the opposing minority of dissenters, to turn around and do the same. . . .

The present need, then, is for de-politicization rather than re-politicization. . . . The task is to de-politicize connections with the right, rather than to re-politicize from the left. . . . If we don't do so, we will experience a polarization of the faculty and the campus, and wherever this has happened, whether under the auspices of the right or of the left, the result has always been a lowering of intellectual tone and the near-impossibility of teaching controversial subjects such as contemporary history.[17]

Genovese, himself a recent victim of political persecution, like Wolff stresses his belief that leftist student efforts to dominate the university will result in rightist control.

The pseudo-revolutionary middle-class totalitarians . . . support demands for student control as an entering . . . wedge for a general political purge of faculties, a purge they naively hope to dominate. . . . But they may very well help to re-establish the principle of the campus purge and thereby provide a moral and legal basis for a new wave of McCarthyism. The disgraceful treatment of Professors Staughton Lynd and Jesse Lemisch, among many who have been recently purged from universities by both liberal and right-wing pressure, has already set a tone of renewed repression, which some fanatical and unreasoning left-wing militants are unwittingly reinforcing. . . .

Universities must resist the onslaught now being made against them by superficially radical bourgeois students who have exploited the struggle over black studies programs to advance their own tactical objectives.[18]

It is important to recognize, as both Hughes and Genovese also point out, that many of the faculty, administrators and trustees who now would emphasize the inherent need for university autonomy against pressures from leftists manifestly to combine politics and scholarship have contributed to the current situation. Since the 1930s, the American university has increasingly become a major center of political involvement. Many faculty have engaged in applied, policy-oriented research, and have not taken care to separate their academic from their policy-adviser role. Professors and institutions have lent their prestige to "establishment" as well as other causes. Universities, through their choice of politically involved men to receive honorary degrees and other indicators of esteem, have implicitly endorsed the value of the work which these men have done. And if the name of the university is used in ways which have clear political consequences, it is difficult to now argue that leftist efforts to use the university should be ruled out, even though they may involve more overt forms of politicization. The argument that the defenders of the status quo can be more subtle in their politically relevant endeavors clearly has merit. Now that the issue of politicization and university autonomy has been joined again, there is a clear need to think through the rationale behind the involvement of academe as such in nonacademic concerns.

Writing as a radical critic of society and the university, Noam Chomsky carries the argument further by pointing out to student activists that they are pressing the university to live up to standards which no institution which operates within a given inegalitarian social system can do.

> Consider, for example, the matter of government contracts for research. . . . [T]here is little doubt that government research contracts provide a hidden subsidy for the academic budget, by supporting faculty research which would otherwise have to be subsidized by the university. Furthermore, it is quite probable that the choice of research topics, in the sciences at least, is influenced very little by the source of funds, at least in the major universities. It is doubtful that scientific education can continue at a reasonable level without this kind of support. Furthermore, radical students will certainly ask themselves why support from the Defense Department is more objectionable than support from

capitalist institutions, ultimately, from profits derived by exploitation — or support by tax-free gifts that in effect constitute a
levy on the poor to support the education of the privileged. . . .
[The university] cannot free itself from the inequities of the
society in which it exists.[19]

Chomsky goes on to argue in terms similar to those of Robert
Wolff that radicals must defend freedom of inquiry within the
university, including the right of faculty to "work on counterinsurgency" if they so choose, for once the principle of interference with research is introduced, it is likely in the long run to
legitimate repression of radical ideas. The leftists, in other words,
have an interest in protecting the right of their campus opponents even to do research which is paid for by oppressive forces
involved in atrocious activities. As Chomsky puts it:

> One legacy of classical liberalism that we must fight to uphold
> with unending vigilance, in the universities and without, is the
> commitment to a free marketplace of ideas. . . . Students are
> right to . . . point out . . . [that] access to funds, power, and
> influence is open to those who undertake . . . work [on counter-
> insurgency], but not, say, to those who would prefer to study
> ways in which poorly armed guerrillas might combat an enemy
> with overwhelming technological superiority. Were the university
> truly "neutral" and "value-free," one kind of work would . . be
> as well supported as the other. The argument is valid, but does
> not change the fact that the commitment is nevertheless under-
> taken with eagerness and a belief that it is right. Only coercion
> could eliminate the freedom to undertake such work. Once the
> principle is established that coercion is legitimate, in this domain,
> it is rather clear against whom it will be used. And the principle
> of legitimacy of coercion would destroy the university as a serious
> institution; it would destroy its value to a free society. This must
> be recognized even in the light of the undeniable fact that the
> freedom falls far short of ideal.[20]

From his experience in universities, Chomsky argues that the
university as it now exists "is highly decentralized and rather

loose in its structure of decision making and administration, hence fairly responsive to the wishes of its members." He suggests that much about the university which radical students dislike "results not from trustee control, not from defense contracts, not from administrative decisions, but from the relatively free choices of faculty and students." Hence he feels that various proposals for "restructuring of the university" will not eliminate the ills which bother the radicals, but rather are "likely to have the opposite effect, namely, they may lead toward a system of enforceable regulations that may appear democratic on paper but will limit the individual freedom that exists. . . ."[21]

Barrington Moore has also pointed out that students in fact do have a great deal of power in the contemporary university. He, therefore, calls on the students to use the traditional methods of scholarly discourse, and warns that reliance on rigid and dogmatic tactics will have less effect in achieving radical ends within the campus.

> Directly and indirectly the students in a university, especially the best students, have a tremendous influence on this general climate of opinion. If imponderable, this climate is probably the most influential single factor in determining individual decisions in a university and thereby deciding what the university really is. Naturally the faculty plays a decisive part as well. But I wonder if the students actually realize how much influence they do possess. . . . I have yet to know a scholar who did not respond in some fashion to the flow of written and oral arguments presented by good students. This situation provides the most significant opening for students who respond critically and negatively to the world about them. If they come to the faculty rigidly and dogmatically prepared to defend radical positions at all costs, they will get nowhere and defeat their own purposes. The consequences of this rigidity are often a tragic waste of essentially fine human materials. On the other hand, if they come in some degree prepared to be convinced as well as to convince, and if they are also willing to do the hard work necessary to demonstrate their intellectual mastery of the evidence, their impact can be enormous.[22]

The issues of university governance, as far as they involve student participation, also relate in part to a comparable set of concerns about politics and scholarship. Since the students in the social sciences and to a lesser extent the humanities are the most radical, the demands for student participation have generally been raised most in these fields. These areas, however, are not only the most politically relevant, they also differ from the natural sciences in that judgments concerning methodological issues and research competence remain highly subjective. There is almost no recognized piece of research, or scholar, in these disciplines whose distinction is not controversial. With few exceptions, it is quite possible to argue that any given work is either methodologically inadequate, that it is following a sterile approach, and/or that its weaknesses stem from biases which have led the researcher to ignore important factors and to come to erroneous conclusions.

In these less precise fields of scholarship, the more committed individuals are to a political role, as distinct from a scholarly one, the more likely they are to judge scholarly work by its presumed political consequences. Obviously such factors, and other sources of personal values as well, affect the way in which academics evaluate each other, regardless of age or institutional status. But in a politicized era, those who have not been fully socialized to the norms of the academy, who are more wont, as students, to feel the primacy of politics, will look for political allies among their professors. Not accepting the worth of the particular discipline in the same terms as its professional practitioners, being less disposed to believe that most scholars try to be objective, students will be more prone to want the university to act in directly political terms than will professors. In dealing with curricular matters, they will be less likely to respect the need for abstract theoretical, methodological, or "basic" fields which do not deal directly with social problems than their elders. An increase in "student power" in matters of faculty appointments or curriculum, therefore, almost inevitably means greater politicization in the methodologically soft disciplines.

There are important arguments against student involvement in the selection of faculty or the research program of other scholars which go beyond the particular issue of politicization. If all intellectuals, including professors, are obligated to stress innovation and creativity according to the standards and logic of their fields, then the questions of who shall take part in a given creative field or what kinds of work shall be considered important cannot be put to a vote of anyone. All intellectuals are in the same position as an artist or serious composer. Talented people will consider the judgments of their audience, of those who buy their paintings, of museum directors, for the reactions of the consumers of their creative product will determine their income. But no creative intellectual worthy of that name will consciously subject the direction of his work to the decision of the marketplace. In any case, innovators, creators, are by definition deviants, who explore unanticipated areas. If students are allowed to vote on the choice of faculty (they should, of course, be consulted), they, like other laymen, will favor what is currently popular. Even in the social sciences, some fields of current "relevance" such as urban studies were of little interest to students during the 1950s. Fellow intellectuals know that they cannot dictate what others should do. Thus, many faculty see the struggle to maintain the rule that only professionals may vote on new members as part of the historic effort of intellectuals to maintain or gain their freedom from interference by patrons, by those with consumer power. A case against student interference with the work of the professor has been effectively made by the British sociologist Ernest Gellner, who himself has been a severe intellectual critic from the left of dominant trends in his discipline.

> What is worrying about the student part of the [New Left] movement is its occasional illiberalism. However libertarian its members may be about legalizing marijuana, they do sometimes put forward proposals such as the student control of "what is taught and how." It does not occur to them that the implementation of this proposal would not involve the *transfer* of power

from one set of people to them, but the *institution* of control
where none exists at present. . . . [A]t least in British universities, teachers . . . are safe and free to teach what and how they
wish, and the students, who also complain, not without cause, of
the quality of teaching, know that there is very little control of
teachers. Those who demand control by themselves over "what" is
taught do not seem to realize the enormity, not of giving *them*
control, but of instituting control *at all*, or rather, of replacing
the present "sociological" controls, working through indirect pressures which can be defied without excessive difficulty by anyone
really wishing to do so — by formal and, presumably, enforced
controls. The present pressures are limited in their effectiveness
precisely because they are held to be illegitimate: they can only
operate in camouflage, and this hampers them. But the rebels
wish to institutionalize and legalize the controls which *they* would
impose, and thus nothing would inhibit *their* effectiveness. They
do not seem to have pondered the institutional implications of
their proposals. What is to happen to teachers who disobey their
instructions? One can only wonder whether they *do* know what
they are saying, and are profoundly illiberal and totalitarian, or
whether they do *not* know what they say, and the proposal is
merely part of . . . general invertebrate thinking.[23]

As I noted earlier, ever since the time American faculty
began to turn increasingly to research, there has been a perpetual
argument of the relative advantages for teaching and intellectual
life of varying emphases and encouragement to research or
teaching. The thesis that research interferes with teaching, that
undergraduates are being short-changed as a result, was present
by the beginning of this century. Suggestions that universities
establish teaching doctorates which do not require a dissertation
as a means of upgrading undergraduate teaching also date back
to that period. The "neglected" undergraduate has been a
favorite article topic for well over three quarters of a century.
And such writings have pointed to the pressures on professors to
engage in extramural activities for almost as long. Thus the
eminent professors of earlier decades were accused of neglecting
their university duties for the lecture circuit and for writing

financially lucrative textbooks or articles for magazines or the popular press.

The issue of teaching versus research, however, did not take on a political character until recently. In fact, if any deduction concerning the ideological correlates of those on different sides of the question may be identified, it is that the conservatives have favored more teaching. The links between intellectuality and political liberalism discussed earlier clearly point in this direction. Conservatives have defended the teaching function of the university that seeks to preserve the classical ideal, to stress the need to absorb the wisdom of the past, the "great books," not to create new knowledge. The pressure to make the university a center of research and innovation has more frequently come from those imbued with the idea of progress, of social change.

Student movements, however, insofar as they represent the "class" sentiments of students, have perceived professors primarily, if not solely, in their role as teachers. They want more time from them. And they have seen grades as mechanisms of social control, as means of getting them to conform to the authority or whims of the teacher. The leftist students have added to this criticism the idea that grades help maintain the "capitalist" emphasis on competition, on the "rat race," on the struggle for success, rather than on learning for its own sake.

The faculty, of course, also divides on these issues. Many younger professors in recent years have accepted the doctrine that research is often self-serving careerism. Some resolve to devote their careers to teaching, to working with students. Those who disagree with this position argue that an emphasis on teaching can be a way of escaping from being judged in the necessarily highly competitive intellectual world. It has also been suggested that a stress on teaching as the primary function of the academic job makes the task of "succeeding" easier. There is less strain in devoting oneself to lectures and discussions with students than in seeking to produce research which is regarded as first-rate.

There would appear to be an "interest" factor in this discussion which is partially generational. The older, more "successful" faculty, who have acquired academic distinction through their research, have an obvious reason for defending the existing system, including the ways in which support has been distributed. Those who have "failed," or are too young to have succeeded, are more prone to stress the virtues of teaching. Yet the inherent requirements of an intellectual career will press many younger faculty to seek jobs which facilitate their concentrating on research and writing. Presumably, it will be precisely those who are high in intellectuality, in scholarly competence, and hence also in political liberalism or radicalism, who will want this. As a group, at the moment, they are clearly in a cross-pressure situation. They, in effect, are the one group in academe who are pressed to resolve the dilemma between degree of emphasis on teaching or research in their own behavior.

Thus far, there is little evidence that the increased concern for undergraduate education which is manifest in the myriad of articles, books, national commissions, and local campus surveys has, in fact, changed the dominant practice of the American academy. Some years ago, the Israeli sociologist Joseph Ben David suggested as a general proposition concerning American academe that any event which reduces the attractiveness of a given university to retain or attract faculty would necessarily result in an increase in the bargaining power of faculty vis-à-vis the administration. A major internal crisis or a change in the ecological environment of a campus meant that the university had to pay more to gain or maintain a high level faculty. His first example was Berkeley after the loyalty oath crisis of 1949–50. He suggested that the cut in the pre-oath teaching load, three courses a semester, six a year, to a four or five course a year load, together with a rapid increase in upper-range salaries, which occurred soon after the oath fight, reflected the need of the university to improve faculty working conditions and income, to make up for the negative image. A similar sharp drop in teaching load and increase in salaries which occurred at the University of Chicago in the late fifties and early sixties seemed linked to the decline in the attractiveness of the neighborhood surrounding that school. And Joseph Ben David, who happened to be a visiting professor at Berkeley during 1964–65, the year of the Berkeley revolt, predicted similar results from that event. History has seemingly validated his prediction. The teaching load at Berkeley which is under the control of departments has been reduced since 1965 in many departments, particularly in the politically vulnerable, and, therefore, competitively less attractive, social science fields.

Few observers of the Berkeley scene who have commented in detail on the various experimental programs designed to improve the quality of undergraduate education there have noted that the biggest change in faculty-student relations is less faculty classroom contact with students than before. Crisis, as Joseph Ben David suggested, means greater bargaining power for faculty, and faculty use such power to reduce their teaching obligations. A similar set of events followed on the Columbia sit-in and student general strike in the spring of 1968. Until that event, the normal teaching load at Columbia was three courses a term; since then, it is two courses. Thus, though many, probably most, of the faculty at these and other institutions honestly believe that they are more interested in and dedicated to teaching since the emergence of student protest in 1964–1965, the evidence as reflected in time given to students at major American institutions does not bear them out. The reasons are obvious, and no amount of moral advocacy that is not accompanied by a change in the reward structure will affect practice. As Jencks and Riesman put it:

> There is no guild within which successful teaching leads to greater prestige and influence than mediocre teaching. . . . No doubt most professors prefer it when their courses are popular, their lectures applauded, and their former students appreciative. But since such successes are of no help in getting a salary increase, moving to a more prestigious campus, or winning their colleagues' admiration, they are unlikely to struggle as hard to create them as to do other things. Indeed, good teaching can be a positive handicap in attempting to meet other payrolls . . . for the able teacher finds students beating a path to his door and leaving him

little time for anything else. If he is really committed to research he may well find that the only way to make free time is to remain aloof.[24]

It is important to recognize that the teaching issue is one in which the student activists can expect more support from ad-ministrators, trustees, alumni representatives, and politicians than from the faculty of major universities. The former are much more disposed to view the university as a school, are more concerned with the way it treats the students than are the professors. The highly competitive, nationally oriented research faculty are seen by the administrative classes of the university in much the same way as the radical students see them, that is, as self-centered, self-serving individuals, who are using the univer-sity to benefit themselves, and who give as little as possible to more campus-centered activities.[25]

Alex Sherriffs, special consultant to Governor Ronald Reagan on higher education, sounded like a radical student in a discus-sion of the activities of the University of California faculty:

> Frustrated, normally idealistic youngsters . . . come up against a faculty which teaches less — and I mean less — than five hours a week. It's symbolic to the kids. If you've got a big name, you're too busy for them. . . . A guy who's an excellent teacher is looked on with some suspicion [by other faculty] as a guy who couldn't make it. They still play the foundation game. That's how you get your grants and your secretary and your prestige. And when they [the faculty] have to cut the budget, they cut out pupils every time. That shows their priorities.[26]

The same criticism of the university faculty has been made up and down the state by Governor Reagan himself. In addition to attacking the radicals on the staff, whom he sees as a small mi-nority, his major explanation for student unrest is what Clark Kerr once called "the faculty in abstentia":

> "Young men and women go to college to find themselves as individuals," the Governor declared in the speech that has be-

come a kind of educational testament. "They see the names of distinguished scholars in the catalogue and sign up for courses with the belief that they will learn and grow and be stimulated by contact with these men. All too often they are herded into gigantic classes taught by teaching assistants hardly older than themselves. The feeling comes that they're nameless, faceless numbers on an assembly line — green cap at one end, cap and gown and an automated diploma at the other."

And on and on the Governor goes with his paraphrase of the FSM, including such classic complaints as the priority of "publish or perish" over concern for teaching and the desire of the students to have someone "know they're there."[27]

A similar political lineup on issues such as these occurs among the faculty. As has been noted, the less research-oriented faculty tend to be more politically conservative and locally oriented in terms of campus affairs, and more concerned with teaching as an institutional function. They, too, deprecate what they consider to be the exaggerated emphasis and rewards given for research. They are the people who staff the committee system, who assist the deans, who keep the place going in normal times. (In a national survey of social science faculty conducted in 1955, Lazarsfeld and Thielens found that conservatives are more disposed to be department chairmen and to be active in campus affairs than liberals, even when age is controlled.)[28] Hence when student groups raise the teaching-research issue, they are likely to confound the basis for faculty political cleavage. The "conservatives" and the establishment agree with them while the more research-oriented "liberals" will, if they honestly speak their minds, be more likely to disagree.

The same apparent "contradiction" exists with respect to outside involvements as consultants for government agencies or business firms. The radical students assume that both sets of institutions are reactionary, and presumably those faculty who are involved with them have "sold out" and should be among the more conservative members of the faculty. But in fact a 1966 national faculty survey conducted by the National Opinion

Research Center indicated that professors who had *never* worked for extramural organizations, whether business or government, were most disposed to *back* government policy on Vietnam. Those who had served government were most opposed to the policy.[29] An even stronger relationship between having been called in as a consultant to business and political liberalism was indicated in the Lazarsfeld-Thielens study of social scientists' reaction to (Joe) McCarthyism. Holding age constant, those who strongly favored academic and civil liberties for Communists and other unpopular minority dissidents were most likely to have been consultants for business. At every age level, the "clearly conservative" had the lowest level of involvement with business.[30]

The "missing" intervening variable in both sets of findings, presumably, is that the most successful scholars are the ones called on to consult, and, as indicated by many surveys, academic success, regardless of how measured, is correlated with degree of leftism in political attitudes. The same results should obtain in any estimate of the relationship between involvement in Defense Department research and political liberalism, or even opposition to the Vietnam war and other American foreign policies. Since the Defense Department has been the largest supporter of basic (non-policy oriented) research in the country, it is likely that its grants have been given largely to the most prestigious scholars in various fields, therefore to the most liberal. This presumed relationship may explain the fact that many of the most prominent faculty radicals and opponents of the Vietnam war have not backed opposition to Defense Department support of basic research when this issue has been raised by student radicals. At Harvard, Berkeley, and MIT, for example, the most radical member of the faculty in terms of public utterances in each case has been a long-term client of the research agencies of the Defense Department.

These differences between the student activists and many of the faculty who stand relatively close to them in general political philosophy or ideology can be conceptualized in another way. Students, including, or especially, the radicals among them, want the university to retain the characteristics of a school and the faculty to behave like teachers in lower levels of education. Many students seek teachers who will tell what they think about life generally. They will see, in professorial claims to seek objectivity by introducing contradictory material, an evasion of their responsibility to take a stand. The faculty, particularly at universities which are major centers of research, who are themselves committed to a life of productive scholarship, see higher education and the role of the professor as highly differentiated, in which teaching is only one of the activities.[31] Florian Znaniecki, in his analysis of the role of the intellectual, pointed up the distinctively different functions of the university and the school:

> . . . [T]he school of higher learning performs the specifically social function of an educational institution only because its main activities are not social but scientific, do not aim to contribute to the maintenance of the social order but to the maintenance of knowledge as a supersocial domain of culture supremely valuable in itself. . . . The school of general education, on the contrary, as an institution of the modern society serves directly the maintenance of social order — whether it be a traditionally static order or a more or less dynamic new order.[32]

It is important to note in Znaniecki's distinction that he describes the institution which advocates radical change and the one which supports the status quo as both being primarily schools rather than scientific organizations. Michio Nagai has pointed out that the teacher-student relationship in the school is one of a parent-substitute to a child, which tends to become particularistic. The teacher in nonuniversity education is expected to consider all aspects of the child's life. He suggests that "the reasons why it is so difficult to establish professional standards for teachers may be found in the diffuseness of the function of the teacher. . . ."[33] Thus, the school is characterized particularly by the diffused content and method of instruction in it as distinct from the highly specialized university.

Given the assumption that schoolteachers have diffuse author-

ity over pupils and that they have a particularistic relationship
with them, it follows that the method of teaching, the very role of
the teacher in the classroom and in personal discussions must be
different:

> While the university professor has authority over the student
> only in a restricted area of human activity, the schoolteacher . . .
> has authority over children in many aspects of their lives. . . .
> The task of the teacher, unlike that of the professor, is not only
> to teach how to learn science, but how to live.[34]

It may be argued that when the activists criticize the educational system today, they seek to retain the status of pupil and to
have teachers rather than to be students of university professors.
Although their demand is now couched in terms of the faculty
taking an activist position in support of radical social change, it
is a demand that their professors act like their schoolteachers,
that they take part in "bull sessions" in which they discuss the
totality of human experience, not simply their subject matter.

The argument concerning grades also cuts across the usual left-
right dimensions, although in recent years it has been raised
largely by student activists.[35] Radicals see in the power to grade
an instrument of coercion which prevents the free interchange of
ideas and opinions between faculty and students. The fact that a
meritocratic grading system has been seen as an instrument of
freedom by those from underprivileged backgrounds is foreign to
them. Felix Frankfurter, who came to Harvard Law School from
CCNY as an immigrant Jewish youth before World War I, never
got over his awe at the democratic implications of the rigorous
grading system:

> What mattered was excellence in your profession to which your
> father or your face was equally irrelevant. And so rich man, poor
> man were just irrelevant titles to the equation of human rela-
> tions. The thing that mattered was what you did professionally.[36]

As Frankfurter saw the situation, the alternative to a rigorous
grading system had to be reliance on faculty "personal likes and

dislikes, or class, or color, or religious partialities or antipathies. . . . These incommensurable things give too much room for personal preferences and on the whole make room for unworthy and irrelevant biases." The young Randolph Bourne, socialist scion of Anglo-Saxon higher status, also argued in similar terms before World War I: "Scholarship is fundamentally democratic. Before the bar of marks and grades, penniless adventurer and rich man's son stand equal."[37] In 1971, radical philosopher Michael Novak was to report that the need of the underprivileged for grades helped to end the experiment in unstructured public higher education in Old Westbury.

> . . . [B]lacks and Puerto Ricans often operated as the most conservative educational forces; desiring grades, clear standards, written assignments, sequences of courses, a firm structure of authority and tests. . . . (They wanted) courses that would get them into law school, graduate school and the arts. "Old Westbury is an interlude for us," one said. "If that degree doesn't mean something, we go back to the streets."[38]

The general issue is how much and under what conditions institutions of higher learning should reflect in their internal structure the different norms and orientations of the worlds of the school and scholarship. In this respect, we meet again a congruence between the Left and the Right. The leftist students agree with many conservative critics of the university. Both want the university to be a school. The Left, however, desires a school which will favor radical social change, while the conservative politicians and alumni want a school which will defend the status quo. Neither wants an institution which is dedicated to subject all simple propositions, all explanations, all reforms, to the test of scientific validity. For in essence the university is the enemy of simplification. The norms which must govern a university make of it a qualitatively different environment than a high school. In shifting from the status of high school pupil to university student, youth must adjust to a highly specialized and segmented system in which their professors will be men for whom undergraduate teaching is necessarily only one of a number of functions, and not even the most important one in the better institutions.

It is essential that those concerned with university life recognize that universities are not schools, that the norms which govern scientific activities are quite different from those which characterize schools. The approach of science and of the university has been analyzed in formal analytical terms by Talcott Parsons and Robert K. Merton. The values they specify describe the "role structure of the scientist" (Parsons) and "the cultural values and mores governing the activities termed scientific" (Merton) in terms which are in variance with the involvement of faculty in indoctrination, in preparation for life, and with the total personality and character found in the school.

Merton emphasizes the neutral, objective, disinterested, and skeptical values inherent in the scientific process. Parsons similarly points out that the ethos of science, which includes functional specificity (professional specialization) and achievement orientation as well as those activities mentioned by Merton, has "above all become embodied in the university as its principal institutionalized frame." These guiding values imply that professors have no general claim to superior knowledge, but must combine organized skepticism and universalism (treatment of all according to impersonal criteria) in their application of objectivity to their specific area of expertise with an understanding of the boundaries of their professional abilities. Further, both men stress that while scientists must conduct themselves commensurate with these values, nonscientists, including students, must reciprocally respect the scientist's inviolable rights in his own field.[39]

These value orientations which are inherent in the scientific ethos contain liberal-left political implications and call for emphasizing the role of the student as apprentice scholar, not as the pupil of a Mr. Chips-type teacher, whether radical or conservative. The values of science emphasize the need for a free society operating under the rule of law. State interference to guarantee that science adheres to a party, national, or religious line, or that scientists are not free to criticize each other, makes for bad science. The stress on universalism, on functional specificity, on achievement orientation, implies opposition to those aspects of stratified societies which limit equality of opportunity. For science, trained intelligence, not family background, race, or wealth, must be the primary quality associated with status and social rewards. Hence, as noted earlier, the more committed an academic to scientific research, the more likely he will oppose those aspects of the social system which appear to perpetuate inequality of opportunity.

Some of the same elements of the scientific ethos which press men in a liberal and left direction politically, also, of course, include the action imperative to treat students in a highly specific, meritocratic manner. To advance scientific knowledge means that all qualified youth must be encouraged and rewarded, but that little reward (or attention) should be given to the unqualified or to the less able. Science is inherently concerned with locating and rewarding the aristocracy of talent. Anyone familiar with the norms of major centers of graduate study in the liberal arts fields knows that this is the way they operate. The faculty are only interested in graduate students who seem to have the ability to make major contributions to knowledge; the inadequate among them are regarded as out of place in such departments. And such values which must be present in major graduate and research centers inevitably inform the treatment of undergraduates in the same institutions. (It may be noted that the leading state universities such as Berkeley or Madison which do not have as highly selective undergraduate admissions policies as the major private institutions, but which maintain an elite research-oriented faculty, have created the optimum condition for fostering neglect of the undergraduates.)

The differences between graduate school university faculty and those at four-year colleges are also to be found among the colleges. Jencks and Riesman have detailed the way in which the ethos of graduate education has affected the entire character of

American academe.[40] In an earlier study, Riesman and Gusfeld have shown how undergraduate schools vary in faculty and student orientation with respect to the different concept of the college they sustain. Some of the consequences of the distinction attempted here between the school and the research institute, graduate-training role of the university, and between the pupil and the student roles open to undergraduates, were developed by Riesman and Gusfield in their analysis of the differences in the activities of undergraduate institutions. They distinguish between the "adult-forming" and "youth-prolonging" aspects of higher education by noting that by using adult standards of performance, universities "weed out" the childlike students. In a limited sense, the highly specialized professor also provides a model of one possible adult role. However, the instructor who views himself less as a specialist and more as a member of a broad intellectual subculture seeks to preserve youthful traits in his students and tends to remain young himself, ". . . young in the sense of being rebellious, open, uncommitted to specific authoritative roles. Correspondingly, they are much less eager than their more didactic colleagues to induct the students into a particular speciality; what they want of them is a greater playfulness, a release of inhibitions imposed by the parochial past and the looming vocational future — in other words a moratorium."[41]

It may be argued that the traits of science enunciated by Parsons and Merton and of "adult-forming" educational functions specified by Riesman and Gusfield are relevant to scientific research and the work of research institutes but not to colleges and universities. The latter are primarily educational not research organizations. Hence the application of scientific traits to the college properly has made for student dissatisfaction and unrest. This argument, made by both students and politicians in authority over universities, clearly is quite valid. Much of what is done in the American system of higher education is closer in function to the work of high schools than it is to graduate centers of education and research. The courses usually taught in lower division, in the freshmen and sophomore years, in most colleges and universities are extensions of high school work, if they are not in fact courses identical to those given in many high schools. Elementary work in languages, in mathematics, in English, in a variety of other subjects, is not on the level of university courses in the sense in which the university has developed in Oxford and Cambridge, in Germany, and elsewhere. The university in much of Europe has ideally at least been closer in requirements to the American graduate school than to the undergraduate college. The *Gymnasium, lycée,* grammar or public schools in Europe cover many of the courses which in this country are included in colleges or universities. The first university degree in Europe is a specialized degree, often in one subject, requiring a thesis. The doctorate is the only degree given in Germany, northern Europe, and many Latin countries. (It is more akin to the American master's degree than the Ph.D.)

As a result of the growth of the research function, American institutions of higher education today are torn between being schools and graduate research centers. When we think of the intellectual or scholarly status of a university, we think of the prestige of its faculty as researchers, not their abilities as teachers. The supremacy of the research function over teaching as a source of institutional status is inherent in the fact that scholarly recognition is a national, often international phenomenon, while the reputation of a man as a teacher is local, limited to people only associated with his campus. Hence, although relatively few institutions are major centers of research, probably the majority of students attending four year degree-granting colleges are in institutions in which the faculty is held to the requirement that they engage in productive scholarship, that they be judged for salary, rank, and local prestige by their presumed research rather than teaching merits. A study of the role of the teaching assistant at major universities indicates that a considerable amount of lower division instruction in such institutions is given by graduate students who are devoting most of their energies to getting a doctoral degree.[42]

Students and faculty are properly in a confused state with

regard to their respective roles. As the importance of the research function for the larger society increased (very few professors were expected to be researchers in the nineteenth century and few were), the more prestigious professors in the centers of graduate training and research took on a variety of activities in addition to research and teaching. A relatively small segment of the American professoriate has been asked to serve as consultants for government, industry, political parties and international agencies. The same men are in demand for extramural lectures, articles, books and editorial consultation. They are invited to participate in the increasing number of international conferences made possible by the jet plane and foundation funds, which are often genuinely necessary to facilitate rapid communication of research results and new ideas. While few schools have separated the graduate from the undergraduate faculty, the number of graduate students increases rapidly. Research in many disciplines now involves the administration of substantial funds and the coordination of the work of various colleagues and assistants. All of these tasks have been added to the work of undergraduate teaching, which was the primary, usually the exclusive, task of professors in the major institutions in the nineteenth century.

To put the whole matter another way, the leading universities and professors have been accumulating more tasks, while they continue to do their old one, undergraduate teaching, as well. These institutions and faculty are judged for eminence and the rewards which go with high status by their research output. The reports on the relative status of academic departments and universities which have been prepared for the American Council on Education and other bodies, and which are made much of by the press, administrators, and faculty themselves, are ratings of these departments as graduate schools, as centers of research, not ratings of undergraduate teaching. This increased pressure on faculty at such institutions for differentiated involvements and the lesser time given to undergraduate education should make the university world an increasingly less happy place for both faculty and undergraduates.

And as we have seen, both the leading faculty and the students at institutions with the highest admission standards tend to be among the most rebellious politically. The political rebellion stems from factors other than the tensions inherent in institutional and faculty role conflict, but a liberal-radical political ideology and "job dissatisfaction" should reinforce one another. The upshot of many politically motivated campus disturbances has been an attack on the governance or other aspects of the university as a place in which to work or learn.

The emphasis on the internal governance of the university to which many faculty and student activists have turned as a "solution" to the problems of higher education seems to be misplaced, as Chomsky suggests. More faculty work, more committees, only make the situation worse. In previous crises, efforts to democratize university government resulted in involvement in "busy" work (committees) of the less research-involved, also more conservative faculty, once the original crisis which activated the concerns of the younger and more liberal-left faculty ended. The increased "democratization" (more elected faculty committees) thereafter increases the importance of the role of the more conservative and scholarly less prestigious "committeemen," since they can claim to be the elected "representatives" of the faculty rather than the appointed consultants of the administration. In effect, faculty elections often serve to give populist legitimacy to locally oriented, relatively conservative professional faculty politicians, who rise to the "top" because the "cosmopolitan," more research-involved liberal faculty see campus politics as a waste of time in normal periods. In a period of renewed crisis, the elected spokesmen of the faculty, chosen before the troubles, usually differ greatly in their political orientations from the dominant faculty mood. The general situation has been well described by William Roth, a leader of the liberal minority on the Board of Regents of the University of California:

> The rhetoric of faculty governance, however, betrays the usual cultural lag. Through an intricate structure of senates, assemblies,

and committees, it maintains the pretense of a self-governing community of scholars. The inaccurate word is "community," for its members are more concerned with doing their own thing than with the general welfare of the particular society which nourishes them. Traditionally, the professor does not want to be bothered by problems of governance. If out of sudden guilt, rage, or embarrassment, he occasionally rises in protest, he soon lapses again into his own affairs. When there is a dramatic, albeit often symbolic, issue to be confronted, the faculty turns out en masse. But the day-to-day business of university government that must be carried on is left to a small minority of concerned people — the scholarly bureaucrats and politicians.[43]

Student participation on a representative basis, as a minority of a campus-wide faculty-student senate, is not likely to give the bulk of the student body any sense of increased participation or involvement. All that they get out of such reforms is the opportunity to vote once a year.

In terms of sheer educational satisfaction, or optimal personal adjustment, there clearly is no "right" form of higher education for everyone. The diverse pluralistic form of American universities and colleges has as one of its advantages the opportunity for students and faculty to sort themselves out, to try to find the best type of school for their personalities and talents. Unfortunately, of course, such a choice is not available to most people.

There does seem to be a set of problems calling for reform stemming from the multiplication of tasks handled by faculty as individuals and by universities as institutions. Differentiation, separation of functions, has been the pattern of response in all institutional life as tasks have multiplied. In the Soviet Union and other communist countries, the research-institute graduate-training set of activities is conducted separately from that of undergraduate teaching. Japan is planning to separate graduate work from other forms of higher education. These alternative systems clearly have liabilities of their own. But if the recent wave of politically induced discontent within the American university is to have any useful function for the life of the university itself, there is a clear and present need to examine the need for, and the possibilities of, a restructuring of the system into a variety of component parts. One important possible reform would be to vary considerably the types of state supported higher education available, as California has done to some extent. This should be combined with much greater encouragement than now exists for students to "try out" different varieties of schools by making transference among institutions easy.

This counsel does not imply the necessity to separate research and teaching. It does suggest, however, the need to recognize and not be afraid to state that a genuine university should not have the attributes of a school in the sense used earlier in this chapter. If a university is to educate for adulthood, it cannot be concerned with continuing to be a *gemeinschaft,* a community which resembles an extended family. Students must learn that intellectual life is complicated and difficult, that professors are also scholars who do not have the time to hold their hands or spoonfeed them with intellectual nourishment. The scholar must share with the student the tentativity of knowledge, his uncertainties about his conclusions, his self-doubts, and his triumphs. The student must be prepared to challenge the findings of his professors, after he has learned the methodology of the field, as another seeker of truth. To communicate the complexities of knowledge to sharp questioning minds is essential to the process of intellectual clarification. Scholarship requires dialogue, controversy, not only among established men in the same field, but with students as well. Those who would turn universities into schools or into research institutes are seeking to escape the intramural conflict by an easy capitulation. The primary function of the university is scholarship, which includes rigorous education, not politics or therapy. This means, of course, that there can only be a relatively small number of universities which have severe standards for faculty and students, although there will be thousands of accredited institutions of higher education.

7

Some Political Consequences of Student Activism in Comparative Perspective

The rise of student protest movements since World War II has been more extensive and more important than in earlier periods. Students played a major role during the 1950s in overthrowing or weakening regimes in the underdeveloped and communist worlds. Thus, student movements were important in the revolts against Perón in Argentina in 1955, against Pérez Jiménez in Venezuela in 1958, in different protest movements in South Korea and South Vietnam during the 1950s, in India, Japan, and many other countries. They helped initiate liberalizing movements in Poland, Hungary, the Soviet Union, and China in 1955–1956. During the 1960s, of course, student protest spread to the developed countries of Europe and the United States.

These movements have a great deal in common in tactics and political style. Student culture is a highly communicable one — the mood and mode of it translate readily from one center to another, one country to another. Yet it would be a mistake to try to interpret the seeming phenomenon of a worldwide student revolt as a response to common social conditions or as an effort to secure a common objective. The sources of student protest must be differentiated among different types of societies: underdeveloped systems, authoritarian regimes, mainly Communist, and the economically developed democratic societies.

The Third and Communist Worlds

In various underdeveloped countries and new states of the third world, the sources of intellectual and student protest may be found in the wide gap which exists between the social outlook of the educated younger part of the population and the more traditional, less educated, older age groups. The gap between the social and political expectations engendered within universities, and the reality of underdeveloped societies, motivates students and intellectuals to accept ideologies which define the status quo as unacceptable and seek drastic institutional changes so as to foster modernization, i.e., the values of the "advanced" societies. This gap is reinforced by the fact that the very logic of the university imposes values of achievement, competitive standards of merit, which are frequently in conflict with the traditional, particularistic values both of the controlling elite and the population at large. Thus, the intellectuals and students of Eastern Europe in the nineteenth century rejected the institutions of their own societies as backward compared to those of France and Britain. Chinese "returned students" in the early years of this century favored the overthrow of the backward Manchu dynasty so as to catch up to the West.

Although the principal source of ideological tensions within such societies involves the conflict between "modern" and "traditional" values, a conflict which opinion surveys suggest is largely linked to differences in education and age, such differences are often tied to positions on international issues. In much of the underdeveloped world the opposition to existing domestic elites and social-cultural-economic systems for being involved in and responsible for national backwardness, is accompanied by support for the Communist model as an example of a successful effort to break through the restrictions on development and modernization. Since the existing social system is often allied

internationally with the United States, the student opposition
movements tend to associate the symbols of the United States,
capitalism, the free world, with the conservative elites of their
own society. Opposition to domestic traditionalism and liberalism becomes translated into support for some form of leftism
which in international terms means opposition to the United
States. Hence, in large measure, leftist student activism in most
of the underdeveloped world is a force against any alignment
with the United States. It is, however, not necessarily a force for
support of the Soviet Union.

The leftist student groups differ considerably from country to
country, and in recent years there has been an increasing growth
of "third force" revolutionary organizations which are both anti-
American and anti-Soviet. Some tend to be Maoist, others identify in a very loose way with Trotskyism, a few are explicitly
anarchist. There is a tendency to take over a variant of what has
come to be know as the New Left ideology, that is opposition to
all power groups. But regardless of the differences among the
leftists, there can be little question that the focus of their hostility in international terms is the United States. This opposition
has become intensified with the escalation of the Vietnamese war
since 1964. In large measure opposition to American intervention
in Vietnam has become the predominant political issue of many
of the left-wing groups.

There is one major variation among the different underdeveloped countries which relates to the image and role of the governing power concerned, i.e., whether it is viewed as leftist or not.
The political movements of students in countries which are
aligned to the Soviet bloc have often opposed Soviet policy.

Two outstanding examples of this phenomenon occurred in
Indonesia under Sukarno and in Ghana under Nkrumah.[1] In
both of these countries led by pro-Communist leaders, the students took a position in opposition to the regime, arguing in
favor of increased liberty within the universities and political life
generally. Their advocacy of greater freedom and their criticism
of various actions of the regime led them to foster the ideologies

of democracy and certain kinds of liberalism. In a sense, the general proposition may be advanced that the most activist student groups tend to be opposed to the existing regime, and consequently take on a political ideology in opposition to it. The situation in the various Communist countries is, of course, a case in point.[2] Where student activism has developed in Communist societies it is critical of the existing regime as oppressive and also critical of its international orientation. To some degree in Eastern Europe, the oppositionist students have favored withdrawal from the Warsaw Pact, have shown signs of being pro-Western, and have taken up the issue of Communist-Israeli relations as a symbolic one. The students in Poland and Czechoslovakia have been strongly in favor of Israel.

The sources of the tensions between the regime and the university and intellectual life which are conducive to student activism in Communist countries are somewhat different from those in the third world. As in the underdeveloped countries, there is an inherent gap between some norms which are an aspect of university and intellectual life, namely, academic and intellectual freedom, and the structure of society. Intellectual and scientific life requires freedom. To simply mouth Party truth, or to limit the problems which one studies or the conclusions which one reaches, to those which are authorized by the regime, places a basic strain on intellectual activity. Lenin and the Bolsheviks, of course, distrusted intellectuals precisely for this reason. It is antithetical for an intellectual simply to be a publicist or spokesman for a given system. Intellectuals, as noted earlier, place a premium on originality as a source of status, and originality means rejecting the verities of the present and past. Hence there is a predisposition among those involved in the world of the intellect, whether inside or outside of the university, to resist authority on such issues, a strain which becomes manifest during periods of crisis. One of the most dramatic examples of the strength of such values among intellectuals and students under Communism surfaced during the brief "hundred flowers bloom" period in China in 1956. The relaxation of controls by the

Maoist regime produced a sudden outburst of critical speeches and statements on the campuses of the country which denounced the government for inhibiting free speech, research, and teaching, and for maintaining an absolutist state. Many of these criticisms pointed to Titoist Yugoslavia as an example of a Communist state which supposedly allowed freedom and which followed an independent policy with respect to the Soviet Union.[3]

Improvements, i.e., a relaxation of controls, serve often to stimulate increased criticism of the system among those who take the values of freedom seriously. For new generations of Eastern European (or Spanish) university students, the fact that there is more freedom than in Stalin's day, or than three years ago, is an ineffective argument. They only know that the present system is not free, that the present rulers are repressive even if they happen to be men who pressed for more freedom a few years earlier. Thus, once the issue of freedom is joined in authoritarian states, we may expect students and intellectuals to fight to drop the existing restrictions, a struggle which can lead either to greater liberalization, or a return to absolutist controls, as recent Czech, Polish and Spanish history unfortunately demonstrate.

The Developed Democracies: The United States and Europe

On the basis of the analyses of the sources of intellectual and student protest in the third and Communist world, it would seem that radical student activism should occur less frequently and be less prevalent in the developed democracies of Europe and the English-speaking states. Since modern industrial societies are largely characterized by their support for a universalistic ethic of merit, of freedom, and of scientific and intellectual creativity and originality, there should be diminished tension between the values of the world of intellect and the larger society. This would be true even recognizing that the universities still place a greater emphasis on egalitarianism and the free competition of ideas than do other institutions. It is worth noting again that the current wave of student unrest in the United States arose as a response to the one issue, race relations, in which the United States has retained an aspect of premodern traditional caste values, which are basically at odds with the norms of a democratic industrial society. Anti-imperialism, that is, opposition to colonial rule, is another example of student identification with the explicit values of democratic society against its own practices. Previous to the emergence of American student protest, the largest post–World War II upheaval in the Western world was occasioned by French student support for the FLN in the Algerian war. The protest against the Algerian war involved many thousands of students, who engaged in fairly drastic measures to sabotage the war effort.[4]

There is, however, another source of the tension between political intellectuals and modern academe, which though not new, is one which has only recently been recognized as a source of political resentment. It involves opposition to the trend toward the growth of hard social science and expertise, the decline of diffuse intellectualism in the social arena. The differentiation of social science knowledge into distinct fields of technical expertise has sharply undermined the role of the humanist intellectual who has traditionally claimed the right to comment on and influence public policy. This phenomenon may be seen most strikingly in economics. Economists now contend that many of the decisions about economic policy require technical knowledge beyond the competence of the informed layman. And as the other social sciences have extended their spheres of competence, and have become more systematically empirical and quantitative, they also question the ability of laymen to understand the factors which affect educational achievement, child-rearing practices, international relations, and the like.

Increasingly, the expert tells the general intellectual that the particular matters under discussion are simply too complicated, too technical, for them to be influenced through advocacy of relatively uncomplicated solutions associated with a particular ideological bent. Those who seek to reform society in some specific way find themselves up against arguments supposedly

derivative from specialized scholarly knowledge. And commitment to the increasing importance of social science and specialization reinforces the ideology of the "end of ideology," i.e., the
position that ideologically dictated positions are basically irrelevant, that governmental decisions should increasingly reflect
expert knowledge, a position which was put strongly in John F.
Kennedy's speech at Yale in the spring of 1963.

These trends have contributed to the rise among left intellectuals and students of a kind of "intellectual *poujadisme*," a backlash opposition to systematic and quantitative social science, to
large-scale social research, to the very conception of the utility of
efforts at objective scholarship in policy-relevant fields. Many
intellectuals react to the emphasis on social science and the concomitant belief in gradualism, expertise, and planning with a
populist stress on the virtues of direct action against evil institutions and practices. They attack the involvement of the university in policy matters as inherently corrupting the values of pure
scholarship and intellectual freedom. The negative reaction to
the application of academic expertise to politics, which ironically
may be found among many natural scientists who are laymen in
fields of race relations, stratification, foreign policy and the like,
has reinforced the hostility of activist students to the "complicat-
ing" social scientists.

The intellectual *poujadiste* reaction is, of course, related to a
much older and continuing source of conflict between intellectuals and the power structure. This is the tension between the
patron or consumer and the intellectuals. The latter tend to view
work which is oriented toward the demands of the marketplace,
rather than to the intrinsic logic of creativity, as corrupt. Such
criticism has taken two forms, a conservative or rightist one
which views democracy as a mass society in which intellectual
elites are pressed to conform to the low taste of the public, and a
leftist one which sees the source of the corruption in the power
held by those who buy and distribute intellectual products, i.e.,
business or government. The conservative critique has in recent
years been absorbed in many countries into the left-wing one.

The view that there is an inherent conflict between the values of intellectuals and those of the marketplace has sustained an anticapitalist ideology among many humanistically inclined intellectuals, one which also affects students preparing for such pursuits.

The Return to Domestic Politics

In Chapter 1, the case was made that the revival of student activism in the United States and other Western countries was fostered by the breakdown in the image of a monolithic internationally unified Communist enemy. Polycentric communism, faced with its own forms of internecine conflict, undercut the rationale inhibiting sharp criticism by left-inclined intellectuals of the social inequities and bad policies of their own societies. Although the Vietnam war became the principal moral issue of the late sixties, in a sense during the decade the Western world returned to a more "normal" political environment in which the main focus of intellectual and student politics has been domestic opponents. The domestic system, including the educational system itself, is held up to criticism for not living up to the ideals fostered by the society. This process has become increasingly evident on both sides of the curtain. The rise of a critical intelligentsia and a New Left student body in the West is a reflection of the change.

The current political scene increasingly resembles that which existed before World War I, in that relatively prosperous conditions have given rise to a growing radicalism. In that earlier age, the mood of liberals and progressives about social change was much more optimistic, in spite of the fact that the socialist movements campaigned against the possibility of international war; there was no real expectation that the prolonged period of peace, economic growth, and the expansion of democracy dating from the 1870s would end. Rather as the economic situation improved, the left, socialist, anarchist, and progressive forces continued to grow, and intellectuals criticized their domestic systems for various internal inequities and inequalities. The first student socialist movements in the United States, Germany, and France date from the period 1900 to 1914. They operated, however, within a much smaller and more elitist student body than at present, and had less impact on society.

It may also be worth recalling again in this connection that students and intellectuals were involved in highly visible activist opposition movements in the underdeveloped countries, particularly in Latin America and parts of Asia, during the 1950s, long before the emergence of university-based opposition movements in the developed states. Anticommunism and cold war ideologies were much weaker in these states. Hence they were less subject to ideological constraints on their propensities to attack the status quo in society or university.

The growth in student opposition during the 1960s was in large measure identified with a left-wing critique of the social welfare planning state in the Western democracies. The available data on the backgrounds of student activists in a number of countries, discussed earlier, suggest that many of the leaders (though not the followers) are the children of relatively affluent, liberal or left-wing parents. They have been reared in progressive households to accept the ideology of equality, democracy, helping the poor, and the like. Their parents represent that part of the elite of their generation who reacted radically to the events of the Depression and the anti-fascist conflict. Right-wing radical critiques of the existing society have to a certain extent been outmoded by the discrediting of fascist doctrines and the reduction of right extreme movements to forms of *poujadisme* based on the outlying provincial declining areas of different societies. The politicized university students have the values of modern egalitarian democracy. That small minority of them who were impelled to be activists often concentrated the fire of their attack on domestic ills.

This domestic concentration, however, has resulted — in foreign policy terms — in a criticism of international collective-security anti-Communist alignments as outmoded and unjustified. The New Left is sympathetic to movements in other countries seeking social change in an egalitarian direction, which means, in the underdeveloped world, Communist or pro-Communist movements of the Castro, Hanoi, Maoist varieties. Since the United States can obviously be identified as a force seeking to maintain the status quo in the underdeveloped countries, as well as a source of support for its own conservative social system, the student left, as noted earlier, is inherently sharply anti-American and against the American alliances. It simply does not accept the underlying theses which justify both alliances such as NATO and SEATO, and the opposition to revolutionary pro-Communist movements.

The Vietnam war with direct armed conflict and intervention by the United States has, of course, exacerbated the extent of the opposition to the United States. The common theme justifying alliances among the student left in different countries has been opposition to American foreign policy. This fact, however, should not lead us to underestimate the extent to which these movements are really primarily domestically oriented or directed against local power structures and universities and the political parties and culture. These are the revolts of activist youth against the older generation in power in their own country. They have the effect, however, of also being a revolt against the system of international alliances and against America's role in the world.

In the Eastern bloc countries, of course, as noted earlier, these revolts are directed to some considerable degree against the system of alliances among the Communist countries. There, the alliance is also a power system in that the Soviet Union keeps control over other countries through it. But basically youth on both sides of the curtain are seeking to reform or revolutionize their own societies and they are opposing the main power to which their country is linked, which they see as a source of support for the status quo at home and abroad. In short, it is the fact that the cold war has declined, that the basis for the system of alliances is no longer as strong as it once was, that made a new international youth movement possible.

The movement which arose in the 1960s differs in a number of significant ways from earlier student movements. As compared to the previous ones, it has almost no relationship to adult organizations. Student and youthful leftist groups, before World War I or during the interwar period before World War II, were to a large extent the youth or student affiliates of adult political parties. They usually were more extreme in their ideology than the adult organizations, but essentially their conception of how to get social change in their country was through their adult party coming into power or increasing its influence. This meant that the primary tasks of the youth group were to recruit support and train leaders for the adult organization, and also to provide the mass base for demonstrations. Insofar as the adult groups were involved in parliamentary activities and tactics, the student groups were as well.

This pattern may still be seen today in the activities of the young Communists in various countries, that is the youth or student sections of the pro-Russian Communist parties. In the West and in many underdeveloped countries, the pro-Russian Communists tend, where possible, to rely on the use of parliamentary and pressure-group tactics. Their student groups also follow the same procedures, essentially the traditional legal methods of demonstrating, striking, picketing, and the like.

Most of the non-Communist left-wing student movements in the underdeveloped states of Latin America and Asia also retain an instrumental orientation towards social change in their own country. That is, they believe in the possibility of progressive social change through policies designed to foster economic development, education, land reform, and political democracy. To achieve these objectives, they favor placing a new adult group in power. Similarly, the student activists in Eastern Europe are concerned with concrete reforms, usually of a political nature.

The student left of the Western democracies, however, is in a postreformist phase. The New Left youth groups initially rejected almost all political parties. For many of them the political parties of the left, both Socialist and Communist, were parties of the parliamentary establishment. They identified these groups as supporters of the domestic or foreign, i.e., Russian, status quo. They saw no adult organizations as genuinely revolutionary, as genuinely resistant to the major trends of the society which they oppose. Hence an international revolutionary movement of students and youth emerged which expressed in almost pure unadulterated form the ethic of absolute ends. They were almost completely uninhibited and uncontrolled, politically, since they had no relations to parties and organizations which had some sort of interest in adhering to the rules of the game and which accepted the need for compromise. Their politics were more expressive than instrumental. The New Left groups also had no clear concept of any road to power, of a way of effecting major social change. They were ready and willing to use tactics which violate the normal democratic game.

It is notable, however, that these tendencies which dominated activist student politics during the 1960s began to change by the end of the decade. In spite of the massive publicity they received and the occasional major demonstrations led by New Leftist groups, particularly in May and June 1968 in France and other parts of Europe, the New Left clearly failed to build a new mass movement and to reach allies outside the campus. Since 1968, most of the European groups have declined greatly. To repeat points made in Chapter 2, the German SDS officially dissolved as a national organization in the spring of 1970. The French groupings are bitterly factionalized and ineffective. The American SDS lives on at the beginning of the 1970s as a shadow of its past self. After a disastrous set of splits, what remains is, in effect, the student section of the Maoist Progressive Labor Party. The Young Socialist Alliance, affiliated to the Trotskyist Socialist Workers Party, was generally recognized by the end of 1970–71 as the largest left-wing youth group, and it has little more than a few thousand members. As noted earlier, American opinion polls were recording a drop-off in the percentage of students identifying themselves as radicals and an increase in conservative backing on campus. Everywhere from California to France and Scandinavia, the New Left parties have secured tiny votes, from one to three percent. The effect of such defeats has been to turn some New Left militants to terrorist tactics as in France and Italy, much like the Weathermen in this country, or to expressive forms of personal protest, of secession from society.

The bulk of the left-inclined students, however, have not followed such forms of despair. Rather, the majority turn passive and the more activist increasingly seem to return to the dominant leftist parties, Communist or Socialist, e.g., in France to the Communists, in Germany to the Social-Democrats. They often do so with the intention to press these parties to support a pure form of communism or socialism. But insofar as these parties operate within the parliamentary and electoral system, the student activism of the 1970s may, in effect, become the radical wing of the more moderate left movements. The same tendency may be seen in the United States in the participation of students in peace- and reform-oriented electoral campaigns.

Assuming a continuation of present trends, both international and domestic, it may also be assumed that the phenomenon of Western student activism is not a temporary one, although it should have peaks and declines. Specific issues which enable the extremist minority to mobilize strength outside their own ranks will result in increased extraparliamentary actions, but such support will largely drift away as specific issues disappear or lose salience.

One example of this phenomenon was the decline of activism after the Algerian war in France. The antiwar movement was very much like the one in the United States today against the Vietnam war. Once the war ended, however, in 1962, the mass support for an activist French student movement fell greatly. This event, of course, cannot be separated from the general decline of political activity that occurred under De Gaulle in the same period, but it does indicate the way in which changing political events can affect the movement, that we are not necessarily dealing with a secular pattern.[5]

A somewhat similar development occurred in Britain in the

late 1950s. The concept of a New Left arose in Britain at this time, seemingly as a reaction against both the Labour and Communist parties. The New Left youth and student movement which emerged in many of the universities was largely concerned with cultural critiques of the larger society rather than with demonstrations, although many of its members were also involved in the Campaign for Nuclear Disarmament. The subsequent electoral victory of the Labour party under Harold Wilson, who was then identified as a left-wing Labourite, sharply reduced the appeal of the British New Left, and it declined during the first few years of the Labour rule.[6] It regained strength, in some part fostered by the impression that the Wilson Labour Government was a failure, that it was conservative in practice. By 1970, however, the largest group of left-inclined students campaigned in the party's ill-fated battle for reelection. And since then, as on the continent, radical British students have shown more concern to build the left wing of the Labour party than to sit-in university buildings.

The Short-term Effects of Student Activism

What has been the effect of this wave of student protest on the politics of the respective countries? The answer clearly is not a simple one. On one hand, the powerful student movement is a force pressing the moderate left and the Communists to move further to the left, to become more militant in order to secure the support of the students. Many adult radicals have begun to identify with the student movement, and this, too, presses on the left parties. Many student demonstrations have been interpreted as reflecting the existence of genuine academic grievances. Various efforts have been made to appease these concerns, particularly by university reform, and occasionally by extramural reform.

On the other hand, the irresponsibility of some of the student movements, their willingness to rely on extraparliamentary, illegal methods, their proclamation that their goal is the revolutionary overthrow of society, their resort to street violence, also have created a backlash among the more moderate and conservative and established parts of the electorate.

In France, the student revolt has had one obvious political consequence; it has given the country its first majority party government in history, one which is right-wing. Thus, it may be argued that student demonstrations strengthen the conservatives within the body politic, that they help place conservatives in power or increase their majority. Such contentions also have been made about California politics and United States politics generally. The Berkeley disturbances were credited with having played an important role in electing Ronald Reagan in California in 1966. The Chicago demonstrators helped elect Nixon in 1968.

The counterproductive character of confrontations with the adult public was brought out strikingly by different surveys of reactions to the battle between Chicago police and antiwar demonstrators at the 1968 Democratic convention. A nationwide Sindlinger telephone sample survey taken soon after the conflict reported overwhelming support for the behavior of the police. A national voting survey conducted by the University of Michigan Survey Research Center two months later found that only 19 percent thought "too much force" had been used against the demonstrators in Chicago; 25 percent said "not enough force," and 32 percent indicated the police had employed the "right amount of force." More significantly perhaps, only 36 percent of McCarthy supporters and 29 percent of Kennedy backers criticized the police for using "too much force." The antagonism to the Chicago demonstrators carried over to antiwar protest generally.

> On a feeling thermometer running from zero to one hundred degrees, 35 percent of the respondents . . . rated "Vietnam War Protestors" at zero. By contrast, the next coldest group — "Liberals" — were rated zero by 5 percent of respondents. One must return to the 1964 Survey Research Center election study to find two groups received more coldly than protestors — the Ku Klux Klan and the Black Muslims.[7]

During the Cambodian incursion in May 1970, the campus demonstrated its antagonism to the war through massive strikes and other forms of protest. Yet, the opinion polls revealed that the electorate as a whole, though overwhelmingly opposed to the war, declared, in a Gallup Poll taken late in May, that the most important problem facing the country was campus unrest.[8] And a variety of opinion surveys completed before the November 1970 state and congressional elections indicated that various politicians who had taken a strong stand against campus unrest gained thereby. Evidence of such reactions, and the scurrying to cover among many liberal Democratic candidates who felt the need to condemn student protest, led Sam Brown, the organizer of the student-based McCarthy campaign in 1968 and of the national antiwar Moratorium movement in the fall of 1969, to write a bitter analytical article in the August 1970 issue of the *Washington Monthly* which strongly argued that much student protest was counterproductive.[9]

Perhaps the most dramatic examples of the negative effect of being identified with student activism on the fortunes of major electoral parties occurred in the Japanese election in December 1969, and in the Finnish one in March 1970. The Japanese Socialist party, which is dominated by its left-wing China-oriented faction, strongly opposed the efforts of the Liberal-Democratic government to enact strong campus control measures, and of the student affiliate of the Communist party to prevent disruptive forms of student protest, while cooperating with efforts at campus reform. In the elections, the Communists gained greatly, while the Socialists lost a third of their seats. In a statement evaluating the election results, the Communists credited the Socialist defeat, in part, to the party's "trailing behind the Trotskyite anti-Communist gangs of thugs and the blind followers of Mao Tse-tung," that is, the militant student groups.[10] In Finland, the coalition Popular Front government of the Communists, Social Democrats and the Center party, supported by a small New Left oriented party, acceded to the demands for increased student power of the Finnish Students' Union. The

Center party Minister of Education brought in a bill to reform the university by providing for heavy student participation in university governance, a proposal strongly opposed by the Professors Union. The March elections, fought on this issue, brought about the greatest shift in votes ever experienced in Finland. The Center party lost over a quarter of its seats, and the more conservative Countryside party, formed to fight it, captured eighteen seats, a gain of seventeen. The New Left TPSL also lost all of its seven seats; the Communists declined greatly, while the party which had most strongly opposed the students' demands, the Conservatives, was the big winner.[11]

The picture, of course, even in electoral terms, is not clear-cut. In Italy, the 1968 national and 1970 provincial elections did not produce any change, although the 1971 provincial elections witnessed startlingly large gains by neo-Fascists. In Germany, the Social Democrats gained in 1969, but they were openly hostile to the SDS, and the small radical leftist party which backed the campus militants took .6 percent of the vote.[12] In general, it seems apparent that one effect of extraparliamentary youth politics in the 1960s was to reinforce the electoral appeal of the conservatives.

The sharp cleavage between the views of university students in the United States and other countries and those of the population is not solely, or even primarily, a function of a "generation gap." As noted earlier in Chapters 2 and 3, young people as such have furnished disproportionate strength to the candidacy of George Wallace, and have *not* been more heavily opposed to the war than older age groups. The gap *within* the youth, the conflict among generation-units, has been greater than that *between* different generations. This conclusion is brought out sharply by reactions to the use of force at the 1968 Democratic convention. Among white respondents, the percentage agreeing that "too much force" was used against the demonstrators was 14 for those who had not graduated from high school, 20 among high school graduates, 32 for those with some college, 50 for college graduates, and 63 percent for those with a graduate degree. Among college students, the proportion was highest, of course, 67 percent.[13]

A similar gulf between student and nonstudent, predominantly working-class, youth with respect to attitudes toward radical change in the political and cultural spheres is indicated by surveys in other nations. Thus the report on a 1969 Italian survey of two samples of youth (17–26), national and university student, indicates that 34 percent of the national sample and 44 percent of the students favored major social changes; 12 percent of the first group and 16 percent of the second agreed that a complete revolution was needed.[14] The picture in Germany based on 1968 surveys of students and youth (18–25) is even more striking. Forty-three percent of all youth as contrasted to 7 percent of students agreed "one should not tolerate criticism towards one's fatherland from foreigners." Fifteen percent of the former and 60 percent of the latter disapproved of capital punishment. Less than a third (29 percent) of the youth sample believed in the right to strike and demonstrate if the public order is endangered, while the majority in two student surveys (54 and 62 percent) agreed with the right. Similar differences occurred with respect to a variety of questions dealing with democratic attitudes, tolerance for opposition, and the like.[15] In Japan, where surveys of students show significant majority sympathy for socialism, a survey in June 1970 of manual workers indicated that those under twenty-two years of age were quite conservative, much more in fact than the older workers. The survey reported that "35.8 percent of the young versus 27.4 percent of the older workers felt a capitalist social system was the best for Japan, while 11.7 percent of the young and 22.3 percent of the older workers preferred a socialist system."[16] A Brazilian survey completed in 1964 just before the military coup d'état indicated that workers generally and young workers, in particular, were "much more conservative than students. . . . The differences between young workers and students are much greater than the differences between young workers and older workers."[17]

The findings of surveys such as these point up the dilemma of activist student movements. While the campus population, both student and faculty, are generally sympathetic to the specific objectives of many demonstrations, and are, therefore, prepared to identify with the protestors in clashes with the police, the general population, including nonstudent youth, are not. Consequently, the provocative tactics often deliberately designed to precipitate violent clashes with the police gain them support within the university community, but alienate those outside, including the workers and other youth. And the practical consequence is to strengthen considerably conservative political tendencies among the electorate.

The strengthening of the Right may actually have also contributed to maintaining the foreign alliances with the United States. Since the conservative parties, France apart, are the more pro-American, collective-security-oriented ones, this paradoxically could have the opposite effect to what the students themselves are striving for internationally. This outcome, however, is not a necessary one.

The dominant political groups in various countries are concerned with maintaining domestic tranquility. Consequently, they should be interested in reducing the size of opposition student movements, and will try to avoid giving the activists any justification for engaging in violence against the government. Many politicians see foreign policy issues as a major source of annoyance for their students. Former German Chancellor Kiesinger explicitly credited the Vietnam war with being responsible for the growth of a violent German student movement and for the alienation of many German youth. Whether he was right or wrong is irrelevant; what is important is that he saw it this way. In Japan, which witnessed a strong New Left–type student movement before the phenomenon occurred in the United States and Western Europe, student opposition to international alliances with the United States, while not upsetting them, has had the effect of reducing the public commitment of the Japanese politicians to such alliances. The United States has withdrawn forces to avoid student protests.

In evaluating the cost to the nation, or to the government and political forces, of a given international policy, those in power have had to count as one of these costs an increase in street opposition to the government, a decline in respect for law and order. Should the other forces pressing for maintenance of the alliance weaken, one may therefore assume that the rise of an activist student movement will become a force for isolationism. If a politician must choose between internationalism and isolationism and if he feels that the international consequences of the choice have become less important, he may opt for the isolationist course to gain domestic tranquility, to maintain law and order, to reduce emotional opposition.

The continuation of the Vietnam war has, of course, made international relations a major source of emotional tension. For those opposed to the war, any alliance with the United States may be perceived as an alliance with murderers, with those who are killing a small country. In the absence of the war, the issue of whether a given country remains part of NATO or has a mutual security treaty with the United States still may remain an important issue for debate and controversy, but presumably will not provoke as intense a set of reactions.

Generation Differences: The Long-term Effects

In the long run, the most important effect of the current wave of student activism on foreign policy may reflect the outcomes of differences in outlook toward politics among different age groups or generations. The experiences which have sustained a strong commitment to the Western alliances are an outgrowth of the struggles against fascism and Stalinism. As noted earlier, Munich, the Hitler-Stalin Pact, the 1948 Czech Coup, the Korean war, the Hungarian Revolution, are all ancient history to the generations which have come of age during the 1960s. Adults often find it hard to understand the extent to which relatively recent events which occurred before a given group of youth reached political and intellectual consciousness simply are not salient to them.

A major consideration of the consequences of political events on a society requires the specification of the role of political generations. Many analysts of politics and cultural styles have stressed the extent to which the concept of the generation must be used as an independent analytical one. The thesis underlying this type of analysis indicates that people tend to form a defined frame of reference in late adolescence or early youth within which they fit subsequent experiences. That is, the first formative political experiences are most important.

A number of scholars have attempted to trace through the participation of different generations in the politics of various nations. They have pointed to the way that workers who came of age during the Great Depression have continued to react to issues of unemployment, economic security, and the like, ever since. The Depression youth, as adults, have been much more likely to be concerned about the welfare state than earlier and subsequent generations. Similarly, as noted earlier, many who were concerned in their youth with foreign policy issues stemming from fascist or Communist expansionism have continued to react along lines stemming from such issues more recently. It is easy to visualize how such processes operate. A small increase in the current unemployment rate will shock someone who has experienced the Depression, while it might not even be noticed by someone who has not. The Soviet Union's military action in Czechoslovakia should have more effect on those who remember the Czech coup or the Hungarian revolution as a major experience of their political youth than those who do not. The events which surround the entry of a generation into politics may continue to have their impact on national life for many decades after these events are forgotten as topics of political discussion, particularly through determining the conceptions of the governing and intellectual strata.

In foreign policy terms, the United States apparently created an isolationist generation out of the events of World War I and the immediate years thereafter. This generation as it grew older, remembering the way it had been "fooled" in World War I, resisted steps toward intervention during the 1930s. Conversely, however, the young people of the later 1930s and early 1940s learned that isolationism and neutralism had led to the rise of fascism and World War II. They presumably have shown up as a much more interventionist group.

To a considerable extent, the contemporary political leaders of the United States and many other Western countries are people who came to political consciousness at a time when foreign policy issues involving the containment of fascism or communism were most salient. This generation of political leaders and their supporters did not need much convincing to react militantly to Communist threats. In this connection it may be important to point out that the United States Government did not feel it necessary to justify the decisions concerning Vietnam taken by Presidents Eisenhower, Kennedy, and Johnson, by exposing the domestic inequities of the North Vietnam regime, its use of force against its own people, or of the terror tactics of the Viet Cong.

This policy was dictated in part by the desire of each administration to keep the United States role in Vietnam as limited as necessary to prevent a Communist takeover in the South, to restrain the pressure of the "hawks" who sought to escalate the war, and thus to risk its widening far beyond the borders of Vietnam. But the reluctance to undertake any significant propaganda campaign in support of the war was also in some part a reflection of the fact that, to those older men in charge of the American information policy, there seemed to be no need for elaborate justifications of efforts to prevent a Communist takeover in another country. All Americans, they thought, recognized that communism is an evil social system, and hence could be expected to back this latest episode in the struggle to contain it.

The internal conflict which developed in the United States over the war illustrates the phenomenon of the generation gap as well as any event that can be presented. For youth, the new generations of college students, the past evils of Stalinism constitute events which have little relevance to the immediate present.

European communism no longer can be identified with Stalinist oppression, with the slaughter of the innocents, or with monolithic power.

Thus, different generations have reacted to a different sense of the nature of, and the political potential of communism. Though those who have dictated American policy in the past decade have been aware of the changes in the Communist system as much as the younger people, there can be little doubt that the variations in the reactions of the generations reflect the fact that the older know from personal experience the potential for evil in communism, while the younger ones only know it as words in the history books. It is perhaps inevitable that they should react quite differently to arguments concerning the need to resist a Communist movement in another country.

The same situation, of course, exists in other countries. It is perhaps more strikingly illustrated in Berlin where until the Berlin Wall, there was considerable support for strong anti-Communist policies among all groups in the city, including the students. The Free University of Berlin, in fact, was founded by refugees from communism. But the Berlin Wall was more successful than those who planned it could have expected. They built it in order to prevent people from leaving East Germany. But by so doing, they destroyed the past relationship to, and function of, West Berlin for East Germany. West Berliners, including students, no longer talk to people who have fled communism. For the Berlin youth communism exists in a society with which they have little contact, while there are many things wrong with the society in which they live. And the student movement of West Berlin, once primarily concerned with the East, is now mainly concerned with changing the society of West Berlin and West Germany.

Recognition that there are generational differences in outlook is not simply relevant to an analysis of any given contemporary scene. For the most important thing about generations is that they may persist. Consequently, any effort to evaluate the consequences of the present political revival of student militancy must include a consideration of its potential impact on future events. Some years ago a private Japanese opinion study of the attitudes and political beliefs of younger members of the Japanese business executive stratum, those under forty, revealed that the majority of such executives had become much more moderate politically over the years, but they still voted for the Japanese Socialist party. Seemingly, the majority of Japanese youth who go to universities, particularly the better ones, become supporters of some brand of Marxism or radicalism. And they continue to identify with the Left for many years after most of them go to work for bureaucratic industry or government, entering ladders which can lead them fairly high up into the Japanese elite.

The Japanese data bear directly on the maxim discussed in Chapter 1: "He who is not a radical at twenty does not have a heart; he who is still a radical at forty does not have a head." This statement expresses a generally expressed consensus that youth may be irresponsible and radical, but as they get older they become more responsible and conservative. There can be little doubt that there is considerable validity to this generalization. The Japanese data, however, indicate that although most Japanese young radicals become more moderate in their opinions and their actions as they get older, many of those who become business executives remain on the left politically, adhering to various doctrines of socialism and, in the Japanese context, anti-Americanism.

Assuming this study is accurate, it suggests that Japan may be moving into a period in which it will have an elite which does not believe in the system which it operates. This more radical elite may not do anything to change the system, but their beliefs may affect the way they react toward radical pressure on them from other groups, as well as their view of new issues as they occur. In a history of czarist Russia, written in 1910, Bernard Pares devoted about two hundred pages to the political activities of the intellectuals and students of the czarist empire.[18] He discussed in great detail the fact that the students were radical and antiregime. Pares, however, then stated that these activities did not mean very much, since the students after graduating went to work for the bureaucracy or entered other sections of the elite and thus became supporters of the system. There is little data on what former Russian radical students did in later years, but clearly there is some possibility that there is some relationship between the radicalism of the Russian students and the weakness of the elite in 1917.

Currently, in the United States, the elite of a more radicalized student generation is gradually moving into the lower and sometimes even the upper rungs of important parts of the society. For example, in the university, in journalism, in other aspects of the communications industry, and in various government agencies, observers have noted that the youthful members of the staffs tend to be much more radical in their reaction to the functions of the organization than older hands. As in Japan, it is probable that many of them retain important parts of the opinions which they formed as students. In spite of the coercive pressures on them to conform which come from participation in the bureaucracy, some aspects of their environment may continue to support their youthful opinions. It is possible, therefore, that the current generation of radical university students will continue to affect the larger body politic in many countries ten, twenty, or even thirty years from now. Their elites may contain a much larger proportion of liberals or leftists than they now do. They may also include many whose image of the United States and its role in the world will be quite different from that of earlier generations.

As another illustration of this process, it may be noted that some analysts of the contemporary American university scene have argued that one of the factors contributing to increased student activism today is the presence on university faculties of many whose political attitudes were formed during the New Deal experience, the Depression, or the struggle against fascism. University faculties are much more liberal or even leftist than they ever have been in the past. It is noticeable that a visibly significant number of senior American university faculty members today are individuals who took part in student movements — liberal and radical politics — during the thirties and early forties. As noted earlier, the current generation of student activists are often the children of people who were active in radical movements in the earlier period. In a sense, these studies indicate that generations sometimes may even appear twice, first in their own right, and second through their influence over their children, who are given a set of ideals which they then try to activate, ideals which stem back to the conditions of their parents' formative political years.

This emphasis on the persistence of political orientations formed in youth does not belie the fact that many, if not most, people do change their beliefs as they grow older and become involved in the responsibilities of career and family, or simply are exposed to a variety of new experiences which may undermine the convictions of their youth. Thus, though the generation of the 1930s has thrown up visible reminders of the effects of the Depression, it is also true that opinion surveys from the 1950s and 1960s indicated that the majority of college graduates of the 1930s had become relatively conservative and usually voted Republican. This fact should be placed alongside the report of the first national survey of American students made in 1936 (see pp. 184–185 in Chapter 5) that most of them were liberal Democrats, that 24 percent identified socialism in positive terms, as contrasted with but 15 percent who were favorable to conservatism. Seemingly most students who had been radicalized in the mid-1930s had given up such views by the 1950s. The conflict of the generations is not simply or even primarily a conflict among generations that have had different formative experiences, it is also a conflict between the young and the older. This conclusion is dramatized by the finding that those who went to college in the conservative, silent, apathetic, conformist, (Joe) McCarthyite 1950s turn out to furnish a higher proportion of voters and supporters for liberal and left candidates and political positions in the late 1960s and early 1970s than do the older alumni of the 1930s, the years of the Red Decade, the Great Depression, and the struggle against fascism. Viewed in the mass, the college experience has not

created "generations" which have continued to display distinctive
political commitments. It is likely that the college cohort that
passed through the radical and activist campus politics of the
late 1960s will not behave as one either, although, like the cohort
of the 1930s, they will probably throw up a visible group of intellectual and organizational leaders who will retain a radical
position.

A change in views is inherent in the differences between college
communities and those in society at large. Colleges are encapsulated communities. Their students have been abruptly removed
from the various constraints of their parental family experience,
and placed in an environment in which peer group pressures are
especially intense and pervasive. For four years they inhabit this
world apart, a remarkably homogeneous and unstratified society,
in which the dominant elite, the faculty, is considerably to the left
of any other in the larger society. After graduation, however,
most — even today when the number rejecting affluence, a
"careerist" outlook and the regular occupational system is far
greater than ever before — reenter the highly differentiated social
system and take part in an affluent middle-class life in job, family,
and community. As we have seen, the intellectual legacies of
college are by no means lost, particularly for those who remain
within the intelligentsia occupationally after leaving school — but
the intense pressures of the encapsulated community which make
for the distinctive and wildly fluctuating bodies of student political opinion are for most removed as abruptly as they had been
introduced.[19]

How the cohort of the late 1960s will behave politically in the
long run will, of course, be affected by factors other than those
associated with aging. The larger political situation may press
them to the right or left. But all the available evidence strongly
suggests that as they grow older they will become *relatively* less
receptive to new change-directed thrusts than those who follow
them through the university. That is, even though American
politics and morals may continue to "liberalize" over time, the

relative relationship of the older to the younger remains "conservative." In this sense, societies like our own, which have a built-in process of enormous social change, also always have a generation gap of some magnitude, particularly between those living in the encapsulated, experiment-oriented campus, and those outside.

No society should find it remarkable that a segment of its student population should be involved in activist student politics that is directed militantly against the status quo. It can be strongly argued, as C. Wright Mills argued, that students are the one group who will continue to supply recruits for such causes, even when no other stratum is available.[20] A completely inactive student body is a much more curious phenomenon historically than one which is involved to some degree in activism. Any efforts to analyze the future of politics, whether on the domestic or international scene, will ignore the students at the peril of being in error.

Chapter Notes

Introduction

1. See S. M. Lipset, "Socialism and Sociology," in Irving Louis Horowitz, ed., *Sociological Self-Images* (Beverly Hills: Sage, 1969), pp. 143–175; and "The Biography of a Research Project: *Union Democracy*," in Philip E. Hammond, ed., *Sociologists at Work* (New York: Basic Books, 1964), pp. 96–120.

2. S. M. Lipset, "Opinion Formation in a Crisis Situation," *Public Opinion Quarterly* (Spring 1953), pp. 20–46.

3. S. M. Lipset, *Political Man* (Garden City: Doubleday, 1960), pp. 416–417.

4. S. M. Lipset, "University Students and Politics in Underdeveloped Countries," *Minerva*, 3 (Autumn 1964), pp. 15–56.

5. See S. M. Lipset and Paul Seabury, "The Lesson of Berkeley," *The Reporter* (January 28, 1965), p. 40; reprinted in revised form in Seymour Martin Lipset and Sheldon S. Wolin, eds., *The Berkeley Student Revolt* (Garden City: Doubleday, Anchor Books, 1965), p. 349.

6. For a statement by Steve Weissman, second to Mario Savio in the leadership of the FSM, boasting of the provocative tactics the FSM radicals had in mind to continue confrontations, see Calvin Trillin, "Letter from Berkeley," in Michael V. Miller and Susan Gilmore, eds., *Revolution at Berkeley* (New York: Dial, 1965), p. 280. See also pp. 277–279.

7. "Stokely Carmichael, Carl Oglesby Talk Strategy and Tactics," *National Guardian* (December 16, 1967), pp. 1, 14.

8. Cited in Eric Ashby and Mary Anderson, *The Rise of the Student Estate in Britain* (London: Macmillan, 1970), p. 125, from *New Left Review* 50 (1968), p. 59.

9. Quoted in Maryl Levine and John Naisbitt, *Right On* (New York: Bantam, 1970), p. 70.

10. Lawrence Eichel et al., *The Harvard Strike* (Boston: Houghton Mifflin, 1970), p. 83 and *passim*.

11. Sam Brown, "The Politics of Peace," *The Washington Monthly* 2 (August 1970), pp. 24–46.

12. For a description of the position of the YPSL during the Harvard crisis of 1969 and a sharp attack on the undemocratic tactics of SDS, see Steven Kelman, *Push Comes to Shove* (Boston: Houghton Mifflin, 1970).

13. See articles in S. M. Lipset, ed., *Student Politics* (New York: Basic Books, 1967); Seymour Martin Lipset and Philip G. Altbach, eds., *Students in Revolt* (Boston: Houghton Mifflin, 1969), and Lipset and Wolin, *The Berkeley Student Revolt*.

14. Typical of attacks on Lipset as a "conservative" in his treatment of student activism are the writings of Tom Bottomore; see "Conservative Man," *New York Review of Books* 15 (October 8, 1970), pp. 20–24; and James Petras, review of *Confrontation: The Student Rebellion and Universities,* in *New Politics* (Fall 1968), p. 88.

15. "Fué Abucheado el Agitador Lipset," *El Universal* (Mexico City: February 12, 1970), p. 1; and Church League of America, "Subversion by the Volume: The Sad State of the Publishing Industry Today," multilithed (New York: August 1970), p. 43.

16. I have discussed the varying reactions to my writings with specific citations to many of them in the preface to the revised paperback edition

of a collection of my essays, *Revolution and Counterrevolution* (Garden City: Doubleday, Anchor Books, 1970).

Chapter 1

1. There is a very extensive literature dealing with student activism comparatively as well as in assorted individual countries. See Philip G. Altbach, *A Select Bibliography on Students, Politics and Higher Education* (Cambridge: Center for International Affairs, Harvard University, 1967); and the bibliography in S. M. Lipset and Philip G. Altbach, eds., *Students in Revolt* (Boston: Houghton Mifflin, 1969), pp. 528–533. Articles dealing with a variety of countries are included in that volume. See also S. M. Lipset, ed., *Student Politics* (New York: Basic Books, 1967); Donald Emerson, ed., *Students and Politics in Developing Countries* (New York: Praeger, 1968); and Julian Nagel, ed., *Student Power* (London: Merlin Press, 1969). The most comprehensive single effort to treat student movements historically and comparatively is Lewis Feuer, *The Conflict of Generations* (New York: Basic Books, 1969).

2. To evaluate the American New Left it is necessary to read various periodicals representing different moderate and extreme leftist groups. These include *New America* (Socialist Party), *The Guardian* (unaffiliated, pro–New Left), *New Left Notes* (two versions put out by different factions), *The Militant* (Socialist Workers Party–Trotskyist), *Challenge* (Maoist), *International Socialist* (Revolutionary Marxist).

3. See, for example, Robert Nisbet, "Who Killed the Student Revolution?" *Encounter* 34 (February 1970), pp. 10–18.

4. Wayne Kind, "Campus Protests Reported on Rise," New York *Times,* March 29, 1970, p. 53. For a report on the previous academic year see Urban Research Corporation, *Student Protests 1969: Summary* (Chicago: 1970). Garth Buchanan and Joan Brackett, *Summary Results of the Survey for the President's Commission on Campus Unrest* (Washington, D.C.: The Urban Institute, September 1970), pp. 9–10.

5. See Urban Research Corporation, *On Strike . . . Shut It Down: A Report on the First National Student Strike in U.S. History* (Chicago: May 1970); and Buchanan and Brackett, *Summary Results,* for statistical data on the extent of the strike.

6. Sam Brown, "The Politics of Peace," *The Washington Monthly* 2 (August 1970), pp. 24–46, especially pp. 24–25.

7. Ernest Gellner, "The Panther and the Dove: Reflections on Rebelliousness and Its Milieux," in David Martin, ed., *Anarchy and Culture: The Problem of the Contemporary University* (London: Routledge and Kegan Paul, 1969), pp. 133–134; Alberto Martinelli and Alessandro Cavalli, "Toward a Conceptual Framework for the Comparative Analysis of Student Movements," (paper presented at the Seventh World Congress of Sociology, Varna, Bulgaria, September 1970), pp. 3–4.

8. Many have written on this phenomenon. See especially Nathan Glazer, *The Social Basis of American Communism* (New York: Harcourt, Brace

and World, 1962), pp. 130–168; Lawrence Fuchs, *The Political Behavior of American Jews* (Glencoe: The Free Press, 1956); Werner Cohn, "The Politics of American Jews," in Marshall Sklare, ed., *The Jews* (Glencoe: The Free Press, 1958), pp. 614–626. See also Charles Liebman, "Toward a Theory of Jewish Liberalism," in Donald R. Cutler, ed., *The Religious Situation: 1969* (Boston: Beacon, 1969), pp. 1034–1061; Nathaniel Weyl, *The Jew in American Politics* (New Rochelle, N.Y.: Arlington House, 1968); Milton Himmelfarb, "Is American Jewry in Crisis?" *Commentary* 47 (March 1969), pp. 33–42; S. M. Lipset, *Revolution and Counter-revolution* (Garden City: Doubleday, Anchor Books, 1970), pp. 375–400. See also for an analysis of the relationship of the Jewish propensity to "intellectuality" to their politics, S. M. Lipset and Everett Ladd, Jr., "Jewish Academics: Achievements, Cultures, and Politics," *The American Jewish Year Book 1971*, vol. 72 (New York: The American Jewish Committee, Philadelphia: The Jewish Publication Society, 1971), pp. 89–128.

9. See articles in James McEvoy and Abraham Miller, eds., *Black Power and Student Rebellion* (Belmont, Calif.: Wadsworth, 1969), especially pp. 222–306, 379–418.

10. Brown, "The Politics of Peace," p. 27.

11. Sol Tax, "War and the Draft," in Morton Fried, Marvin Harris, and Robert Murphy, eds., *War* (Garden City: Doubleday, The Natural History Press, 1968), pp. 199–203. Actually Tax concluded that there were seven wars out of twelve fought by the United States which were less popular than the Vietnam one. The twelve, however, include various Indian wars, the Civil War, and the Revolutionary War.

12. Samuel Eliot Morison, "Dissent in the War of 1812," in Samuel Eliot Morison, Frederick Merk and Frank Freidel, *Dissent in Three American Wars* (Cambridge: Harvard University Press, 1970), pp. 3–31.

13. Alice Felt Tyler, *Freedom's Ferment* (New York: Harper, Torchbooks, 1962), p. 407.

14. Frederick Merk, "Dissent in the Mexican War," in Morison et al., *Dissent in Three American Wars*, pp. 33–63; Edward S. Wallace, "Notes and Comment — Deserters in the Mexican War," *The Hispanic American Historical Review* 15 (1935), p. 374.

15. David Donald, "Died of Democracy," in David Donald, ed., *Why the North Won the Civil War* (Baton Rouge: Lousiana State University Press, 1960), pp. 85–89; James McCague, *The Second Rebellion: The New York City Draft Riots of 1863* (New York: Dial, 1968); Basil L. Lee, *Discontent in New York City, 1861–65* (Washington: Catholic University of America Press, 1943).

16. Frank Freidel, "Dissent in the Spanish-American War and the Philippine Insurrection," in Morison et al., *Dissent in Three American Wars*, pp. 65–95, especially p. 77.

17. H. C. Peterson and Gilbert C. Fite, *Opponents of War, 1917–1918* (Seattle: University of Washington Press, 1957), pp. 39, 123–135, 234; Daniel Bell, "The Background and Development of Marxian Socialism in the United States," in Donald Drew Egbert and Stow Persons, eds.,

Socialism and American Life, vol. 1 (Princeton: Princeton University Press, 1952) , pp. 314–315.

18. Hazel Erskine, "The Polls: Is War a Mistake?" *Public Opinion Quarterly* 34 (1970) , pp. 138–141; Edward Suchman, Rose K. Goldsen and Robin Williams, Jr., "Attitudes Toward the Korean War," *Public Opinion Quarterly* 17 (1953) , pp. 173, 182.

19. I have discussed these elements in the relationship of American Protestantism and American political morality elsewhere. See *The First New Nation: The United States in Historical and Comparative Perspective* (Garden City: Doubleday, Anchor Books, 1967) , pp. 184–187; *Revolution and Counterrevolution* (New York: Basic Books, 1968) , pp. 255–258, 299–303; and, with Earl Raab, *The Politics of Unreason: Right-Wing Extremism in the United States, 1790–1970* (New York: Harper & Row, 1970) , pp. 61–67.

20. See especially Feuer, *Conflict of Generations;* Lipset and Altbach, *Students in Revolt;* and Nagel, *Student Power.*

21. Kingsley Davis, "The Sociology of Parent-Youth Conflict," *American Sociological Review* 5 (August 1940) , p. 535 and passim; for more recent versions of this approach, see Margaret Mead, *Culture and Commitment: A Study of the Generation Gap* (Garden City: Doubleday, Natural History Press, 1970) , especially pp. 51–76; Kenneth Keniston, "The Fire Outside," *The Journal* 9 (September–October 1970) , pp. 5–7.

22. Norman Birnbaum, *The Crisis of Industrial Society* (New York: Oxford University Press, 1969) , p. 148.

23. Feuer, *Conflict of Generations,* p. 528; Edward Shils, "Comments," in François Duchêne, ed., *The Endless Crisis: America in the Seventies* (New York: Simon and Schuster, 1970) , pp. 171–172.

24. [Aristotle,] *Rhetoric,* in *The Basic Works of Aristotle,* edited by Richard McKeon (New York: Random House, 1941) , p. 1404.

25. Erik H. Erikson, *Identity, Youth and Crisis* (New York: Norton, 1968) , pp. 128–129.

26. Gordon W. Allport, *Pattern and Growth in Personality* (New York: Holt, Rinehart, and Winston, 1961) , pp. 283–304; Erikson, *Identity, Youth and Crisis,* pp. 139–140.

27. See especially the recent works of Alain Touraine, *Le mouvement de mai ou le communisme utopique* (Paris: Seuil, 1968) , especially pp. 14–15; *La société post-industrielle* (Paris: Denoel, 1969) , p. 26 and passim.

28. John and Margaret Rowntree, "The Political Economy of Youth," *Our Generation* 6 (May-June-July 1968) , p. 173.

29. Ernest Mandel, "The New Vanguard," in Tariq Ali, ed., *The New Revolutionaries* (New York: Morrow, 1969) , p. 47.

30. For a summary, see S. M. Lipset and Philip G. Altbach, "Student Politics and Higher Education in the United States," in Lipset, *Student Politics,* pp. 234–237.

31. "Prudence is really a hateful thing in youth. A prudent youth is prematurely old." Randolph S. Bourne, *Youth and Life* (Boston: Houghton Mifflin, 1913) , p. 10.

32. I have developed this point at length in my book *The First New Nation: The United States in Historical and Comparative Perspective.*

33. Max Weber, *From Max Weber: Essays in Sociology,* edited by Hans H. Gerth and C. Wright Mills (New York: Oxford University Press, 1946), pp. 120–128.

34. David K. Cohen, "Public Education: The Coming Decade," mimeographed (Center for Educational Policy Research, Harvard University, April 30, 1970), pp. 7–9.

35. Charles Hampden-Turner, *Radical Man* (Cambridge, Mass.: Schenkman, 1970), p. 364; for a similar analysis to those of Cohen and Hampden-Turner, see Richard Flacks, "Who Protests: The Social Bases of the Student Movement," in Julian Foster and Durward Long, eds., *Protest: Student Activism in America* (New York: Morrow, 1970), pp. 151–152.

36. S. N. Eisenstadt, *From Generation to Generation* (Glencoe: The Free Press, 1956), pp. 163–166.

37. David Easton and Robert D. Hess, "Youth and the Political System," in S. M. Lipset and Leo Lowenthal, eds., *Culture and Social Character* (New York: The Free Press, 1961), pp. 244–247.

38. S. N. Eisenstadt "Archetypal Patterns of Youth," *Daedalus* 91 (Winter 1962), pp. 28–46; and Eisenstadt, "Changing Patterns of Youth Protest in Different Stages of Development of Modern Societies," *Youth and Society* (December 1969), pp. 135–148; Talcott Parsons, *Social Structure and Personality* (New York: The Free Press, 1964), pp. 150–153; 172–180; Talcott Parsons, "Age and Sex in the Social Structure of the United States," *American Sociological Review* 7 (1942), pp. 604–616; Bennett M. Berger, "On the Youthfulness of Youth Cultures," *Social Research* 30 (Autumn 1963), pp. 319–342; Jack D. Douglas, *Youth in Turmoil* (Chevy Chase, Md.: National Institute for Mental Health, 1970), pp. 17–80.

39. César Graña, *Modernity and Its Discontents* (New York: Harper Torchbooks, 1964), pp. 73–74. For excellent as yet unpublished analyses of rebellious youth in Germany and France in the first half of the nineteenth century, see the papers by Anthony Esler of the History Department of William and Mary College: "Rebellious Younger Generations as a Force in Modern History," and "Youth in Revolt: The French Generation of 1830."

40. D.M.W. [Donald Mackenzie Wallace], "Nihilism," *Encyclopaedia Britannica,* 11th ed., vol. 19, pp. 686–688.

41. Ludwig Von Mises, *Bureaucracy* (New Haven: Yale University Press, 1944), pp. 94–95.

42. Donald G. MacRae, "The Culture of a Generation: Students and Others," in Walter Laqueur and George L. Mosse, eds., *Education and Social Structure in the Twentieth Century* (New York: Harper Torchbooks, 1967), pp. 7–8.

43. Eisenstadt, "Changing Patterns of Youth," p. 136.

44. Herbert Moller, "Youth as a Force in the Modern World," *Comparative Studies in Society and History* 10 (April 1968), p. 238.

45. Feuer, *Conflict of Generations,* p. 511.

46. Engels to Marx, April 25, 1870, as quoted in Shlomo Avineri, "Feuer on Marx and the Intellectuals," *Survey*, no. 62 (January 1967), p. 154.

47. D.M.W., "Nihilism," pp. 687–688.

48. Daniel Guerin, *Fascism and Big Business* (New York: Pioneer, 1939), pp. 47–50, 62–63; Karl Bracher, *Die Auflösung der Weimarer Republik* (Villingen, Schwarzwald: Ring Verlag, 1964), pp. 146–149; Hans Peter Bleuel and Ernst Klinnert, *Deutsche Studenten auf dem Weg ins Dritte Reich* (Gütersloh: Sigbert Mohn, 1967).

49. Letter from Max Weber to Herman Baumgarten, July 14, 1885, in Max Weber, *Jugendbriefe* (Tübingen: Mohr, 1930), p. 174, as presented in Reinhard Bendix and Guenther Roth, *Scholarship and Partisanship* (Berkeley: University of California Press, 1971).

50. Walter Laqueur, "Reflections on Youth Movements," *Commentary* 47 (June 1969), pp. 34, 35, 36.

51. See Klara Zetkin, *Reminiscences of Lenin* (London: Modern Books, Ltd., 1929), pp. 55–60.

52. "Report of Commission on Campus Unrest," *The Chronicle of Higher Education* 5 (October 5, 1970), pp. 7, 8–9. Other recent variants of this position may be found in Edgar Friedenberg, "Current Patterns of Generational Conflict," *Journal of Social Issues* 25, no. 2 (1969), pp. 21–38; Friedenberg, "The Generation Gap," *The Annals of the American Academy of Political and Social Science* 382 (March 1969), pp. 32–42; John Seeley, "Youth in Revolt," *Britannica Book of the Year.* (Chicago: University of Chicago Press, 1969), pp. 313–315.

53. Laqueur, "Reflections on Youth Movements," pp. 36–37.

54. For a summary of the many studies dealing with the politics of faculty, see S. M. Lipset, "The Politics of Academia," in David C. Nichols, ed., *Perspectives on Campus Tensions* (Washington, D.C.: American Council on Education, 1970), pp. 85–118. See chap. 6, pp. 197–235 of this book for an elaboration on some of the themes in that article.

55. Kenneth A. Feldman and Theodore M. Newcomb, *The Impact of College on Students*, vol. 1 (San Francisco: Jossey-Bass, 1969), especially pp. 8–10, 19–28, 30–32, 99–100, 101–102; and Feldman and Newcomb, vol. 2, pp. 19–36, 49–56, for summaries of results of the large number of separate studies.

56. For a detailed description of those processes that predicted a student revolt directed against faculty neglect of undergraduates, see Clark Kerr, *The Uses of the University* (Cambridge: Harvard University Press, 1964). A more recent analysis and denunciation of the consequences of these trends which focuses on the University of California as its prototype example is Robert Nisbet, *The Degradation of the Academic Dogma* (New York: Basic Books, 1971), esp. pp. 69–111.

57. See Christopher Jencks and David Riesman, *The Academic Revolution* (New York: Doubleday, 1968), especially pp. 236–250, 531–535.

58. Lawrence Veysey, *The Emergence of the American University* (Chicago: University of Chicago Press, 1965), pp. 295–299.

59. David Matza, "Position and Behavior Patterns of Youth," in Robert

E. L. Faris, ed., *Handbook of Modern Sociology* (Chicago: Rand McNally, 1964) , p. 210.
60. Max Weber, *From Max Weber,* pp. 84–85.
61. Daniel and Gabriel Cohn-Bendit, *Obsolete Communism* (New York McGraw-Hill, 1968) , p. 47. "The student, at least, in the modern system of higher education, still preserves a considerable degree of personal freedom, if he chooses to exercise it. . . . He can, if he so chooses, take extreme political positions without any personal danger; in general, he is not subjected to formal sanctions or even reprimands."

Chapter 2

1. For a discussion of youth backing for Wallace and racism see S. M. Lipset and Earl Raab, *The Politics of Unreason: Right-Wing Extremism in America 1790–1970* (New York: Harper & Row, 1970) , pp. 367–367, 371–372, 394, 418, 513.
2. Hazel Erskine, "The Polls: Is War a Mistake?" *Public Opinion Quarterly* 34 (Spring 1970) , p. 134.
3. Philip E. Converse and Howard Schuman, " 'Silent Majorities' and the Vietnam War," *The Scientific American* 222 (June 1970) , p. 22. See also Milton J. Rosenberg, Sidney Verba and Philip E. Converse, *Vietnam and the Silent Majority* (New York: Harper & Row, 1970) , pp. 65–73.
4. "The Student Revolution — A Special Report," *Gallup Opinion Index,* no. 66 (June 1970) , p. 15.
5. "Campus '65," *Newsweek,* March 22, 1965, p. 53.
6. Samuel Lubell, "The People Speak" (news releases reporting on a study of American college students) .
7. Gallup Poll release, July 1966.
8. "Results of a New Gallup Survey of College Students," *Gallup Opinion Index,* no. 55 (January 1970) , p. 16.
9. "Special Survey of College Students," Gallup Poll release, June 29, 1968.
10. Samuel Lubell, "Where the New Left Dissidents Come From," Boston *Globe,* October 10, 1968.
11. Gallup Poll release, June 29, 1968.
12. "Profile of a Generation," multilithed report of a survey prepared for CBS News (New York: Daniel Yankelovich Associates, April 1969) , p. 158.
13. "Aversion to Vietnam War Reaches High Among College Students," Harris Survey, June 30, 1969.
14. "Young Hawks on Decrease," National Gilbert Youth Poll (newspaper release through Newspaper Enterprise Association, December 12, 1969) ; "A Study of Youth and the Establishment," multilithed report (New York: Daniel Yankelovich Associates, December 1970) , p. 76.
15. "Special Report on the Attitudes of College Students," *Gallup Opinion Index,* no. 48 (June 1969) , p. 42.
16. "The New Mood on Campus," *Newsweek,* December 29, 1969, p. 42.
17. "Results of a New Gallup Survey of College Students," *Gallup Opinion Index,* no. 55 (January 1970) , p. 16.

18. National Gilbert Youth Poll.

19. *"Playboy's* Student Survey," *Playboy* 17 (September 1970) , p. 182; report of the May 1970 Harris Survey, p. 49.

20. *Playboy* Student Poll news release, November 1965.

21. Report of May 1970 Harris Survey, p. 20.

22. Ibid., p. 35.

23. Ibid., p. 51.

24. Anthony Ripley, "Survey Finds Spring Campus Protests Were Greatest in History," New York *Times,* October 3, 1970.

25. Kenneth Gergen and Mary K. Gergen, "Vietnam and the Students: A Brief Summary of Research Results" (mimeographed report, Department of Psychology, Swarthmore College, June 1970) , p. 2.

26. Report of May 1970 Harris Survey, p. 140. See table in chap. 3, p. 93.

27. Gergen and Gergen, "Vietnam and the Students," p. 1.

28. Samuel Lubell, "Unresolved Crises Cause Youth Dissension," Boston *Globe,* October 9, 1968.

29. *A Study of the Beliefs and Attitudes of Male College Seniors, Freshmen, and Alumni* (New York: Roper Research Associates, May 1969) , p. 5.

30. Yankelovich, "Youth and the Establishment," p. 35.

31. Gilbert Marketing Group, February 1970 Omnibus Youth Survey, Table 22.

32. A report on this study was published as "Youth in College," *Fortune* 13 (June 1936) , pp. 99–102, 156–162. The data reported here, however, are from the unpublished report prepared by the Roper Research Associates. I am indebted to Burns Roper for a copy of this report.

33. A preliminary journalistic account of the findings of the Rossi study may be found in Malcolm G. Scully, "Students Found Tolerant on Sex, Marijuana, Even 'the System,' " *The Chronicle of Higher Education* 5 (February 15, 1971) , p. 6.

34. Lubell, "The People Speak," no. 6, pp. 1–3.

35. "A Study of the Inward Generation," special report published by *Psychology Today,* October 1969.

36. Yankelovich, "Profile."

37. James A. Foley and Robert K. Foley, *The College Scene* (New York: Cowles, 1969) , p. 128.

38. Ibid., p. 132.

39. Ibid., p. 19.

40. Ibid., p. 36.

41. Yankelovich, "Youth and the Establishment," pp. 67–68, 73–74.

42. Gilbert Marketing Group, February 1970 Survey, Tables 31, 24, 25.

43. Scully, "Students Found Tolerant," p. 6.

44. "The Student Revolution," *Gallup Opinion Index,* no. 55, pp. 22, 23.

45. Report of May 1970 Harris Survey, p. 88.

46. Ibid., p. 112.

47. Ibid., p. 110.

48. Ibid., p. 114.

49. Ibid., p. 163. *"Playboy's* Student Survey," p. 184.

50. Report of May 1970 Harris Survey, pp. 165, 167, 171.

51. For report on this survey see "Students Avoid Party Labels; Also Reject Radical Politics," Gallup Poll release, Sunday, February 14, 1971; "The U.S. Campus Mood, '71: A Newsweek Poll," *Newsweek,* February 22, 1971, p. 61.

52. Louis Harris and Associates, *Youth Attitudes for* Life *Magazine Year End Issue* (New York: November 1970) , passim.

53. The College Poll surveys are published weekly in various Sunday newspapers. Those cited here are from releases of January 10 and 24, April 14, and May 23, 1971. The Campus Poll reports are carried in newspapers across the country on Thursdays. Those reported here are from the releases of November 12, 1970, November 26, 1970, January 14, 1971, and March 11, 1971.

54. See Philippe Bénéton and Jean Touchard, "Les Interprétations de la Crise de Mai-Juin 1968," *Revue Française de Science Politique* 22 (June 1970) , pp. 520, 525, for summary of and references to various French surveys. See also F. Netzler and J. La Brousse, *Diverses Opinions et Attitudes des Etudiants de la Faculté des Lettres de Nanterre* (Paris: Institut Français d'Opinion Publique, June 1970) , p. 20.

55. Enzo Montillo, "Italy: The Youth of the Opinion Surveys," *SIPE* [International Student Press Service], 2 (July 1, 1970) , pp. 13–14.

56. Michiya Shimbori, "The Sociology of a Student Movement — A Japanese Case Study," in Seymour M. Lipset and Philip G. Altbach, eds., *Students in Revolt* (Boston: Houghton Mifflin, 1969) , p. 309, n. 12.

57. See report on nineteenth-century student conflicts in chap. 4; Veysey's analysis is discussed on page 135.

58. Bryan Wilson, *The Youth Culture and the Universities* (London: Faber and Faber, 1970) , p. 227.

59. Robert H. Somers, "The Mainsprings of the Rebellion: A Survey of Berkeley Students in November, 1964," in S. M. Lipset and Sheldon S. Wolin, eds., *The Berkeley Student Revolt* (Garden City: Doubleday, Anchor Books, 1965) , pp. 549–550.

60. Kathleen Gales, "A Campus Revolution," *British Journal of Sociology* 17, (March 1966) , p. 14.

61. Glen Lyonns, "The Police Car Demonstration: A Survey of Participants," in Lipset and Wolin, *The Berkeley Student Revolt,* pp. 525–527.

62. Robert H. Somers, "The Berkeley Campus in the Twilight of the Free Speech Movement: Hope or Futility?" in James McEvoy and Abraham Miller, eds., *Black Power and Student Rebellion* (Belmont, Calif.: Wadsworth, 1969) , p. 427.

63. Gergen and Gergen, "Vietnam and the Students," p. 1.

64. Roper Research Associates, *Beliefs and Attitudes,* p. 52.

65. Daniel Yankelovich, "The Generation Gap — A Misleading Half-Truth" (New York, Spring 1970) , pp. 10–11, and Table 4.

66. Ibid., Table 4.

67. "The New Mood on Campus," *Newsweek,* December 29, 1969, p. 43.

68. For the results of the 1969 Carnegie Survey, see Philip W. Semas, "Students 'Satisfied' with Education, Most of Them and Teachers Agree," *The Chronicle of Higher Education* 5 (January 18, 1971) , p. 1.

69. Harris and Associates, *Youth Attitudes,* p. 53.
70. Gallup Poll release on student survey, May 25, 1969. Yankelovich, "The Generation Gap."
71. Marshall W. Meyer, "Harvard Students in the Midst of Crisis," mimeographed (New York State School of Industrial Relations and Department of Sociology, Cornell University, 1970) , p. 43, Table 8.
72. Robert B. Smith, "Campus Protest and the Vietnam War" mimeographed (Department of Sociology, University of California, Santa Barbara, 1970) , pp. 1, 46–47; for a summary of evidence from various studies at different institutions which comes to similar conclusions, see Riley Dunlap, "A Comment on 'Multiversity, University Size, University Quality, and Student Protest: An Empirical Study,' " *American Sociological Review* 35 (June 1970) , pp. 525–528.
73. Richard Peterson, *The Scope of Organized Student Protest in 1967–68* (Princeton: Educational Testing Service, 1968) , pp. 10–11; Alan E. Bayer and Alexander W. Astin, *Campus Disruption During 1968–1969* (Washington, D.C.: Office of Research, American Council on Education, ACE Research Reports, August 1969) , pp. 22–23; Urban Research Corporation, *Student Protests 1969: Summary* (Chicago: 1970) , pp. 4, 6–8; Wayne King, "Campus Protest Reported on Rise," New York *Times,* March 29, 1970; Garth Buchanan and Joan Brackett, *Summary Results of the Survey for the President's Commission on Campus Unrest* (Washington, D.C.: The Urban Institute, September 1970) , pp. 36, 43.
74. See chap. 1, n. 61.
75. Gilbert Marketing Group, Tables 20A and 27A.
76. Kenneth Keniston, "Heads and Seekers," *The American Scholar* 38 (Winter 1968–69) , pp. 97–112.
77. Roper Research Associates, *Beliefs and Attitudes,* p. 198.
78. "The New Mood on Campus," *Newsweek,* December 29, 1969, p. 44.
79. Foley and Foley, *The College Scene,* p. 66.
80. Yankelovich, "A Study of Youth," p. 65.
81. *"Playboy*'s Student Survey," p. 236.
82. "Twice as Many College Students Today as in 1969 Admit They Have Tried Marijuana," Gallup Poll release, Sunday, January 17, 1971.
83. Harris and Associates, *Youth Attitudes,* p. 58.
84. "Special Report on the Attitudes of College Students," *Gallup Opinion Index,* no. 48, p. 26; Gallup Poll release, February 26, 1971.
85. Yankelovich, *"Profile,"* pp. 74, 77.
86. Ibid., p. 151.
87. "Student Protests Focus on Domestic Injustices," Boston Sunday *Globe,* January 24, 1971.
88. See, for example, Charles A. Krause, "Campaign Help Unexpected. Students Stun Conservatives," Washington *Post,* October 25, 1970, p. 1; Thomas Oliphant, "Students in Politics: Fewer Than Expected," Boston Sunday *Globe,* October 25, 1970, p. 1; Nina Housman, "Adam Smith and John Wayne: Gurus of the New Student Right," *New America,* January 27, 1971, p. 8; Stephen Schlesinger, "The Buckley Kids," *New York,* November 2, 1970, pp. 8, 10.

89. Nicholas Bagnall and Duff Hart-Davis, "What Happened to the Oxbridge Revolution? Student Radicals Run Out of Steam," (London) *Sunday Telegraph*, March 14, 1971, p. 19; Ellen Lentz, "Student Disorder Ebbs in Germany," *New York Times*, April 11, 1971, p. 19; Masuru Ogawa, "Student-Gangsters," *Japan Times Weekly*, April 3, 1971, p. 3; Raymond Boudon, "Sources of Student Protest in France," *The Annals of the American Academy of Political and Social Science* 395 (May 1971), pp. 148–149; Michiya Shimbori, "Student Radicals in Japan," in ibid., pp. 154–156.

90. Milton Mankoff and Richard Flacks, "The Changing Social Base of the American Student Movement," *The Annals of the American Academy of Political and Social Science* 395 (May 1971), p. 62. n. 10.

91. Kenneth Keniston, "The Chilling Shame of Violence," Boston *Globe*, June 7, 1971, p. 10.

92. The Rossi survey taken in the spring of 1970 found that 29 percent of the female freshmen and 36 percent of the juniors "said they had had sexual intercourse." Scully, "Students Found Tolerant," p. 6.

Chapter 3

1. Richard Flacks, "The Liberated Generation: An Explanation of the Roots of Student Protest," *Journal of Social Issues* 23, no. 3 (1967), pp. 66, 68. Kenneth Keniston, "Notes on Young Radicals," *Change* 1 (November–December, 1969), p. 29. For a summary of various studies bearing on this point, see also Richard G. Braungart, "Family Status, Socialization and Student Politics: A Multivariate Analysis" (Ph.D. thesis, Department of Sociology, Pennsylvania State University, 1969), p. 61; Kenneth Keniston, "The Fire Outside," *The Journal* 9 (September–October 1970), pp. 9–10.

2. See Richard Flacks, "Who Protests: The Social Bases of the Student Movement," in Julian Foster and Durwood Long, eds., *Protest: Student Activism in America* (New York: Morrow, 1970), pp. 147–152; and S. M. Lipset, *Political Man* (New York: Doubleday, 1960), pp. 109–110, 285–294. On the Jewish contribution to activism, see Nathan Glazer, "The New Left and the Jews," *The Jewish Journal of Sociology* 11 (December 1969), pp. 122, 127–131; Flacks, "The Liberated Generation," p. 65; Nathan Glazer, "The Jewish Role in Student Activism," *Fortune* 79 (January 1969), pp. 112–113, 126–129; Lipset, *Revolution and Counterrevolution*, rev. ed. (New York: Doubleday, Anchor Books, 1970), pp. 375–400.

3. Michiya Shimbori, "Zengakuren: A Japanese Case Study of a Student Movement," *Sociology of Education* 37 (Spring 1964), pp. 232–233; C. J. Lammers, "Student Unionism in the Netherlands," mimeographed (Leyden: Institute of Sociology, University of Leyden, 1970), pp. 25–26, 31; Walter Korp, "Vansterstudenterna: Barn ar bongare el ler proletaria at," *Sociologiska Forskning* 4 (1969), pp. 286–287, 292–293; Ted Goertzel, "Political Attitudes of Brazilian Youth" (paper presented at session on politics of students and young workers, Seventh World Congress of Sociology, Varna, Bulgaria, September 1970), p. 3; Klaus R. Allerbeck, "Alternative Explanations of Participation in Student Move-

ments" (paper prepared for the Seventh World Congress of the International Political Science Association, Munich, September 1970), pp. 13–14; Tessa Blackstone, Kathleen Gales, Roger Hadley and Wyn Lewis, *Students in Conflict* (London: Weidenfeld and Nicolson, 1970), p. 200.

4. Allerbeck, "Alternative Explanations," p. 14.
5. Reports on the membership of the YAF may be found in David L. Westby and Richard G. Braungart, "Class and Politics in the Family Backgrounds of Student Political Activists," *American Sociological Review* 31 (October 1966), pp. 690–692; Braungart, "Family Status," p. 142; David L. Westby and Richard G. Braungart, "The Alienation of Generations and Status Politics: Alternative Explanations of Student Political Activism," in Roberta S. Sigel, ed., *Learning About Politics* (New York: Random House, 1970), pp. 476–488; David G. Jansen, Bob B. Winborn and William D. Martinson, "Characteristics Associated with Campus Social-Political Action Leadership," *Journal of Counseling Psychology* 15 (November 1968), pp. 552–562.
6. Bruno Bettelheim, "The Anatomy of Academic Discontent," *Change* 1 (May–June 1969), pp. 23–24.
7. Lipset, *Revolution and Counterrevolution,* pp. 310–342; Lipset, "The Politics of Academia," in David C. Nichols, ed., *Perspectives on Campus Tensions* (Washington, D.C.: American Council on Education, 1970), pp. 85–118; see also chap. 6 of this book.
8. Roger M. Kahn and William J. Bowers, "The ·Social Context of the Rank-and-File Student Activist: A Test of Four Hypotheses," *Sociology of Education* 43 (Winter 1970), pp. 39, 45–47, 48–49; Braungart, "Family Status," pp. 61–62; Flacks, "The Liberated Generation," pp. 69–70; Paul Heist, "Intellect and Commitment: the Faces of Discontent," in O. W. Knorr and W. J. Minter, eds., *Order and Freedom on Campus* (Boulder, Colo.: Western Interstate Commission for Higher Education, 1965), pp. 61–69.
9. For a summary of the literature see Kenneth A. Feldman and Theodore M. Newcomb, *The Impact of College on Students,* 1 (San Francisco: Jossey-Bass, 1969), p. 161; see also Kahn and Bowers, "Social Context," pp. 39, 46–48.
10. Hanan Selvin and Warren Hagstrom, "Determinants of Support for Civil Liberties," in S. M. Lipset and Sheldon S. Wolin, eds., *The Berkeley Student Revolt* (New York: Doubleday, Anchor Books, 1965), p. 513.
11. Morris Rosenberg, *Occupations and Values* (Glencoe: The Free Press, 1957), pp. 19–22; see also James A. Davis, *Undergraduate Career Patterns* (Chicago: Aldine, 1965), pp. 52–53.
12. Westby and Braungart, "Class and Politics," pp. 690–692.
13. Braungart, "Family Status," p. 142.
14. Milton Mankoff and Richard Flacks, "The Changing Social Base of the American Student Movement: Its Meaning and Implications," *The Annals of the American Academy of Political and Social Science,* May 1971; for an earlier presentation of a similar thesis with more limited data, see A. Riley Dunlap, "Radical and Conservative Student Activists: A Com-

parison of Family Backgrounds," *Pacific Sociological Review* 13 (Summer 1970), pp. 178–179.

15. For more detailed discussion of and evidence for this thesis, see S. M. Lipset, *Agrarian Socialism*, rev. ed. (Garden City: Doubleday, Anchor Books, 1968), pp. 201–207, 214–217, 221–242; and Lipset, *Political Man*, pp. 116–121.

16. For example, see "Profile of a Generation" multilithed report of a survey prepared for CBS News (New York: Daniel Yankelovich Associates, April 1969).

17. Charles V. Hamilton, "Minority Groups," in Robert H. Connery, ed., *The Corporation and the Campus*, Proceedings of the Academy of Political Sciences, vol. 30, no. 1, pp. 20–21.

18. Anthony M. and Amy W. Orum, "The Class and Status Bases of Negro Student Protest," *Social Science Quarterly* 49 (December 1968), p. 528, n. 30, and references to other works there included.

19. Mary K. and Kenneth J. Gergen, "How the War Affects the Campuses," *Change* 3 (January–February 1971), p. 70.

20. Report of Harris Survey, May 20–28, 1970, pp. 155–156.

21. Yankelovich, "Profile," pp. 159–172 and passim.

22. See Report of Harris Survey, and Yankelovich, "Profile."

23. For a summary of the evidence, see Lipset, "The Politics of Academia."

24. Alexander W. Astin, "Personal and Environmental Determinants of Student Activism," *Measurement and Evaluation in Guidance* 1 (Fall 1968), pp. 161–162; Alan E. Bayer and Alexander W. Astin, "Violence and Disruption in the U.S. Campus, 1968–1969," *Educational Record* 50 (Fall 1969), p. 341. Another study of the characteristics of schools which had protests in 1969 indicated that larger ones "with student bodies that had high scholastic aptitudes were more likely to face protests than other schools." Urban Research Corporation, *Student Protests 1969: Summary* (Chicago: 1970), pp. 14, 13.

25. Bayer and Astin, "Violence and Disruption," p. 341; see also Urban Research Corporation *Student Protests 1969*, p. 13; Joseph W. Scott and Mohamed El-Assal, "Multiversity, University Size, University Quality and Student Protest: An Empirical Study," *American Sociological Review* 34 (October 1969), pp. 702–709.

26. Harold Hodgkinson, "Student Protest — An Institutional and National Profile," *The Record* 71 (May 1970), p. 537.

27. Ibid., pp. 540–542, 547–548.

28. Anthony Ripley, "Survey Finds Spring Campus Protests Were Greatest in History," New York *Times*, October 3, 1970, p. 35; Garth Buchanan and Joan Brackett, *Summary Results of the Survey for the President's Commission on Campus Unrest* (Washington, D.C.: The Urban Institute, 1970), pp. 18–21.

29. Hodgkinson, "Student Protest," pp. 549–550.

30. Quotations are from Kenneth Keniston and Michael Lerner, "Campus Characteristics and Campus Unrest," *The Annals of the American Academy of Political and Social Science* 395 (May 1971), pp. 49, 52.

31. See George R. Stewart, *The Year of the Oath* (Garden City: Doubleday, 1950) ; David P. Gardner, *The California Oath Controversy* (Berkeley: University of California Press, 1967) ; S. M. Lipset, "Opinion Formation in a Crisis Situation," *Public Opinion Quarterly* (Spring 1953) , pp. 20–46.

32. Glen Lyonns, "The Police Car Demonstration: A Survey of Participants," in Lipset and Wolin, *The Berkeley Student Revolt*, p. 522.

33. Jürgen Habermas, *Toward a Rational Society: Student Protest, Science, and Politics* (Boston: Beacon, 1970) , p. 20.

34. Alexander W. Astin and Alan E. Bayer, "Antecedents and Consequents of Disruptive Campus Protests," *Measurement and Evaluation in Guidance* 4 (April 1971) , pp. 22–24; and Astin, "New Evidence on Campus Unrest," *Educational Record* 52 (Winter 1971) , pp. 44–46.

35. Peter M. Blau and Ellen L. Slaughter, "Institutional Conditions and Student Demonstrations" (mimeographed paper, Department of Sociology, Columbia University, 1970) .

36. Keniston, "Notes on Young Radicals," pp. 31–32; R. William Cowdry and Kenneth Keniston, "The War and Military Obligation: Attitudes, Actions and Their Consistency" (mimeographed paper, Department of Psychiatry, Yale University, 1969) , pp. 22, 26–27, 30; Jeanne H. Block, Norma Haan and M. Brewster Smith, "Socialization Correlates of Student Activism," *Journal of Social Issues* 25, no. 4 (1969) , pp. 164–165. The latter study differentiates between "activists" and "dissenters."

37. Lyonns, "The Police Car Demonstration," in Lipset and Wolin, *The Berkeley Student Revolt*, p. 521.

38. Flacks, "The Liberated Generation"; Braungart, "Family Status."

39. Lamar E. Thomas, "Family Congruence in Political Orientations of Politically Active Parents and Their College-Age Children (Ph.D. thesis, Committee on Human Development, University of Chicago, 1968) , p. 46. Liberal parents were much more "cause-oriented" than conservatives. Whether the children of the former were activist or not correlated strongly with degree of cause orientation rather than child-rearing practices.

40. Block et al., "Socialization Correlates," pp. 163–164 and Table 7. It is not clear from the report whether the investigators inquired as to respondents' religion or that of their parents. Left-oriented people tend to say "none" for their own religion. Hence, when family religious background is probed, many of the "none" turn out to in fact come from Jewish backgrounds.

41. Keniston, "Notes on Young Radicals," p. 31.

42. David Matza, "Subterranean Traditions of Youth," *Annals of the American Academy of Political and Social Science* 338 (November 1961) , p. 106; David Matza, "Position and Behavior Patterns of Youth," in Robert E. L. Faris, ed., *Handbook of Modern Sociology* (Chicago: Rand McNally, 1964) , pp. 209–214.

43. Kenneth Keniston, "The Sources of Student Dissent," *Journal of Social Issues* 23, no. 3 (1967) , pp. 110–115; Kenneth Keniston, "The Fire Outside," *The Journal* 9 (September–October 1970) , pp. 9–10.

44. Alvin W. Gouldner, *The Coming Crisis of Western Sociology* (New York: Basic Books, 1970), p. 78.
45. Keniston, "Notes on Young Radicals," p. 32.
46. Block et al., pp. 146–147, 163–165.
47. Richard Blum, "Epilogue: Students and Drugs," in Richard Blum and Associates, *Students and Drugs: Drugs II* (San Francisco: Jossey-Bass, 1969), p. 366.
48. Blum, "Prologue: Students and Drugs," ibid., p. 8.
49. James W. Trent and Judith L. Craise, "Commitment and Conformity in the American College," *Journal of Social Issues* 23 (1967), p. 39; a more recent work of this sort is Robert Liebert, *Radical and Militant Youth* (New York: Praeger, 1971).
50. S. M. Lipset and Philip G. Altbach, "Student Politics and Higher Education in the United States," *Comparative Education Review* 10 (June 1966), pp. 320–349. The review of the literature is on pages 331–334. This article was reprinted and updated in S. M. Lipset, *Student Politics* (New York: Basic Books, 1967); see pp. 222–224. See also Braungart, "Family Status," pp. 331–332; and Larry C. Kerpelman, "Student Political Activism and Ideology: Comparative Characteristics of Activists and Non-activists," *Journal of Counseling Psychology* 16 (1969), pp. 8–13.
51. Larry C. Kerpelman, *Student Activism and Ideology in Higher Education Institutions* (Washington, D.C.: Bureau of Research, Office of Research, U.S. Department of Health, Education, and Welfare, March 1970), pp. xv, 79, 85.
52. Cowdry and Keniston, "The War and Military Obligation," pp. 21–23.
53. Roy E. Miller and David H. Everson, "Personality and Ideology: The Case of Student Power" (paper presented at the Midwest Political Science Association, April 30–May 2, 1970, Public Affairs Research Bureau and Department of Government, Southern Illinois University), p. 36.
54. Kerpelman, *Student Activism and Ideology,* pp. 5–6, 42, 80; for a similar point, see Lipset and Altbach, "Student Politics and Higher Education," pp. 223–224; for recent data on this, see Block et al., "Socialization Correlates," p. 31.
55. Kerpelman, *Student Activism and Ideology,* p. 80; see also Lipset and Altbach, "Student Politics and Higher Education," p. 250, n. 61.
56. Enunciated as a possibility in S. M. Lipset, "The Activists: A Profile," in Daniel Bell and Irving Kristol, eds., *Confrontation: The Student Rebellion and the Universities* (New York: Basic Books, 1969), p. 56.
57. Miller and Everson, "Personality and Ideology," pp. 35, 38–39.
58. Blum, "Epilogue: Students and Drugs," p. 377.
59. Dennis H. Wrong, "The Case of the *New York Review*," *Commentary* 50 (November 1970), pp. 62–63. The Keniston review of the book by Kelman was published in the *New York Review of Books,* September 24, 1970.
60. Glaucio A. D. Soares, "The Active Few: Student Ideology and Participation in Developing Countries," in S. M. Lipset, ed., *Student Politics* (New York: Basic Books, 1967), pp. 124–147.

61. Paul Goodman, "The New Reformation," *New York Times Magazine*, September 14, 1969, pp. 33, 143, 144. Similar criticisms have been advanced by Norman Birnbaum, the Amherst sociologist, who was founding editor of the *New Left Review* in London, and who is both an identified Marxist scholar and a disciple of C. Wright Mills.

"The ahistoricism and pragmatism of American thought has found a parody in the disdain for political thinking exhibited by most of the militants of the American student left. An unreflected doctrine of immediacy, an explicit fear of academicism (and an implicit incapacity, engendered by a defective university system, for sustained thought), a considerable ignorance of nearly everything and especially of the history of socialism, combine in the jargon, the slogans, and the bewilderment of the *avant-garde* of the new American left." Norman Birnbaum and Marjorie Childers, "The American Student Movement," Julian Nagel, ed., *Student Power* (London: Merlin, 1969), p. 139.

62. "Rightists Launch Offensive," *The Guardian* 21 (February 8, 1969), p. 8.

63. *The Campaigner* 1 (September 1968), p. 9.

64. C. LaRouche and L. Marcus, "The New Left, Local Control and Fascism," *The Campaigner* 1 (September 1968), pp. 10–33, passim.

65. Irving Louis Horowitz, *The Struggle Is the Message* (Berkeley: The Glendessary Press, 1970), pp. 84–85, 97, 101. (Emphasis mine. S.M.L.)

66. Peter L. Berger, "Between System and Horde," in Peter L. Berger and Richard J. Neuhaus, *Movement and Revolution* (New York: Doubleday, Anchor Books, 1970), pp. 44–45.

67. Daniel Guerin, *Fascism and Big Business* (New York: Pioneer, 1939), pp. 47–50, 62–63; Guido Martinotti, "The Positive Marginality: Notes on Italian Students in Periods of Political Mobilization," in Lipset and Altbach, *Students in Revolt*, pp. 173–175; Karl Bracher, *Die Auflösung der Weimarer Republik* (Villingen, Schwarzwald: Ring Verlag, 1964), pp. 146–149; Peter Gay, *Weimar Culture* (New York: Harper & Row, 1968), pp. 139–140; Fritz K. Ringer, *The Decline of the German Mandarin* (Cambridge: Harvard University Press, 1969), pp. 250–251; John Orr, "The Radical Right," in Julian Nagel, *Student Power*, pp. 73–90; Lewis Feuer, *The Conflict of Generations* (New York: Basic Books, 1969), pp. 284–291.

68. Randolph S. Bourne, *Youth and Life* (Boston: Houghton Mifflin, 1913), pp. 23, 266, 304, 305.

69. [Aristotle,] *Rhetoric*, in *The Basic Works of Aristotle*, edited by Richard McKeon (New York: Random House, 1941), p. 1404. Aristotle goes on, of course, to say equally unflattering things about the character of the "Elderly," who err on the side of caution, small-mindedness, cynicism, concern for the useful rather than the noble, and so forth. Typically, the best are those in the middle, "Men in their Prime," who tend to have the "right amount" of each relevant trait. The Prime age for "the mind [is] about forty-nine," pp. 1405–1406.

70. See S. M. Lipset and Earl Raab, *The Politics of Unreason: Right-

Wing Extremism in the United States 1790–1970 (New York: Harper & Row, 1970) , chaps. 1, 11, and 12, for this discussion.

71. "Poll Finds Voters Aged 18 to 21 Favor Democrats and Kennedy," New York *Times,* April 18, 1971, p. 37.

72. This discussion of the youth support for Wallace and the ideology of the National Youth Alliance is taken from Lipset and Raab, *The Politics of Unreason,* pp. 418–419, 513–514.

73. "Rightists Launch Offensive," p. 8.

74. Dennis C. McMahon, "The National Youth Alliance," *The American Mercury* 105 (Spring 1969) , p. 63.

75. National Youth Alliance leaflet headed "Lost and Alone."

76. Ralph Blumenthal, "Infusion of Youth Strengthens Radical Rightist Party in West Germany," New York *Times,* March 2, 1969.

77. Boris Kidel, "German Rightists Shift to Disruption," Boston Sunday *Globe,* December 27, 1970.

78. Noël-Jean Bergeroux, "Shot in the Right Arm," *Le Monde — Weekly Selection,* March 25, 1970, p. 2.

79. Cosimo Di Fazio, "Italy: The Menace of the Extremist Groups of the Right," *SIPE* 3 (March 10, 1971) , pp. 3–6.

Chapter 4

1. S. M. Lipset, "University Students and Politics in Underdeveloped Countries," in S. M. Lipset, ed., *Student Politics* (New York: Basic Books, 1967) , pp. 3–53; "Introduction: Students and Politics in Comparative Perspective," and "The Possible Effects of Student Activism on International Politics," in S. M. Lipset and Philip G. Altbach, eds., *Students in Revolt* (Boston: Houghton Mifflin, 1969) , pp. xv–xxiv, 495–521.

2. Richard Holfstadter, *Academic Freedom in the Age of the College* (New York: Columbia University Press, 1961) , p. 206. See also Samuel Eliot Morison, *Three Centuries of Harvard* (Cambridge: Harvard University Press, 1936) , pp. 132–148. A recent historian of American education suggests that from the early nineteenth century on, students through their protest activities and extracurricular institutional innovations have been the "most creative and imaginative force in the shaping of the American college and university" (Frederick Rudolph, "Neglect of Students As a Historical Tradition," in Lawrence E. Dennis and Joseph F. Kaufman, eds., *The College and the Student* [Washington: American Council on Education, 1966], p. 47; see also pp. 47–58) .

3. Morison, *Three Centuries of Harvard,* p. 138.

4. W. H. Cowley, unpublished "Notes on Universities," chap. 11, "Student Participation," pp. 11–25.

5. Granville Stanley Hall, *Adolescence: Its Psychology* (New York: D. Appleton, 1904) , p. 138.

6. Ibid.

7. Morison, *Three Centuries of Harvard,* p. 185; Frederick Rudolph, *The American College and University: A History* (New York: Knopf, 1962) , p. 38.

8. Harry P. Bowes, "University and College Student Rebellion in Retrospect and Some Sociological Implications" (Ed.D. thesis, School of Education, University of Colorado, 1964), p. 96; see also Charles A. Wagner, *Harvard: Four Centuries of Freedom* (New York: Dutton, 1950), p. 87.

9. Morison, *Three Centuries of Harvard*, pp. 252–253.

10. Bowes, "Rebellion in Retrospect."

11. Cowley, "Notes on Universities," chap. 11, p. 15.

12. Bowes, "Rebellion in Retrospect," pp. 75–76.

13. Thomas Jefferson, *Writings* (Washington: Thomas Jefferson Memorial Association, 1890), vol. 11, p. 455.

14. Morison, *Three Centuries of Harvard*, pp. 179–180.

15. Bowes, "Rebellion in Retrospect," p. 84; see also Rudolph, *The American College*, pp. 96–97; and Oscar and Mary Handlin, *The American College and American Culture* (New York: McGraw-Hill, 1970), pp. 37–38.

16. Bowes, "Rebellion in Retrospect," p. 76; T. J. Wertenbaker, *Princeton, 1846–1896* (Princeton: Princeton University Press, 1946), p. 136.

17. E. Earnest, *Academic Procession: An Informal History of the American College 1636 to 1953* (Indianapolis: Bobbs-Merrill, 1953), p. 31; Hofstadter, *Academic Freedom*, pp. 241–242.

18. Sister M. Kennedy, "The Changing Academic Characteristics of the Nineteenth Century American College Teacher" (Ph.D. thesis, Department of Education, St. Louis University, 1961), p. 52.

19. Ibid., p. 72; see also John Brubacher and Willis Rudy, *Higher Education in Transition* (New York: Harper, 1958), p. 53.

20. Morison, *Three Centuries of Harvard*, pp. 211–212.

21. John R. Bodo, *The Protestant Clergy and Public Issues: 1812–1848* (Princeton: Princeton University Press, 1954), pp. 39–43; Anson P. Stokes, *Church and State in the United States* (New York: Harper, 1950) vol. 2, pp. 12–20.

22. Richard M. Johnson, "Sunday Observance and the Mail," reprinted in George E. Probst, ed., *The Happy Republic* (New York: Harper Torchbooks, 1962); pp. 250–254.

23. S. M. Lipset and Earl Raab, *The Politics of Unreason: Right-Wing Extremism in America, 1790–1970* (New York: Harper & Row, 1970), chap. 2.

24. Bowes, "Rebellion in Retrospect," pp. 104–105, 108.

25. Wagner, *Harvard*, p. 87.

26. Bowes, "Rebellion in Retrospect," pp. 115–116.

27. A Graduate of '69 [Lyman H. Bagg], *Four Years at Yale* (New Haven: Charles C. Chatfield, 1871), p. 516.

28. Handlin and Handlin, *American College*, pp. 40–41.

29. C. A. Bristed, *Five Years in an English University* (New York: G. P. R. Putnam, 1874), p. 61.

30. Howard H. Peckham, *The Making of the University of Michigan: 1817–1967* (Ann Arbor: University of Michigan Press, 1967), p. 46.

31. Russel Nye, *Fettered Freedom: Civil Liberties and the Slavery Controversy* (East Lansing: Michigan State University Press, 1949), p. 93; Hofstadter,

Academic Freedom, pp. 259–261; Earnest, *Academic Procession,* pp. 66–68, 85, 90.

32. Cowley, "Notes on Universities," chap. 11, p. 26.
33. Bowes, "Rebellion in Retrospect," p. 126.
34. Laurence R. Veysey, *The Emergence of the American University* (Chicago: University of Chicago Press, 1965), pp. 295, 299.
35. Laurence R. Veysey, "The Emergence of the University" (Ph.D. thesis, Department of History, University of California, Berkeley, 1962), p. 101.
36. Erik H. Erikson, *Identity: Youth and Crisis* (New York: Norton, 1968), pp. 237–240, 258.
37. Veysey, "Emergence of the University," pp. 101–103.
38. Walter Laqueur, *Young Germany* (New York: Basic Books, 1962).
39. George E. Peterson, *The New England College in the Age of the University* (Amherst: Amherst College Press, 1964), p. 146.
40. *The Autobiography of Lincoln Steffens* (New York: Harcourt, Brace, 1931), pp. 117–118. See also Lewis S. Feuer, *The Conflict of Generations* (New York: Basic Books, 1969), pp. 327, 332; and Peterson, *The New England College,* pp. 113–148.
41. Feuer, *Conflict of Generations,* p. 332.
42. Veysey, "Emergence of the University," p. 279. Although third-party groups were to attain more support in 1912 and subsequent years than they did earlier, the majority of students seemingly continued to vote Republican, following family patterns, until 1932. For Harvard student preferences in 1912, see "University Notes," *Harvard Graduates' Magazine* 21 (December 1912), p. 364; for 1908, see "Student Life," ibid. 16 (June 1908), p. 705: and in earlier years, Francis G. Caffey, "Harvard's Political Preferences Since 1860," ibid. 1 (April 1893), pp. 407–415.
43. Merle Curti and Vernon Carstensen, *The University of Wisconsin: 1848–1925* (Madison: University of Wisconsin Press, 1949), pp. 412–418.
44. Winton U. Solberg, *The University of Illinois 1867–1894* (Urbana: University of Illinois Press, 1968), pp. 207–213, 319–326.
45. Ibid., p. 211.
46. Ibid., p. 318.
47. Ibid., p. 275.
48. Feuer, *The Conflict of Generations,* p. 341.
49. Peterson, *The New England College,* pp. 139–140.
50. Walter P. Metzger, *Academic Freedom in the Age of the University* (New York: Columbia University Press, 1961), p. 36.
51. Peckham, *The Making of the University of Michigan,* p. 62.
52. "College Discipline," *The Critic* 1 (July 30, 1881), p. 204. Yet thirty years later, an analyst of the American university scene who contended as of 1909 that "almost every educator, [who] if asked what was the main fault of our large colleges, would . . . [reply] that it was the loss of personal relationship between instructor and student," also argued that the "less personal attention they [students] get from professors the better some of them like it." (Edwin E. Slosson, *Great American Universities* [New York: Macmillan, 1910], pp. 76, 386).

53. Hugo Münsterberg, "Productive Scholarship in America," *The Atlantic Monthly* 87 (May 1901), p. 624.

54. G. S. Hall, "Research: The Vital Spirit of Teaching," *The Forum* 27 (July 1894), p. 570.

55. Münsterberg, "Scholarship in America," p. 624.

56. Hall, "Research," p. 569.

57. Peterson, *The New England College*, pp. 145–146.

58. N. S. Shaler, "The Problem of Discipline in Higher Education," *The Atlantic Monthly* 54 (July 1889), p. 35.

59. Francis Wayland and H. L. Wayland, *A Memoir of the Life and Labors of Francis Wayland* (New York: Sheldon and Co., 1867), vol. 1, p. 264. A Graduate of '69 assumes in his book on life at Yale "that no peeler can lawfully enter . . . the college yard," *Four Years at Yale*, p. 516.

60. S. C. Bartlett, "College Disturbances," *The Forum* 4 (December 1887), p. 427.

61. "Professor Wilson's Address," *Johns Hopkins University Celebration of the Twenty-Fifth Anniversary* (Baltimore: The Johns Hopkins Press, 1902), pp. 39, 41; see also comments to the same effect by President Dabney of the University of Tennessee, and William Rainey Harper of the University of Chicago, ibid., pp. 54, 59–60.

62. See summary and excerpts of an article by Charles Ramsey in *The Educational Review* for January 1895, in "Needed Reforms in College Teaching," *The Review of Reviews* 11 (February 1895), p. 21.

63. "The Decline of Teaching," *The Nation* 70 (March 8, 1900), p. 18; "For Better Teaching and Better Research," *The World's Work* 2 (July 1901), p. 913.

64. B. P., "College Professors and the Public," *The Atlantic Monthly* 89 (March 1902), p. 284.

65. Abraham Flexner, "The Problems of College Pedagogy," *The Atlantic Monthly* 103 (June 1909), p. 844.

66. E. E. Slosson, *Great American Universities* (New York: Macmillan, 1910), pp. 17–18.

67. B. P., "College Professors," pp. 284–285.

68. Ibid., p. 286.

69. Metzger, *Academic Freedom*, pp. 43–44; for a detailed analytic account of the shift see Veysey, *Emergence of the University*, pp. 121–179.

70. Alexander Francis, *Americans: An Impression* (London: Andrew Melrose, 1909), pp. 228–229.

71. Randolph S. Bourne, *Youth and Life* (Boston: Houghton Mifflin, 1913), pp. 48, 295, 325–326.

72. David A. Shannon, *The Socialist Party of America* (Chicago: Quadrangle, 1967), pp. 55–56; Ira Kipnis, *The American Socialist Movement 1897–1912* (New York: Columbia University Press, 1952), pp. 259–260.

73. Upton Sinclair, *The Goose-Step* (Pasadena: "The Author," 1923), p. 460.

74. John Reed, "The Harvard Renaissance," *The Harvard Progressive* (March 1939), pp. 8, 10, 22. The 1917 essay was somewhat similar in tone: "Students themselves criticized the faculty for not educating them. . . . Some

men, notably Walter Lippmann, had been reading and thinking and talking about politics and economics, not as dry theoretical studies, but as live forces acting on the world, on the university even. . . . [The members of the Socialist Club] . . . wrote articles in the college papers challenging undergraduate ideals, and muckraked the university. . . . The result of this movement upon the undergraduate world was potent. All over the place radicals sprang up, in music, painting, poetry, the theater, etc. The more serious college papers took a socialistic, or at least, progressive tinge. . . ." John Reed, "Almost Thirty," *New Republic* 86 (April 29, 1936), pp. 332–333. For other contemporary accounts of the activities of the Harvard Socialists, see Francis B. Thwing, "Radicalism at Harvard," *Harvard Graduates' Magazine* 20 (December 1911), pp. 260–263; Gerard C. Henderson, "The College and the Radicals," ibid. 20 (March 1912), pp. 463–465.

75. Randolph S. Bourne, "The Price of Radicalism," *The New Republic* 6 (March 11, 1916), p. 161.
76. E. Earnest, *Academic Procession* (Indianapolis: Bobbs-Merrill, 1953), p. 249.
77. S. William Rudy, *The College of the City of New York: A History 1847–1947* (New York: City College Press, 1949), p. 346.
78. Peterson, *The New England College,* pp. 179–184.
79. A. G. Bowden-Smith, *An English Student's Wander-Year in America* (London: Edward Arnold, 1910), p. 267.
80. Allen F. Davis, *Spearheads for Reform: The Social Settlements and the Progressive Movement 1890–1914* (New York: Oxford University Press, 1967), pp. 35–36.
81. Henry F. May, *The End of American Innocence: A Study of the First Years of Our Own Time, 1912–1917* (Chicago: Quadrangle, 1964), p. 281.
82. Ibid., p. 304.
83. Ibid., p. 282.
84. Ibid., pp. 304–308.
85. Davis, *Spearheads for Reform,* p. 183.
86. James H. Leuba, *The Belief in God and Immortality* (Boston: Sherman, French, 1916), pp. 221–288.
87. Paul F. Lazarsfeld and Wagner Thielens, Jr., *The Academic Mind* (Glencoe: The Free Press, 1958), pp. 144–146, 150–151, 161–163.
88. Leuba, *God and Immortality,* pp. 202–203.
89. Cornelia A. P. Comer, "A Letter to the Rising Generation," *The Atlantic Monthly* 107 (February 1911), pp. 147–148, 149.
90. Randolph S. Bourne, "The Two Generations," *The Atlantic Monthly* 107 (May 1911), pp. 592, 596.

Chapter 5

1. Henry May, "Shifting Perspectives on the 1920s," *The Mississippi Valley Historical Review* 43 (1956–57), p. 425.
2. Cited in William Leuchtenberg, *The Perils of Prosperity* (Chicago: University of Chicago Press, 1958), p. 176.

3. Martin J. Sklar, "On the Proletarian Revolution and the End of Political-Economic Society," *Radical America* 3 (May–June, 1969), p. 33; for a general analysis and description of the radical young intellectuals see pp. 23–36.

4. Frederick J. Hoffman, "Philistine and Puritan in the 1920s," *American Quarterly* 1 (Fall 1949), pp. 249–250, 251–252. *See also* Henry May, *The Discontent of the Intellectuals: A Problem of the Twenties* (Chicago: Rand McNally, 1963).

5. Cited in Arthur M. Schlesinger, Jr., *The Crisis of the Old Order, 1919–1933* (Boston: Houghton Mifflin, 1957), p. 49, from Arthur Pound and S. T. Moore, eds., *They Told Barron* (New York, 1930), pp. 13–14.

6. Calvin Coolidge, "Are the Reds Stalking Our College Women?" *The Delineator* (1921), as cited in "Mr. Coolidge on Direct Action," *The Freeman* (June 1, 1921), p. 268, and citations from the Coolidge article in Robert W. Iversen, *The Communists and the Schools* (New York: Harcourt, Brace, 1959), p. 14.

7. Ibid., p. 13.

8. Upton Sinclair, *The Goose-Step* (Pasadena: "The Author," 1923), p. 130; see also pp. 412–424.

9. Harold Lewack, *Campus Rebels* (New York: Student League for Industrial Democracy, 1953), p. 8.

10. E. Earnest, *Academic Procession* (Indianapolis: Bobbs-Merrill, 1953), p. 265; Oscar Handlin and Mary F. Handlin, *Facing Life* (Boston: Little, Brown, 1971).

11. George Santayana, "America's Young Radicals," *The Forum* 67 (May 1922), pp. 373–374. A comprehensive attack on the spreading collegiate socialist movement by a conservative group which advocated suppression of its rights may be found in Henry Campbell Black, "Socialism in American Colleges," *Bulletin of the National Association for Constitutional Government*, no. 4 (December 1920), pp. 3–46.

12. Herbert Adolphus Miller, "Youth and Age," *The New Student* 2 (November 4, 1922), p. 1.

13. C. Hartley Grattan, "The College Student and Contemporary Writers," *The New Student* 4 (February 28, 1925), pp. 8–12.

14. D.P.H., "This Paper," *The New Student* 3 (October 20, 1923), pp. 1–2.

15. W. H. Cowley, unpublished "Notes on Universities," chap. 11, pp. 32, 36.

16. See "Coolidge Carries Colleges," *The New Student* 4 (November 1, 1924), pp. 1–4.

17. "The Students Buck the Drill-Master," the New York *World* (November 18, 1925), as reprinted in *The New Student* 5 (December 9, 1925), p. 15.

18. *Students in Revolt* (New York: League for Industrial Democracy, 1933), p. 7.

19. Earnest, *Academic Procession*, p. 279.

20. Ibid., pp. 281–282. For contemporary accounts of campus activities on behalf of Sacco and Vanzetti, see articles in *The New Student* 6 (1927), e.g., "Proper Case for Clemency" (April 27, 1927), p. 1; "Students for Sacco, Vanzetti" (May 4, 1927), p. 1; "Sacco-Vanzetti Pleas" (June 1, 1927), p. 2.

21. S. P. Fullinwider, *The Mind and Mood of Black America* (Homewood, Ill.: Dorsey, 1969), p. 128.

22. Edmund D. Cronon, *Black Moses: The Story of Marcus Garvey and the Universal Negro Improvement Association* (Madison: University of Wisconsin Press, 1955).

23. John Davis, "Unrest in Negro Colleges," *The New Student* 8 (January 1929), pp. 13–14.

24. Edward K. Graham, "The Hampton Institute Strike of 1927: A Case Study in Student Protest," *The American Scholar* 38 (Autumn 1969), pp. 673, 677.

25. Alfred C. Kinsey et al., *Sexual Behavior in the Human Female* (Philadelphia: Saunders, 1953), pp. 298–302; R. R. Bell, *Premarital Sex in a Changing Society* (Englewood Cliffs, N.J.: Prentice-Hall, 1966), pp. 33–40; I. R. Reiss, "America's Sex Standards — How and Why They are Changing," *Trans-action* 5 (March 1968), pp. 26–32.

26. Earnest, *Academic Procession*, pp. 264–265.

27. Robert Gorham Davis, "Rimbaud and Stavrogin in the Harvard Yard," *New York Times Book Review* (June 28, 1970), p. 2.

28. Oscar Handlin and Mary Handlin, *The American College and American Culture* (New York: McGraw-Hill, 1970), p. 69.

29. Earnest, *Academic Procession*, p. 249.

30. John Palmer Gavit, *College* (New York: Harcourt, Brace, 1925), pp. 237, 241, 244, 262.

31. Christian Gauss, *Life in College* (New York: Scribner's, 1930), pp. 111, 113.

32. Alvin Toffler, *Future Shock* (New York: Random House, 1970).

33. Gauss, *Life in College*, pp. 101, 108.

34. "The Faculty and Teaching — the Heart of the Dartmouth Report," *The New Student* 5 (November 11, 1925), pp. 4–5. Other parts of the report are reprinted in *The New Student* (October 3, 1925), pp. 3–6, and (February 3, 1926), pp. 11–13. See also "What the Undergraduate Wants," *The New Republic* 39 (July 30, 1924), pp. 258–260.

35. " 'Too Big' Our Higher Education Is Overgrown — and End of Student Influx Is Not in Sight," *The New Student* 5 (November 11, 1925), p. 1.

36. The Editors of *The Vagabond*, "Gigantism and the University," *The New Student* 4 (January 24, 1925), p. 7.

37. Grant Showerman, "Intellect and the Undergraduate," *School and Society* 13 (February 26, 1921), pp. 241–242.

38. Frank E. Spaulding, "The Passing of Great College Teachers," *The Forum* 75 (March 1926), p. 447.

39. See the report of his speech in the *Bulletin of the A.A.U.P.* 11 (March–April 1925), p. 156.

40. Addison Hibbard, "Our Truant Professors," *Outlook* 150 (December 5, 1928), pp. 1267, 1269.

41. As cited by W. H. Cowley in his unpublished "Notes on Universities," chap. 12, p. 22. I am very grateful to Professor Cowley for this reference.

42. Robert M. Hutchins, "Training Professors and Paying Them," *The Review of Reviews* 81 (February 1930), p. 99.

43. Somnia Vana, "College Education: An Inquest, II," *The Freeman* 4 (March 1, 1922), pp. 584–585. There is no relationship between *The Freeman* of the 1920s, and the ultraconservative magazine of the same name, which began publication in 1950.

44. Milton Mankoff and Richard Flacks, "The Changing Social Base of the American Student Movement: Its Meaning and Implications," *The Annals of the American Academy of Political and Social Science* 395 (May 1971), p. 62.

45. C. Michael Stanton, "Student Protest: Youth Response to Depression and Affluence," unpublished ms., Boston College, chap. 2, p. 7. William R. McIntyre, "Student Movements," *Editorial Research Reports* 2 (December 1957), p. 925; Murray Kempton, *Part of Our Time* (New York: Simon and Schuster, 1955), pp. 302–303.

46. George P. Rawick, "The New Deal and Youth" (Ph.D. thesis, Department of History, University of Wisconsin, 1957), pp. 281–282, and *"Digest Helps Poll Articulate College Generation,"* *The Literary Digest* 119 (January 12, 1935), p. 38; "League Loses by Slim Margin in College Vote," *The Literary Digest* 119 (February 16, 1935), p. 7. For results of the *Literary Digest* poll on Roosevelt, see Harold Seidman, "How Radical Are College Students?" *The American Scholar* 4 (Summer 1935), p. 327.

47. Norman Birnbaum and Majorie Childers, "The American Movement," in Julian Nagel, ed., *Student Power* (London: Merlin, 1969), p. 132.

48. Martin McLaughlin, "Political Processes in American National Student Organizations" (Ph.D. thesis, Department of Political Science, Notre Dame University, 1948), pp. 17–20; Rawick, "The New Deal and Youth," pp. 308–311, 317–322, 335–337; Hal Draper, "The Student Movement of the Thirties: A Political History," in Rita James Simon, ed., *As We Saw the Thirties* (Urbana: University of Illinois Press, 1967), pp. 172–182; Birnbaum and Childers, "The American Movement," pp. 132–133.

49. Kempton, *Part of Our Time*, 320–321.

50. Irving Howe and Lewis Coser, *The American Communist Party* (Boston: Beacon, 1957), p. 529; Morris L. Ernst and David Loth, *Report on the American Communist* (New York: Holt, 1952), p. 14.

51. Ibid., p. 2.

52. Ibid., pp. 3–4.

53. Nathan Glazer, *The Social Basis of American Communism* (New York: Harcourt, Brace and World, 1961), pp. 114–118.

54. Ernst and Loth, *Report on the American Communist*, p. 3.

55. Glazer, *The Social Basis of American Communism*, p. 130.

56. Gardner Murphy and Rensis Likert, *Public Opinion and the Individual* (New York: Harper, 1938), pp. 71–87.

57. Ibid., pp. 110–111.

58. Ibid., pp. 107–108, (emphasis mine. S.M.L.)

59. "The A.S.U. . . . established radical traditions at certain universities . . . which were to be revived a generation later — often by the very children of A.S.U. members." Birnbaum and Childers, "The American Movement," p. 133.

60. "Youth in College," *Fortune* 13 (June 1936), pp. 99–102, 155–162.
61. Unpublished report of 1936 national college student study prepared by Cherington, Roper and Wood. I would like to thank Burns Roper for making this report available to me.
62. "Youth in College," pp. 100, 158.
63. Edward Suchman, Rose K. Goldsen and Robin Williams, Jr., "Attitudes Toward the Korean War," *Public Opinion Quarterly* 17 (1953), pp. 173, 182.
64. Norman Miller, "Social Class and Value Differences Among American College Students" (Ph.D. thesis, Department of Sociology, Columbia University, 1958). This study is based on a comprehensive analysis of a sample of thirteen schools gathered by a Cornell group of sociologists. Similar conclusions in analyzing these materials are reported in Arthur Liebman, "The Active and Silent Generation: Student Politics in the 1950s and 1960s" (draft memo: Center for International Affairs, Harvard University, 1970), p. 9. A study of Berkeley students' reactions to the effort to impose a loyalty oath in 1950 found similar relationships between academic class and liberalism. S. M. Lipset, "Opinion Formation in a Crisis Situation," *Public Opinion Quarterly* 17 (1953), pp. 20–46.
65. Lawrence C. Howard, "The Academic and the Ballot," *School and Society* 86 (November 22, 1958), p. 416. For a summary of the variety of research results bearing on the political orientations and voting behavior of American professors, see S. M. Lipset, "The Politics of Academia," in David C. Nichols, ed., *Perspectives on Campus Tensions* (Washington, D.C.: American Council on Education, 1970), pp. 85–118.
66. Paul F. Lazarsfeld and Wagner Thielens, Jr., *The Academic Mind* (Glencoe: The Free Press, 1958), p. 402.
67. M. Stanton Evans, *Revolt on Campus* (Chicago: Regnery, 1961), p. 217.
68. Liebman, "The Active and Silent Generation," pp. 8–9.
69. See Margaret Mead, *Culture and Commitment: A Study of the Generation Gap* (Garden City: Doubleday, Natural History Press, 1970); Kenneth Keniston, "The Fire Outside," *The Journal* 9 (September–October 1970), pp. 5–6; for a general critique of this approach, see S. M. Lipset, "The Banality of Revolt," *Saturday Review* (July 18, 1970), pp. 23–26, 34.
70. Claude Bowman, *The College Professor in America* (Philadelphia: privately printed, 1938). See especially p. 185. The comparison of literature dealing with the role of the professor between 1900 and 1910, and after World War II, found almost total similarity in content and tone, much to the surprise of the author.

"Although the nation underwent rapid and extensive change between the turn of the century and the post–World War II period, the arguments and incantations echoing through the university sounded surprisingly similiar in both eras. The force and scope of the major problems affecting the professor may have increased by the late 1940s, but the rhetoric describing them was identical to that employed prior to World War I.

"Appearing again as a prominent issue was the avowed decline in the quality of teaching, especially in undergraduate courses, and the apparent supremacy of research men in the eyes of university administrators. The loss of prestige accorded teachers was blamed on elective courses and the departmental system. Only the researcher was felt to gain recognition and advancement, and many charged that this resulted in the neglect of teaching in favor of the laboratory, library, or field. Research and publication were the invidious bases of promotion. . . .

"The second major issue reappearing in the second period involved the *content* of university courses. Some observers of the academic scene felt that a major responsibility had been abrogated by the universities in their refusal to instruct youth in the moral and spiritual values of American culture. Countervailing opinions suggested that professors could not be expected to survey contemporary life, reduce its complexity to classroom proportions, and derive a single set of values acceptable to all. Such efforts approached indoctrination rather than education and fell beyond the province of the university. Some felt that the values attending liberal arts courses did not, in fact, liberalize but instead inflicted upon students prejudice and disdain for many aspects of American life.

"A third major source of tension remained in relationships between university faculties and administrations. The pyramiding of administrative personnel and power had deprived the teacher of prestige and authority. The administrative chores forced upon the professor detracted from his major responsibility, that of teaching." (Donald F. Allen, "Changes in the Role of the American University Professor" [Ph.D. thesis, Department of Sociology, University of Texas, 1962], pp. 168–169, 171.)

71. Laurence R. Veysey, *The Emergence of the American University* (Chicago: University of Chicago Press, 1965) , pp. 294–302.

72. See Max Ways, "The Faculty Is the Heart of the Trouble," *Fortune* 79 (January 1969) , pp. 94–97, 161–164; William F. Baxter, "Faculty and Government Roles in Campus Unrest," *The Educational Record* 50 (Fall 1969) , pp. 411–419; John P. Roche, "Retreat of the Faculty," *The New Leader* 52 (November 10, 1969) , pp. 15–61. Such claims are, of course, not new. Randolph Bourne discussed the efforts to explain pre–World War I student radicalism as a consequence of the activities of "these agnostic professors who unsettle the faith of our youth, these 'intellectuals who stick a finger in everybody's pie in the name of social justice,' . . . these remorseless scientists who would reveal so many of our reticences." (Randolph Bourne, *History of a Literary Radical* [New York: Huebsch, 1920], pp. 109–110.)

Chapter 6

1. Robert F. Boruch, "The Faculty Role in Campus Unrest," *ACE Research Reports* 4, no. 5 (1969) , pp. 50, 21.

2. S. M. Lipset, "The Politics of Academia," in David C. Nichols, ed., *Perspectives on Campus Tensions* (Washington, D.C.: American Council on Education, 1970) , pp. 85–118. Much of this chapter is taken from the

original, much longer draft of that paper, which was prepared for the ACE's Special Committee on Campus Tensions.

3. "Text of a Pre-Inauguration Memo from Moynihan on Problems Nixon Would Face," New York *Times*, March 11, 1970.

4. "The Scholar in Politics" (a commencement address delivered at Dartmouth and Amherst colleges, and before the alumni of Miami University), *Scribner's Monthly* 6 (1873), pp. 613–614. (Emphasis in original). Twenty-eight years later, speaking at Stanford in 1901, an older Reid saw the same behavior by American academics as bad. "It is a misfortune for the colleges, and no less for the country, when the trusted instructors are out of sympathy with its history, with its development, and with the men who made the one and are guiding the other." Whitelaw Reid, *American and English Studies* (New York: Scribner's, 1913), vol. 1, pp. 241–242.

5. George Stigler, unpublished memorandum, as quoted in Milton Friedman, "The Ivory Tower," *Newsweek* (November 10, 1969), p. 92. For a similar comment from the Left, see Noam Chomsky, "Philosophers and Public Policy," *Ethics* 79 (October 1968), pp. 5–61. "Perhaps the most important role of the intellectual since the enlightenment has been that of unmasking ideology, exposing the injustice and repression that exists in every society that we know, and seeking the way to a new and higher form of social life that will extend the possibilities for a free and creative life." Chomsky goes on to argue that the intellectual will cease this role when he becomes an "administrator" in the postindustrial society.

6. See Lipset, "The Politics of Academia," for documentation based on the large number of studies from 1912 to 1969. For reports on the analysis of the recent massive (60,000 sample) Carnegie Commission on Higher Education survey of the professoriate, see S. M. Lipset and Everett Ladd, Jr., ". . . And What Professors Think," *Psychology Today* 4 (November 1970), pp. 49–51, 61, and "The Divided Professoriate," *Change* 3 (May-June 1971), pp. 54–60.

7. Everett C. Ladd, Jr., "Social Scientists and Opposition to the Vietnam War: The Petition Campaign Revisited" (mimeographed), pp. 28–30.

8. Christopher Lasch, *The Agony of the American Left* (New York: Knopf, 1969), p. 21.

9. Max Weber, *The Methodology of the Social Sciences* (Glencoe: The Free Press, 1949), p. 6.

10. Ibid., p. 81.

11. Ibid., p. 76.

12. Ibid., p. 55.

13. Ibid., p. 84.

14. From the *Critique of the Gotha Programme (1875)*, as quoted in Noam Chomsky, "The Function of the University in a Time of Crisis," in Robert M. Hutchins and Mortimer J. Adler, eds., *The Great Ideas Today: 1969* (Chicago: Encyclopaedia Britannica, 1969), p. 58.

15. Robert Paul Wolff, *The Ideal of the University* (Boston: Beacon, 1969), p. 75.

16. Barrington Moore, Jr., "Barrington Moore Asks for Student Restraint," *Harvard Crimson* 146 (November 8, 1967).
17. H. Stuart Hughes, "The Need Now Is to De-politicize the University," *Harvard Alumni Bulletin* 71 (September 15, 1969), p. 37.
18. Eugene D. Genovese, "Black Studies: Trouble Ahead," *The Atlantic* 223 (June 1969), pp. 38–39, 41. Another leftist historian, William Appleton Williams, whose graduate students at Wisconsin had started the earliest New Left journal, *Studies on the Left,* also has commented in extremely critical terms about the recent crop of campus New Leftists. "They are the most selfish people I know. They just terrify me. They are acting out a society I'd like to live in as an orangutan.

    . . . "They say: 'I'm right and you're wrong and you can't talk because you're wrong.' They think the university president should be leading the revolution — it's ludicrous." Quoted in Nan Robertson, "The Student Scene: Angry Militants," New York *Times,* November 20, 1967.
19. Chomsky, "Function of a University," pp. 58–59. At the December 1969 meeting of the A.A.A.S., Chomsky "surprised the radical students and faculty members in the audience at a discussion about academic research and the military. . . . Chomsky, an outspoken critic of the Vietnam war and of military research, argued that chemical and biological warfare research should be conducted on university campuses so that the students and faculty members could keep track of what is going on. . . . Chomsky argued that students should be 'effective revolutionaries' and that 'breaking locks has brought practically no new information.' As an example of why he thinks military research should be conducted on university campuses, Chomsky said the recent revelations about the physical deformations in animals caused by 2, 4, 5-T had gone over 'like a lead balloon' on university campuses because there were no CBW departments to alert people to the importance of these issues. The herbicide 2, 4, 5-T has been widely used in Vietnam as a defoliant." (Los Angeles *Times,* December 19, 1969.)
20. Chomsky, "Function of a University," p. 59.
21. Ibid., p. 60.
22. Moore, "Student Restraint," p. 5.
23. Ernest Gellner, "The Panther and the Dove: Reflections on Rebelliousness and Its Milieux," in David Martin, ed., *Anarchy and Culture: The Problem of the Contemporary University* (London: Routledge and Kegan Paul, 1969), pp. 143–144 (emphases in the original).
24. Christopher Jencks and David Riesman, *The Academic Revolution* (Garden City: Doubleday, 1968), p. 531.
25. For an analysis and description of faculty activities along these lines, see Clark Kerr, *The Uses of the University* (Cambridge: Harvard University Press, 1963). One of the key documents of the Berkeley revolt, one that outlined student grievances, drew heavily on Kerr's analyses of faculty behavior. See Bradford Cleveland, "A Letter to Undergraduates," in S. M. Lipset and Sheldon S. Wolin, eds., *The Berkeley Student Revolt* (New York: Doubleday, Anchor Books, 1965), pp. 66–81.
26. A. H. Raskin, "Where It All Began — Berkeley, 5 Years Later, Is

Radicalized, Reaganized, Mesmerized," *New York Times Magazine,* January 11, 1970, p. 85.

27. Ibid.
28. Paul F. Lazarsfeld and Wagner Thielens, Jr., *The Academic Mind* (Glencoe: The Free Press, 1958) , pp. 151–152, 443.
29. C. Edward Noll and Peter H. Rossi, *"General Social and Economic Attitudes of College and University Faculty Members"* (private report; Chicago: National Opinion Research Center, University of Chicago, November 1966) , p. 58.
30. Lazarsfeld and Thielens, *The Academic Mind,* p. 443.
31. In the following discussion, I am highly indebted to the brilliant analysis by Michio Nagai, "The Problem of Indoctrination: As Viewed from Sociological and Philosophical Bases" (Ph.D. thesis, Department of Sociology, Ohio State University, 1952) .
32. Florian Znaniecki, *The Social Role of the Man of Knowledge* (New York: Columbia University Press, 1940) , p. 155.
33. Nagai, "The Problem of Indoctrination," p. 46.
34. Ibid., p. 52.
35. Robert S. Powell, Jr., "Participation Is Learning," *Saturday Review* 53 (January 10, 1970) , p. 58.
36. *Felix Frankfurter Reminisces* (Garden City: Doubleday, Anchor Books, 1962) , p. 43.
37. Randolph S. Bourne, *Youth and Life* (Boston: Houghton Mifflin, 1913) , p. 318.
38. Michael Novak, "Battles of Old Westbury," New York *Times,* July 17, 1971, p. 23.
39. Robert K. Merton, *Social Theory and Social Structures* (Glencoe: The Free Press, 1949) , pp. 308–314; Talcott Parsons, *The Social System* (Glencoe: The Free Press, 1951) , pp. 342–344, 434.
40. Jencks and Riesman, *The Academic Revolution.*
41. David Riesman and Joseph Gusfield, "Style of Teaching in Two New Public Colleges," in Robert Morrison, ed., *The Contemporary University: USA* (Boston: Houghton Mifflin, 1966) , pp. 257–258.
42. Robert Dubin and Frederic Beisse, "The Assistant: Academic Subaltern," *Administrative Science Quarterly* 11 (March 1967) , pp. 521–527.
43. William M. Roth, "The Dilemmas of Leadership," *Saturday Review* 53 (January 10, 1970) , p. 68.

Chapter 7

1. David J. Finlay, Roberta E. Koplin, and Charles A. Ballard, Jr., "Ghana," in Donald K. Emmerson, ed., *Students and Politics in Developing Countries* (New York: Praeger, 1968) , 64–102; Harsja W. Bachtiar, "Indonesia," ibid., pp. 180–214.
2. David Burg, "Observations on Soviet University Students," *Daedalus* 89 (Summer 1960) , pp. 520–540; Lewis S. Feuer, *The Conflict of Generations* (New York: Basic Books, 1969) , pp. 298–312; Richard Cornell, "Students and Politics in the Communist Countries of Eastern Europe," *Daedalus* 97 (Winter 1968) , pp. 166–183; Miluse Kubickova, "Students in Czechoslo-

vakia," in Philip G. Altbach, ed., *The Student Revolution* (Bombay: Lalvani, 1970), pp. 267–285.

3. Dennis J. Doolin, *Communist China: The Politics of Student Opposition* (Stanford: Hoover Institution on War, Revolution, and Peace, 1964); John Israel, "Reflections on the Modern Chinese Student Movement," in Seymour M. Lipset and Philip G. Altbach, eds., *Students in Revolt* (Boston: Houghton Mifflin, 1969), pp. 324–331.

4. A. Beldon Fields, *Student Politics in France* (New York: Basic Books, 1970), pp. 32–40.

5. Ibid., pp. 166–169.

6. A. H. Halsey and Stephen Marks, "British Student Politics," in Lipset and Altbach, eds., *Students in Revolt*, pp. 43–55; Stephen Hatch, "From C.N.D. to Newest Left," in David Martin, ed., *Anarchy and Culture* (London: Routledge and Kegan Paul, 1969), pp. 122–128.

7. John P. Robinson, "Public Reaction to Political Protest: Chicago 1968," *Public Opinion Quarterly* 34 (Spring 1970), pp. 1–3.

8. "Student Unrest Seen as Nation's Top Problem," *The Gallup Political Index*, no. 61 (July 1970), p. 3.

9. Sam Brown, "The Politics of Peace," *The Washington Monthly* 2 (August 1970), pp. 24–46.

10. Kiyoaki Murata, "The JCP-JSP Dispute," *The Japan Times Weekly*, August 29, 1970, p. 4.

11. Pekka Puska and Seppo Naumanen, "Finland: The Struggle for a Democratic University," SIPE [International Student Press Service] 2 (May 5, 1970), pp. 7–12.

12. S. M. Lipset, *Revolution and Counterrevolution*, rev. ed. (New York: Doubleday, Anchor Books, 1970), chap. 9.

13. Robinson, "Public Reaction to Political Protest," p. 7.

14. Enzo Montillo, "The Youth of the Opinion Surveys," SIPE [International Student Press Service] 2 (July 1, 1970), pp. 13–14.

15. Max Kaase, "Determinants of Political Mobilization for Students and Non-Academic Youth" (paper prepared for session on the politics of students and young workers, Seventh World Congress of Sociology, Varna, Bulgaria, September 14–19, 1970), pp. 5–7; Max Kaase, "Democratic Attitudes in the Federal Republic of Germany: Students, Non-Academic Youth and Total Population" (paper prepared for session on youth and politics, (Eighth World Congress of Political Science, Munich, Germany, August 31–September 5, 1970), pp. 4–6.

16. "New Values for Young Workers," *The Japan Times Weekly*, September 19, 1970, p. 12; Neville Meaney, "The Crises in Japanese Universities, 1969," *Vestes: The Australian Universities' Review* 13 (November 1969), pp. 225–231.

17. Ted Goertzel, "Political Attitudes of Brazilian Youth" (paper prepared for session on the politics of students and young workers, Seventh World Congress of Sociology, Varna, Bulgaria, September 14–19, 1970), p. 14.

18. Bernard Pares, *Russia Between Reform and Revolution* (New York: Schocken, 1962; first published in 1910), pp. 161–282.

19. Irving Louis Horowitz, ed., *Power, Politics and People: The Collected Essays of C. Wright Mills* (New York: Ballantine, 1963) , pp. 257–258.
20. Much of this discussion is taken from S. M. Lipset and Everett C. Ladd, Jr., "What Happens to College Generations Politically?" *The Public Interest,* no. 25 (Fall 1971) , pp. 99–113. This article also presents the results of a variety of opinion surveys.

Indexes

Subject Index

Name Index